4

Blueprint

Capturing global environmental value

David Pearce

CENTRE FOR SOCIAL AND ECONOMIC RESEARCH ON THE GLOBAL ENVIRONMENT

CSERGE

EARTHSCAN
Earthscan Publications Ltd, London

First published in the UK in 1995 by
Earthscan Publications Limited

A catalogue record for this book is available from the British Library

ISBN: 1 85383 184 0

Typeset by DP Photosetting, Aylesbury, Bucks
Printed and bound by Clays Ltd, St Ives plc
Cover design by Dominic Banner

For a full list of publications please contact:

Earthscan Publications Limited
120 Pentonville Road
London N1 9JN
Tel: 0171 278 0433
Fax: 0171 278 1142

Earthscan is an editorially independent subsidiary of Kogan Page Limited and
publishes in association with WWF–UK and the International Institute for
Environment and Development.

Contents

Part III Capturing global value

Boxes

Preface

This is the fourth volume in the 'Blueprint' series. Blueprint 1 – *Blueprint for a Green Economy* (1989) addressed the issue of environmental conservation and improvement from the perspective of the environmental economist. It argued that many, if not most, environmental problems have their origins in the inefficient workings of the economy. Accordingly, to solve these problems requires addressing those economic forces directly through the creation of economic incentives for sustainable development. *Blueprint* did not argue, as some people thought, that there is no role for our traditional forms of regulation, often called 'command and control', such as standard-setting and outright prohibition. It did argue that there is a balance between the use of economic incentives and command and control and that the existing balance is far too heavily in favour of the latter. Since *Blueprint* was written major advances have been made in the introduction of incentive systems – environmental taxes, the removal of environmentally damaging subsidies, tradeable pollution permits and resource quotas, deposit-refund systems, and so on. Progress in the United Kingdom in this respect has been slow, but all the main political parties now acknowledge the role that economic instruments must play in future environmental policy. The 'ideological' battle, if we can call it that, has been won. The challenge is to design incentive systems in practice, and that is undeniably difficult but eminently worth pursuing.

Blueprint 3 – *Measuring Sustainable Development* (1993) – returned to the theme of Blueprint 1 and focused again on the UK economy. Blueprint 3 showed that the definitions of sustainable development advanced in Blueprint 1 were not only robust, but that sustainable development was itself capable of measurement. Blueprint 3 developed a simple 'savings rule' for measuring sustainable development, a rule no more complex than the one that any business person would use in deciding whether or not his or her business was sustainable. Essentially, the savings rule argues that nations must set aside funds to offset the depreciation on capital assets. The assets in question must, however, include capital in the conventional sense – machinery, roads, factories – and capital in the form of knowledge and skills, and capital in the form of environmental assets ('natural' capital). Applied to the

UK such a rule revealed some interesting outcomes. Ignoring the capital invested in humans in the form of knowledge, the UK was actually unsustainable for part of the 1980s due, in the main, to depleting oil and gas reserves without reinvesting the proceeds adequately in other forms of capital. There is a warning here that is quite familiar to students of resource-dependent economies: do not *consume* the proceeds from exploiting natural resources, *reinvest them*. But Blueprint 3 developed other indicators of environmental change in individual economic sectors – water, transport, waste management, agriculture and the countryside – and showed that in many respects the UK's record is not a good one. The measures developed in Blueprint 3 are now becoming increasingly commonplace. The World Bank, for example, has adopted the savings approach to measuring sustainable development.

Blueprint 2 – *Greening the World Economy* – was published in 1991 and applied the same techniques and approach to world environmental issues – global warming, ozone layer depletion, the tropical forests. Blueprint 2 argued that exactly the same set of procedures is required. The most effective way forward is to construct economic incentives that make parties to any environmental concern better off with conservation than without it. All too often, this is not the way that international policy (or, for that matter, domestic policy) proceeds. The 'rightness' of an action is pursued regardless of whether one or more stakeholders in the issue lose from the action. Inevitably, the losers then block the agreement or render it ineffective. It is the original design of the agreement that is wrong. Too little attention is paid to designing incentives that, as far as possible, make all parties see the sense in the agreement. That problem has not gone away – even recent international environmental agreements suffer from the same syndrome. Sadly, some environmentalists are to blame for the under-commitment to pragmatic solutions: they prefer to identify the villains and make them pay because that is the 'right' solution. The short-sightedness and counter-productive nature of these approaches appears to stem from a wider supposedly moral view that if something is wrong it should be corrected regardless of cost, regardless of who loses. Yet, failure to appreciate the fact that there are virtually always costs of conservation is what accounts for the almost derisory scale of funds the rich world appears willing to allocate to solving the environmental problems that affect the Earth in general. Without doubt, environmentalists' pressure helped generate the Rio agreements of 1992. Also without doubt, a great many constructive and effective solutions have been ignored or played down because of their desire not just to win but to win in their own way.

This volume, Blueprint 4, returns to the theme of Blueprint 2. It argues that saving the world's environment will involve an extensive, imaginative search for 'global bargains' – deals between the rich and poor and, for that matter, between the rich and rich and the poor and poor, that give everyone a self-interested incentive to improve the environment. Like Blueprint 2, Blueprint 4 does not reject arguments that call for a change in the 'moral view' of our obligations to the Earth as life-support system. It does take a pragmatic stance: while we wait for the moral view to take hold, and that wait is likely to be a very long one indeed, our environments are degrading around us. It is better to acknowledge that people will act when their own self-interest is served. And it is not difficult to construct schemes that achieve this mutual gain while benefiting the environment.

Future Blueprints will turn their attention to various sectors of the economy and to more detailed assessments of the kinds of environmental polices needed in those sectors. Blueprint 5, for example, will look at the social costs of road transport. Other volumes will address solid waste management and air pollution.

David Pearce
London and Duddenhoe End, January 1995

Acknowledgements

Like Blueprint 3, Blueprint 4 bears the imprint of CSERGE – the Centre for Social and Economic Research on the Global Environment. CSERGE was established in 1991 as a joint research centre of University College London and the University of East Anglia in the UK. CSERGE's core funding comes from the UK Economic and Social Research Council (ESRC) and the Directors of CSERGE (David Pearce, Kerry Turner and Tim O'Riordan) and the staff of CSERGE owe a considerable debt of thanks to the ESRC, and in particular to Howard Newby, ESRC's past Chairman, for their financial statement of belief in us. CSERGE also secures funding from many other sources and some of those sources have helped us develop the ideas in this volume. Particular thanks go to the UK Overseas Development Administration for sponsoring work on incremental cost under the Rio Conventions, and to the UK Department of the Environment for continued support for work on acid rain control (as well as many other issues not addressed in Blueprint 4). Needless to say, none of these institutions is responsible for the views expressed here or for any mistakes.

My intellectual debts are numerous. Chapter 11 on incremental cost is a joint product of Raffaello Cervigni and myself. Raffaello is now with the Global Environment Facility in Washington DC. Chapter 5 on 'causes' draws on the volume edited by Kate Brown and myself. Kate was Senior Fellow at CSERGE to 1994 and is now with the School of Development Studies in the University of East Anglia, whilst retaining her close links with CSERGE. Parts of Chapter 2 draw on work carried out for the Intergovernmental Panel on Climate Change by Sam Fankhauser, a previous Fellow of CSERGE and now also with the Global Environment Facility. I am indebted to my co-authors for their stimulating cooperation.

Jonathan Sinclair-Wilson of Earthscan has retained his customary coolness in the face of repeated broken promises on deadlines. To all the staff of Earthscan a special word of thanks is owed. They have been faithful to the Blueprint series, often producing finished products from manuscripts in unbelievably short periods of time, have always been accommodating with respect to publicity, and, in Zoe Davenport, have a talented designer of covers that have done much to give the Blueprints their distinctive appearance. Ed Calthrop assisted with the final preparation of the manuscript and Kirsty Powell produced the index: many thanks Ed and Kirsty.

Blueprint 4 was prepared during a major house move. If it is ragged at the edges I hope readers will understand the trauma of buying and selling property in England's antiquated market system. As always, Blueprint the cat and his mate, Floss, have been a source of amusement and comfort. Let Blueprint 4 be in memory of their friend, Dill, who sadly did not live to see her new home.

PART I

Global issues

━━━━━ ◆ ━━━━━

Chapter 1

The global commons

OWNERSHIP AND CARE OF THE ENVIRONMENT

The owner of a property has an incentive to look after and care for that property. If the property is neglected, it will fail to yield a continued flow of services (or 'rents') and may ultimately not sustain the owner's lifestyle, or even the owner's very existence. One of the features of many environmental problems is that they occur in contexts where there are no owners, or where there are owners who have only limited 'security of tenure'. So it is with global resources like the atmosphere, the stratosphere, the oceans, and many of the world's forests and rangelands. Lack of ownership, or 'property rights', gives rise to neglect and over-use. Because the atmosphere belongs to no-one (at least until recently), it is treated as a free resource and hence one for which no one individual or nation has responsibility. Free resources tend to be abused and that is what has happened to the atmosphere. It has become a dumping ground for the waste gases of fossil fuel combustion and for other gases – the so-called 'greenhouse gases'. The same is true of the stratosphere – it too became the dumping ground for chlorofluorocarbons (CFCs), just as the oceans are also dumping grounds for ship waste, oil pollution, nuclear waste, sewage sludge and other waste. Much of the recent development of international environmental agreements can be seen as an effort to confer property rights on these resources, to make them owned by someone rather than leaving them as owned by no-one.

A useful distinction is between 'open access' and 'common property' resources. It is important to understand that these terms refer to the way the resources are managed (or not managed). Garret Hardin's famous essay *The Tragedy of the Commons* (Hardin, 1968) did much to confuse the two. An open access resource has no owner. A common property resource does have an owner: it may be a local community or a community of nations. The distinction is crucial because, while common property does have some in-built risks of over-exploitation, it often is a perfectly viable and sustainable form of resource management. This is because the common owners mutually agree to limit use of the resource. Under open access, there is no such agreement on limiting use. Common property regimes also tend to have defined management groups, individuals or institutions with a special responsibility for caring for the resource. Hardin's 'tragedy' is really the tragedy of open access. Box 1.1 explains why an open access resource will tend to be abused and may be destroyed altogether. But the risks of over-exploitation are very much less with common property.

Box 1.1
THE PRISONER'S DILEMMA

Why should an open access resource be over-exploited, perhaps to the point of extinction? One way of understanding the process is to see the problem as one of *game theory*. In game theory each individual's actions are determined by what they think the other person will do or decide. Since the classic example of the misnamed 'tragedy of the commons' was that of grazing livestock on a piece of land, we borrow that example here. The matrix below shows what happens if two livestock owners, 1 and 2, add cattle to the land. In each case they have the option to add an animal to the land or not to add an animal to the land. Suppose neither of them adds any further animals. Then the gains to each of them are zero since neither suffers nor gains. This is shown by the sequence 0,0 in the lower right hand corner of the matrix. The sequence 0,0 refers to the sequence of gains (losses) for owners 1 and 2 respectively.

		Owner 2	
		Adds an animal	Does not add an animal
	Adds an animal	−2,−2	+1,−3
Owner 1			
	Does not add an animal	−3,+1	0, 0

Now suppose owner 1 adds an animal but owner 2 does not. Then we are in the right-hand upper corner of the matrix. Owner 1 gets a net gain of +1 which comes about because the initial gain he gets (say +4) is partly offset by the effect of the extra crowding on his own herd (−3). Owner 2 has not added any animal so suffers a net loss of −3. The bottom left-hand corner of the matrix is the mirror image of the top right-hand corner: owner 2 gets the net gain but owner 1 loses. Finally, if both owners add cattle they both lose – the top left-hand corner. The entries here reflect the fact that owner 1 gets +4 from adding an animal, but loses 3 because of the crowding effect, *and* loses a further 3 because of the crowding effect of owner 2's animal. Hence owner 1's overall gain is +4 −3 −3 = −2. The same applies to owner 2.

How will each owner behave if they do not in fact cooperate, i.e. if each one operates in their own interests? If owner 2 adds an animal, owner 1 suffers −3 without adding an animal, but −2 by adding one. So, owner 1 will add an animal to minimise their losses. If owner 2 does *not* add an animal, owner 1 will still add an animal, to get +1 rather than 0 (without adding an animal). This means that whatever owner 2 does, owner 1's decision ('dominant strategy') is always to add an animal. Since the same analysis applies for owner 2 in response to owner 1's decision, a failure to cooperate will always produce the top left-hand corner of the matrix in which both suffer a loss of –2. But this means that their *collective losses* are –4, compared to collective losses of –2 if they operated in the top right-hand corner or bottom left-hand corner, or zero if they agreed that neither should add an animal. In other words, the failure to come to an agreement makes them both worse off. This is the so-called 'prisoner's dilemma'. It provides a very simple way of understanding why individuals acting in their own self-interest and sharing a resource will tend to over-use it, where over-use means that all concerned actually lose.

(The example is adapted from Stevenson, 1991)

There is, of course, a third property regime – private property. If common property is confused with open access it is easy to jump to a false conclusion, namely that private property is the only solution to environmental problems. And there are many who believe that, perhaps because they have confused communal management with no management at all. Private property will often be a good solution, but it will often not be. The reason for that is simple: the single owner has no incentive to take account of the costs that his or her activities impose on other private owners – no incentive to account for what the economist calls an 'externality'. Under common property, however, the externality generated by A is suffered by B who is a member of the same community. The managers of common property then invoke the mutual rules of behaviour governing the common property. The externality is 'internalised' within the community. 'Conferring property rights' is widely advocated as an essential pre-requisite of managing environmental problems. This is correct as long as it is realised that it does not entail conferring private property rights rather than communal control. The balance between private and communal control needs to be assessed in each case. Private management may generate externalities and also, incidentally, strong inequalities because one person or one corporation secures the asset and others secure nothing. Communal management tends to be fairer and may avoid the externalities, but it also has some risks in the face of forces such as rapid population growth. Indeed, many communal management schemes have broken down precisely because rapid population growth has led to repeated subdivision of the asset.

The global commons – the atmosphere, oceans outside territorial waters, stratosphere – should therefore be better classified as the global open access resources. When nations come together to agree on limits to the abuse of these resources they are effectively turning those open access resources into global common property resources. And they also establish a global management regime by setting up monitoring and sanctioning devices. These might range from specific threats – trade sanctions perhaps – against those who seek not to fulfil their obligations under the agreement (as is the case with the Montreal Protocol), or they may be less well defined. Nations have regular occasions on which they need to speak to other nations and secure favours. Breaking one agreement may therefore mean that they are denied what they want in some future agreement. In other words, no international agreement can be seen in isolation. It is always part of a wider set of bargains and deals, 'repeated games' as the game theorists call them, that act as sanctions against breaking a single agreement.

GLOBAL GOODS, GLOBAL BADS

Global resources like the atmosphere have other important features apart from the way they tend to be managed. Management regimes for global resources tend to be either open access (no management) or international common property (management by international agreement). But the *nature* of global resources also matters, for they tend to have the characteristics of what economists call *public goods*. A public good may be contrasted with a private good. A private good is something we might buy in a supermarket. If I buy it, you cannot buy the same unit of the good that I have purchased. We are said to be '*rivals*' in the market place. One of the features of a public good, however, is that my consumption of the good does not diminish your consumption of the good. It is said to be 'non-rival'. Clean air is a public good because the benefit I get from breathing in clean air does not diminish the benefit you get as well. We can immediately see that many global resources have this 'non-rival' feature: the ozone layer protects me as well as you against ultraviolet radiation; avoiding global warming benefits you as well as me (although we need to modify this statement shortly); and keeping the oceans free of pollution is also likely to benefit everyone. Of course, these benefits need not be shared in any absolutely equal sense. You may value clean air more than I do. Global warming may affect country A more than country B: imagine the case of low-level island countries versus more mountainous countries – the former are far more at risk from sea-level rise. The opposite of a public good is a public 'bad': something that affects people adversely and which, if suffered by one individual tends to be suffered by others as well, without any one person's suffering reducing the suffering of others. So, global warming is a public bad, but the control of global warming is a public good.

There is a second feature of public goods and bads. With private goods it is usually possible to devise a mechanism whereby others can be *excluded* from their benefits. A very common exclusion mechanism is the charging of a price. But some private goods are rationed in different ways – by quotas for example. With a public good, however, exclusion is difficult and may be impossible. Suppose we instituted a charging mechanism for clean air with the aim that everyone should pay for the benefits of a cleaner ambient environment. Such a mechanism would quickly fail because there is no way we can prevent people enjoying the benefits of clean air without paying – the so-called *'free riders'*. So, if just a few nations responsible for most of the pollution of the stratosphere, say, agreed to reduce their emissions, the benefits of that reduction would accrue to others as well, even though they have not borne any of the cost of resolving the problem. Of course, we could argue that those who are responsible for the pollution should be the ones who pay for its control. Rather than have an agreement based on the 'beneficiary pays' principle, the agreement should be based on the 'polluter pays principle'. As we shall see, this is exactly how the Rio agreement on climate change was formulated: rich countries contribute most of the greenhouse-gases that cause global warming, therefore rich countries are having to pay for greenhouse-gas control. The fact that many other nations benefit from the control explains why they are party to the agreement but why they do not bear any of the burden of cost. This issue of responsibility makes the analysis of global public goods more complex than the usual public good analysis.

Public goods, then, have two characteristics – non-rivalry and non-exclusion. By contrast, private goods have rivalry and excludability. In reality there is a spectrum of goods and resources in between these 'pure' examples. Many environmental resources are not truly 'public'. Think of a pristine beach or a fine wildlife viewing point. With just a few tourists, we could argue that the good is non-rival: your appreciation of the beach does not reduce mine, your appreciation of the wildlife does not diminish mine. But as soon as the beach gets crowded, and as soon as the wildlife is surrounded by many vehicles (visitors to some wildlife parks in Africa will recognise the problem), there is rivalry. The extra individual does diminish the benefit obtained by others. The beach and the wildlife park can of course be made excludable – charges can be made for entry to both, and very often are, depending on where in the world the asset is. In some countries, for example, all beaches are public beaches with effective open access. In other countries most of the beaches are privately owned, and in still others private ownership may be tempered by some rights of access for the public. In this way, many potentially public goods cease to be public goods because of over-use. In turn, over-use may stimulate controls on access: they become the subject of common property management regimes.

Why do these distinctions and classifications matter?

The first observation to make is that no individual nation has an incentive to 'go it alone' to correct the over-use of a global resource exhibiting public good characteristics, even if that country is a 'big player' in terms of its contribution to the global problem in question. The reason for this lies in the 'free rider' phenomenon: others will reap the benefit but will not bear part of the burden of cost. They can be free riders because the global resource in question is non-rivalrous and because it is virtually impossible to exclude others from obtaining the benefit. This explains why it is necessary to have an international agreement and why special incentives have to be designed. If the issue was left to the 'free market' it would not be resolved.

The second observation has already been alluded to. If the problem lies with the open access nature of the resource, then what has to be done is to confer property rights through either 'privatisation' – turning the public good into a private good in the way that beaches or parks might be converted (single ownership), or through communal management. It is not clear what single ownership of the atmosphere or stratosphere would mean, so that global communal management of the atmosphere and the stratosphere becomes the solution. And that is exactly how the issue has been approached under the Montreal Protocol (concerning the ozone layer) and the Framework Convention on Climate Change (concerning global warming). Biological diversity is somewhat more complex and is discussed below. Box 1.2 also explains why the amount of the public good that would be supplied by a privatized agency will be positive – i.e. some of the public good certainly gets supplied – but the amount that is supplied is not the amount that *should* be supplied.

The third point to make is that communal management can be, and often is, extremely effective. While there may be a 'tragedy of open access' there need be no 'tragedy of the commons'. But there are risks with communal management for, unless the sanctions for breaking the communal agreement are strong, the incentive remains for any one individual to break the agreement. This is why the analysis of international agreements is so important. The Rio agreements are particularly complex in this respect, as we shall see.

How does *biological diversity* fit into this picture? It is, after all, the

Box 1.2
WHY THE FREE MARKET WILL NOT PROVIDE ADEQUATE AMOUNTS OF A PUBLIC GOOD

The diagram below shows two demand curves. The first, D1, is for individual 1 and shows how that individual's demand for the public good varies with its price. The second curve, D2, shows individual 2's demand for the public good. D1 and D2 are also (marginal) *willingness to pay* curves because they trace out how much each individual is willing to pay for an extra unit of the public good. The overall demand for the public good is obtained by summing the two curves. The usual way of summing demand curves is to add them horizontally, but for a public good the curves are added vertically. This is because the provision of a unit of the good to 1 also entails its provision for individual 2. The summed demand curve is therefore Da = D1 + D2. Suppose the cost of supplying the public good is given by MC, where MC stands for marginal cost, the extra cost of supplying one extra unit of the public good.

How much of the public good *should* be provided? The answer is Qa. This is where supply and demand match. A more sophisticated answer is that Qa maximizes the excess of willingness to pay over cost, or 'consumers' surplus'. This is the area under Da and above MC.

But how much *will* be supplied? If individual 1 makes a decision on her own, she will purchase Q1. This is where the net benefits from the public good (willingness to pay minus the cost) are maximized for individual 1. Now individual 2 makes a choice, but does so knowing that individual 1 has already chosen an amount Q1. If individual 2 ignored 1's choice, he would choose Q2, and the total amount supplied would be Q1 + Q2 which equals Qa, the right answer. But individual 2 will not ignore 1's choice, for if 1 buys Q1, Q1 will also be supplied to individual 2 by virtue of the public goods 'joint supply' – whatever is supplied to 1 is supplied to 2. So, 2 will in fact offer to buy Q2 *minus* Q1, knowing that he will get Q1 anyway. The total supplied will therefore be Q1 + (Q2–Q1) = Q2. But Q2 is less than Qa. The public good is *undersupplied* because of the free-rider phenomenon.

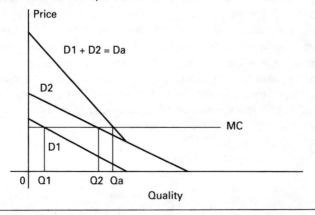

subject of the second Rio agreement, the Convention on Biological Diversity. Is biological diversity – the diversity of living things – a public good as well? In many respects it is. For example, without it, it would not be possible to cross-breed plants to ensure their resistance against diseases. Repeated cross-breeding between cultivated and wild species, for example, is the way that crop breeders 'race against time' to overcome the emergence of new threats to crops as their resistance to disease is weakened. Genetic diversity, then, is rather like information and it is very difficult to exclude others from the benefits of information. On the other hand, diversity resides in biological resources, and the richest sources of those resources are confined to certain areas of the world, especially the tropical forests. This means that individual countries can try to 'own' the information value of the biodiversity. This is essentially what securing *intellectual property rights* means. In the Convention on Biological Diversity, much is made of the need for the rich countries to pay the poor countries for the diversity in the resources they extract and which may then be processed into valuable products such as medicinal drugs. Here again, then, we have an example of a resource with public good characteristics that begins as an open access resource but which becomes the subject of property rights regimes.

Biodiversity is a public good in a much grander sense, however. For many ecologists argue that it is the very basis of life on Earth itself. Without biodiversity we would not have ecological processes that process wastes, recycle nutrients and regulate the very environments in which we all live. By reducing diversity, then, the argument is that we expose everyone – the entire global population – to increasing risks of some form of 'collapse'. That collapse need not be the end of life itself, as some 'doomsters' argue. Collapses could (and do) take the form of greater risks of disease, fewer amenities to enjoy (e.g. disappearing coral reefs) and so on.

But a considerable part of the benefits of the conservation of biodiversity accrue not to the world as a whole, but to the individual nations in which those resources reside. Countries with diverse species, for example, can usually gain from eco-tourism and from sales of diverse products. In effect, biodiversity becomes a 'mixed good', yielding benefits that have many of the characteristics of a private good, and other benefits that accrue as public goods.

Chapter 2
Climate change

SOME GLOBAL WARMING SCIENCE

The Framework Convention on Climate Change (FCCC) was negotiated in 1992 and was designed to address the problem of *global warming*. The Convention came into force in March 1994 and its contents are discussed in Chapter 10. This section briefly reviews the nature of the global warming problem and ways in which it might be viewed.

The 'greenhouse effect' is a natural phenomenon. Certain 'greenhouse gases' are emitted from the Earth and reside in the atmosphere. There they absorb radiation going from the Earth but permit incoming solar radiation to pass through to the Earth, just like a greenhouse. The effect is to keep the Earth warmer than it otherwise would be. The problem of global warming arises because it is thought that anthropogenic emissions of greenhouse gases have reached such a level that they are *accelerating* the warming effect. The main greenhouse gases are carbon dioxide (CO_2), methane (CH_4) and nitrous oxide (N_2O). Other trace gases are also implicated in global warming, notably ozone (O_3) and CFCs, but whereas CFCs were originally thought to be very powerful greenhouse gases, they may have a more minor role to play once allowance is made for possible feedback effects (see below). Carbon dioxide is the main greenhouse gas and probably accounts for 50 per cent of the problem, with methane and nitrous oxide making up another 23–25 per cent. Carbon dioxide emissions come from two main sources: the burning of fossil fuels (coal, oil and gas) and the burning of tropical forests. The exact contributions are disputed, but of the CO_2 contribution, about 80 per cent probably comes from fossil fuel burning and 20 per cent from forest burning. Methane emissions come from various sources: wetlands, rice paddies, ruminants, landfill sites, fossil fuel burning, mining, (even termites!). Nitrous oxide comes from cultivated land and from fossil fuel burning.

Recent scientific assessments by the Intergovernmental Panel on Climate Change (IPCC) has modified earlier assessments of climate change. First, while the climate sensitivity parameter range remains at 1.5–4.5°C for equilibrium $2 \times CO_2$, transient realized global mean surface temperature is now expected to rise by a central estimate of roughly 0.25°C/decade, or by 2.5°C by 2090 over the 1990 base. (Because of lags in the climate system, primarily the time lag due to the warming of the oceans, any increase in radioactive forcing takes time to work through to an equilibrium change in temperature.) The corresponding central estimate in the 1990 report was 0.3°C/decade, for a cumulative 4.2°C over the preindustrial base by the year 2100. This diminution is attributable to consideration of terrestrial uptake, incorporation of the effect of ozone stripping in the evaluation of radiative forcing from CFCs, and the influence of aerosol sulphates.

Second, there is increasing emphasis on regional differences. These stem importantly from the differential impact of ocean thermal lag. In the northern hemisphere, with greater land mass relative to oceans, realized warming may be 0.5°C/decade, twice the pace of the global mean. Centres of land masses may have warming two to three times the global mean. Of specific interest for social cost estimates is the effect of increasing land–ocean temperature differentials.

Third, a central estimate for sea level rise by the year 2100 is now placed at 45cm, compared to 66cm in earlier IPCC assessments.

The broad thrust of these changes is to moderate the expected pace of mean global warming, but to intensify the role of variability and surprises at the regional level. For mid-continental areas in the northern hemisphere, the new estimates would seem to leave even the mean pace of warming close to that in the earlier IPCC estimates. Increasing ocean–land differentials suggest greater precipitation changes and higher storm damages. Importantly, the new incorporation of aerosol sulphates also carries the implication of potential acceleration from baseline warming if there is greater progress than expected in the reduction of urban pollution and thus reduction in these aerosols.

In view of these considerations, it would seem that increased damage associated with variability and unpredictability, as well as greater attention to the high regional warming coefficients for the northern hemisphere and for mid-continental areas, would broadly compensate reduced damages from the standpoint of the timetable of mean warming. This would mean that the time path for mean global warming over the next century would be reduced only modestly (from 0.3°C/decade to 0.25°C/decade). On this basis, there would appear to be little reason for altering the broad orders of magnitude of the damage estimates in the economic effects literature reviewed below. At most, the revised assessment might imply somewhat later damages for the southern hemisphere (and thus, broadly, for developing countries).

Few scientists would argue that global warming is a proven phenomenon. This is because, although increased rates of warming are observable, as are increased atmospheric concentrations of greenhouse gases, global temperatures are not stable over time. They fluctuate and past fluctuations appear only partly related to carbon dioxide concentrations. The observed rate of warming may therefore be part of a 'cycle' rather than a definite trend. Another problem is that the science of the carbon cycle is still not perfectly understood. As noted above, some of the science is under fairly continuous revision. Analyses of the amounts of carbon released do not 'square up' with atmospheric concentrations: somewhere carbon is being absorbed by a carbon 'sink'. This might be in forests, since growing trees absorb carbon dioxide, but there is scientific disagreement over this issue. Yet another problem is that there are various confounding effects and 'feedback' mechanisms which are also not well understood. Various factors may be at work. Sulphur dioxide emissions also come about because of the burning of fossil fuels. But the formation of sulphate aerosols may actually *diminish* global warming because these aerosols act as a coolant. CFCs are known to deplete the stratospheric ozone layer, which is a problem in itself, but this depletion effect may also be a coolant because the ozone layer acts as a heat trap. There are other confounding factors, but the general point is that the science of global warming is uncertain and hence the issue becomes one of how to behave in the context of this uncertainty. If global warming is proven, then its effects could be dramatic for some countries, particularly the low-lying ones and those with fertile deltas because of the effects of warming on the thermal expansion of the seas and therefore sea level rise.

The other feature of global warming is that, while its effects may be present now, most of the damage it will cause will be borne by future generations. This is because the greenhouse gases are 'cumulative pollutants', the damage they do is a function of the cumulated stock in the atmosphere rather than of current emissions. This combination of uncertainty and 'futurity' is one of the reasons why some people think global warming is relatively unimportant. They argue that we should not incur significant costs now for the sake of benefits that are very uncertain, and which will accrue to people in the future who are likely to be much richer than we are today. While there is some force in this argument it is not persuasive, as we shall see.

POLICY PERSPECTIVES ON CLIMATE CHANGE

Two broad perspectives have emerged on ways to analyse decisions which have adverse effects on generations yet to be born: the benefit-cost framework and the sustainability framework. While they initially appear to be very divergent, they have features in common.

The *benefit-cost framework* requires that the future damages be weighed up, integrated into an overall assessment, and then compared to the costs of measures undertaken now by the current generation. In turn, there are two perspectives on the way in which benefits and costs should be compared:

1 The *judgemental benefit-cost* framework, in which gains and losses are compared but without reducing them to common units. On this approach, the monetary costs of control might be compared with some wide-ranging environmental impact statement representing the best state of knowledge about climate change impacts, together with assessments of the distributional incidence of those impacts both geographically and across time.

2 The *monetized benefit-cost* framework. On this approach, the common unit of money is used to 'reduce' the benefits of climate control to the same units as costs to permit direct comparison, but only as far as 'monetisation' is credible.

Approach 2 is characterized by the following features:

- Benefits and costs are defined in terms of human preferences. A benefit is anything that improves an individual's wellbeing; a cost is anything that reduces that wellbeing The philosophy underlying this approach is given in *Blueprint for a Green Economy* (Pearce *et al.*, 1989) and in Pearce (1993).
- Those preferences are expressed in the market-place by willingness to pay (WTP) for a benefit and willingness to accept compensation (WTAC) for a cost.
- Where markets do not exist – for example with respect to ecosystem change – WTP and/or WTAC are measured through 'surrogate markets' or 'created markets'. Surrogate markets are real markets in which environmental change has an influence: a house price or land value may be higher because of an environmental amenity for example (the hedonic property price method). Created markets reflect people's responses to questions put to them about their willingness to pay (the contingent valuation method). Although controversial, these approaches are well established.
- The 'intrinsic' values of other species and ecological systems may be captured at least in part by created markets since people may be expressing their understanding of intrinsic values when they express their willingness to pay for the continued existence of an environmental asset even though they may make no use of it, nor do they intend to use it ('passive use', or 'existence' value).
- Future generations' preferences count at least in so far as they are assumed to want what current generations want. If there is

evidence that they will want more environmental assets affected by climate change, then this 'rising relative preference' can be accommodated by benefit-cost approaches by allowing benefits or cost to rise through time.

- A technical point: future generations' preferences may count equally with current generation preferences if the *pure time preference* component of the *discount rate* is zero (see Box 2.1). If it is positive, their preferences count less in the benefit-cost framework.
- Since WTP is constrained by income, it is likely to be less for low income groups than for high income groups. This may appear to give rise to an unfairness since the preferences of low income groups (countries) will carry less weight than the preferences of high income groups. One way to address these ethical issues is to give different weights to different income groups in the aggregation process. See also Box 2.2.
- Aggregation of damages is also a hallmark of benefit-cost studies. Care has to be taken in interpreting such aggregate figures since they clearly mask: (a) substantial regional variations in impact within a country and between countries; and (b) dislocation costs in adapting to changed local impacts. The aggregation of sectoral impacts also tends to imply that losses in one sector are compensated for by gains in other sectors.

The second overall perspective – the *sustainability approach* – gives the highest priority to the avoidance of 'unacceptable' damage to future generations. Rationales for avoiding this harm follow a sequence like the following:

- There is reasonable evidence to suppose that actions now in emitting greenhouse gases could cause significant damage to future generations, including unborn generations.
- Future generations are defenceless against actions taken now in the knowledge that those actions may cause harm.
- Current generations have obligations to future generations at the very least through a set of links from parents to children, from children to their children, and so on, or, more generally, because future generations have rights even when those generations are not identifiable, and even when their existence is contingent on actions taken now.
- Probable improvements in the wellbeing of future generations cannot be treated as 'compensation' for harm knowingly inflicted on future generations by current generations, any more than harming the poor now can be excused by paying them compensation after the event.

Box 2.1

FUTURE GENERATIONS AND THE DISCOUNT RATE

Discounting is a procedure whereby future gains and losses are regarded as being less important than a nominally equal current gain or loss. Discounting is not peculiar to benefit-cost analysis: it is widely used in most decision-making procedures. Its basic rationale lies in the fact that people appear to prefer their benefits now and to postpone their costs. There is some evidence to suggest the opposite: everyone is familiar with 'getting it over with' – bearing a cost immediately in order to savour the relief later on. But there is also a vast amount of human behaviour that is consistent with discounting. But is discounting fair to future generations? After all, if the person making the decision does not have to bear the cost later on, they have an in-built incentive to undertake actions which yield benefits now and costs later. Global warming control appears to have the opposite characteristics – the costs are borne now and the benefits not only accrue later but accrue to different people, future generations. This is why some people find discounting to be ethically impermissible. Nonetheless, such moral views suffer a similar problem to the sustainability principle – they tend to overlook the fact that there are costs to such decisions. A failure to discount may mean not undertaking profitable investments that build up new technology and capital which will also be of benefit to future generations. The discounting issue is therefore very complex.

A 'standard' formula for determining the size of the discount rate is

$$s = p + u.g$$

where s is the discount rate for society, p is the 'pure time preference rate' – the rate at which the future is discounted simply because of time, u is the 'elasticity of the marginal utility of income' and g is the expected growth rate in consumption per capita. u measures the rate at which utility or wellbeing declines as income grows, the basic idea being that an extra \$1 to someone who has a \$100,000 p.a. income is 'worth' less than an extra \$1 to someone with an income of \$50,000 say. There is a controversy over the 'real' nature of u, but it is widely accepted that it can be estimated from careful analysis of savings behaviour. While popular estimates of s for economies such as the UK and USA lie in the region of about 5 per cent (in real terms, i.e. with inflation netted out) recent work suggests that a defensible discount rate for the UK is actually only about 2.5 per cent (Pearce and Ulph, 1995).

- Hence doing harm is not reversible by doing good. Benefits and costs cannot be 'traded off' in the sense advocated by benefit-cost analysis regardless of whether the benefit-cost analysis is monetised or not. There is a duty to avoid future harm.

As with the benefit-cost approaches, all the propositions in the sustainability approach are open to dispute. Controversial assumptions

Box 2.2
UNFAIRNESS AND WILLINGNESS TO PAY

Benefit-cost analysis assumes that the monetary values of damage can be aggregated across (a) individuals, and (b) countries. This aggregation process raises an important problem of so-called *interpersonal comparisons of utility*, where utility is simply another word for 'welfare' or 'wellbeing'. Basically, introspection allows any one individual to assess his or her own preferences, but perhaps not others' preferences. Each individual knows by how much he or she is better off in situation X compared to situation Y, but he or she cannot assess how this change compares to the extent to which someone else is better off for the same change of situation. This inability to assess other minds produces the theorem that it is impossible to make comparisons of wellbeing between individuals, and hence by extension, between countries. There is therefore an endless number of ways in which individuals' assessment of their own wellbeing can be aggregated to yield a measure of social welfare change. But while the problem of interpersonal comparisons of utility tends to be received wisdom in economics it is far from clear that it should be: we all make judgements about others' wellbeing all the time.

Measuring social welfare change requires ethical judgements about individuals' preferences. Such judgements could include one to the effect that preference measures should not be unduly influenced by income differences. In this case, the individual measures of preference – willingness to pay – could be weighted so as to reflect the preference of someone with an average income. One way to proceed is to indicate the outcomes of the benefit-cost analysis according to differing value judgements about the weights attached to preferences – a kind of 'value sensitivity analysis'. Thus, whether a change in the state of the world raises or lowers social welfare depends on the impacts on individual welfare as well as on normative criteria for making interpersonal welfare comparisons. Measures of social welfare change are, therefore, not objective but normative.

Global warming damage formulations usually present total damages (D) as the sum of individual impacts (d_i):

$$D = \sum_i d_i$$

An alternative formulation could be to present the results in the following way,

$$D = \sum_i d_i \cdot \left(\frac{Y_a}{Y_i}\right)^E$$

where Y_a is now some reference level of income, say the global average income, or the income of the richer countries, and E is a factor correcting for differences in the utility of income between countries. In the literature, E is usually either the income elasticity of demand or the elasticity of the marginal utility of income. Other ways of determining equity weights, e.g. using factors other than income, could of course also be used.

An example will indicate how the measures differ. Suppose there are just two countries. In country A, damage d_A is $50 and in country B it is $30. Country A has an income of $5000 and in country B it is $1000. The unweighted approach would make the global damage $80. As a percentage of world income this is $80/6000 \approx 1.33$ per cent. Note, however, that A's damage is 1 per cent of its income, and B's is 3 per cent.

Setting Y_a at the average world income of $3000, and $E = 1$ for convenience, the weighted procedure would produce the following result:

$$D = 50 \cdot \left(\frac{3000}{5000}\right) + 30 \cdot \left(\frac{3000}{1000}\right) = 30 + 90 = 120$$

Damage is now in 'equity weighted' terms, and expressed as a fraction of world income it is 2 per cent. The share of B's income has risen to 9 per cent and the effect of equity weighting is therefore to make B's damage much more important.

How is the value of E selected? If logarithmic utility functions are chosen and E is interpreted as the elasticity of the marginal utility of income, then $E = 1$, and we have the results shown above. Various alternative weights could be chosen, e.g. to reflect income elasticities of demand.

There are many problems involved in such procedures, but they illustrate the idea of 'value sensitivity'. There is the question of what per capita income figure to use. Here the answer is probably purchasing parity rather than exchange-rate-based per capita income. For low-income countries, the former tend to be about three times as high as the latter, whereas the two are approximately equal for rich countries. The use of exchange-rate-based per capita income would inappropriately increase still further the multiple of the developing country welfare weight relative to the industrial country welfare weight. Further, what is the time reference of the per capita income? In principle it should be in the year for which the damage is calculated, and thus, say, 2050 and beyond in the climate-change context. By then the ratio of the per capita income of rich relative to poor nations should have diminished because of the rapid growth in the latter, reducing the differences among relative welfare weights from trade in greenhouse effects. Income available is based on country shares in global income, whereas utility effects essentially involve population weighting. In a cooperative international abatement pro-gramme, there is a resulting opportunity for efficient trades in which rich countries allocate some of their income to defray the losses of poorer coun-tries that are equivalent in absolute terms to the income transferred but much larger in terms of utility otherwise sacrificed. Of course, this same dynamic suggests that a utility-oriented approach would counsel larger amounts of grant aid to poor countries already today, irrespective of the greenhouse effect. That such larger flows do not presently occur (they would have to eliminate per capita income differences completely to remove the gain from utility trade) is not an argument for failing to consider welfare weighting in greenhouse damage analysis, if only because there is a qualitative and ethical difference between refraining from assisting on the one hand and imposing damage on the other.

include: (a) that harm can accrue to individuals whose existence is contingent on actions now; but, more importantly, (b) that trade-offs can be avoided, since any action now incurs a cost of abatement, and any abatement cost involves losses for others which in turn implies that other individuals' rights may be impaired. This latter point tends generally to be ignored by those who advocate 'rights-based' approaches.

Within the sustainability approach, two views are:

1 That since the obligation to avoid harm is absolute, the cost of avoiding harm is irrelevant: the benefits of control are so large that inspection of costs is unhelpful. This is the *absolute standards* approach.
2 That harm should be avoided subject to a constraint that avoiding harm does not itself impose 'unacceptable cost' – the *safe minimum standards* approach.

The sustainability approach takes a long-term view and stresses the need to sustain a viable global ecological system. It therefore tends to be characterized by:

● the avoidance of unacceptable risk where risks are known;
● the 'precautionary principle' – whereby actions giving rise to *possible* but quantitatively unknown and potentially very large risks are avoided or corrected;
● the view that what is unacceptable is only partly measured by reference to individuals' preferences since: (a) individuals are not well informed about climatic risks, (b) experts are similarly not well informed due to uncertainty about climate change and its effects; and (c) human preferences may not capture other values, e.g. intrinsic values;
● very low discount rates of the order of a few percentage points, and maybe even zero.

Whereas the benefit-cost approach seeks to measure the scale of damage, the sustainability approach assumes that damage will be 'significant', so much so that action is warranted regardless of quantification.

The sustainability approach often tends to have as its objective a concern to avoid exceeding some target rate of temperature rise, often quoted as $0.1°C$ per decade, and some absolute overall rise in temperature of $2-3°C$. Examples include Krause *et al.* (1989) and Rijsberman and Swart (1990). The costs of achieving these constraints are assumed to be worth incurring in order to avoid the risks to future generations (Box 2.3).

With reference to the benefit-cost approach, it is well known that a time path in which the present value (i.e. the discounted value) of benefits minus costs is maximized need not be a sustainable path, and that a sustainable path could, in turn, be unacceptable in terms of its implied living standards for each generation (Pearce *et al.*, 1994) The choice between benefit-cost approaches and sustainability approaches therefore depends crucially on: (a) attitudes to uncertainty; (b) the degree of concern for the wellbeing of future generations; and (c)

Box 2.3
PERSPECTIVES ON CONTROLLING CLIMATE CHANGE

The diagram below illustrates the various perspectives on controlling climate change. The horizontal axis shows the rate of warming in degrees centigrade per decade. The latest IPCC assessment suggests that 'business as usual' warming will be around 0.25°C per decade. MD is the *extra* (or marginal) damage caused as the rate of warming increases and it is assumed here that this will increase as warming rates increase. MAC is the (marginal) abatement cost of controlling global warming. This curve slopes in the opposite direction because, as warming is reduced, more and more expensive policies may need to be undertaken. MAC is shown as beginning below the horizontal axis to illustrate the idea that there may be 'win-win' policies for controlling warming, i.e. measures which have no cost in the sense that greenhouse gas control is an incidental effect of a measure that pays for itself any way. Many people feel that energy conservation fits this picture.

The benefit-cost approach is shown by looking at the intersection of the MD and MAC curves. This is the benefit-cost 'optimum' level of control because at any other point the extra benefits of control outweigh the extra cost (points to the right of X) or the costs outweigh the benefits (points to the left of X). The sustainability approach, on the other hand, sets a constraint on 'allowable' warming. In the diagram this is shown as 0.1°C per decade simply because this is a figure suggested by a number of people. The cost of achieving this sustainability objective is the whole shaded area under MAC, whereas the cost of achieving the benefit-cost objective is seen to be lower – the lightly shaded area.

Uncertainty can be introduced by making the MD curve 'fuzzy'. Policy is then a matter of deciding how to respond to the risk of being wrong. Secondary benefits can also be introduced by lowering the MAC curve, since a benefit is simply a negative cost. The net cost of reducing global warming is therefore less than the cost in terms of resources.

Of course, the benefit-cost approach could produce the same result as the sustainability approach if the MD curve sloped upwards sharply at 0.1°C.

Note that the curves are hypothetical – the diagram only illustrates the different policy approaches.

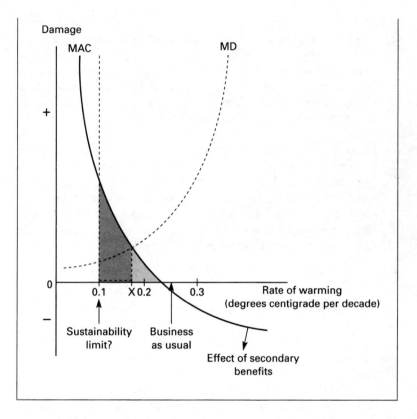

beliefs about the damage function, i.e. the way in which warming relates to damages.

A consensus viewpoint stresses the following common features of both the sustainability and the benefit-cost approaches:

- The existence of uncertainty cannot justify 'business as usual', i.e. doing nothing. Action on climate change is justified since the damage costs could be very high, the 'coefficient of concern' for the future is not zero, and there are costs of delayed action since greenhouse gas impacts may not be reversible.
- The right benefit-cost perspective is one which investigates the benefits and costs of taking actions. Such actions are likely to yield benefits of a similar order of magnitude as the costs of the actions for some time to come, since avoided climatic damages are not the only benefits of those actions. This underlines the difference between *damage estimation* and *abatement* benefits: the latter include the avoided damages estimated by the former concern, but also include other benefits from greenhouse gas abatement.

● Neither sustainability nor 'maximizing net benefits' is an obviously non-controversial objective. Sustainability cannot be an overriding objective independent of the quality of life that is sustained or the costs of achieving it. Maximizing net benefits cannot be an overriding objective since it may be consistent with an approach which discriminates against future generations. This suggests an approach in which the best features of both approaches are taken: a concern for the wellbeing of future generations, the wellbeing of Earth itself, and acknowledgement of the limited resources that all societies have at their disposal to tackle global problems. Such approaches come closest to the 'safe minimum standards' approach: taking a precautionary approach in favour of the environment unless the demonstrated costs of so doing are very high. Precaution would have its justification in very high damage costs: damage costs must therefore be investigated.

Box 2.3 summarizes the various standpoints in one diagram.

ESTIMATING GLOBAL WARMING DAMAGE

Box 2.4 summarizes the principal existing estimates of global warming damage for major regions of the world. In the United States, losses from benchmark $2 \times CO_2$-equivalent warming reach over 1 per cent of GDP in the Cline, Fankhauser and Tol compilations, and some 2.5 per cent of GDP in the central Titus estimates. Titus specifies a lower and upper end of his range of estimates, at 0.8 per cent and 5.4 per cent of GDP, respectively. The Titus estimates are based on General Circulation models (GCMs) with average warming parameters of about 4°C, higher than the IPCC's best guess of 2.5°C.

Estimates for other OECD countries are mostly within the same order of magnitude of 1–2 per cent of GDP.

Early estimates by Nordhaus (1991a,b), again for the US, arrived at a direct calculation of only 0.26 per cent of GDP, primarily from sea level rise; but Nordhaus also sets 1 per cent of GDP as a reasonable central estimate. The CRU/ERL (1992) estimates for the European Union, on the other hand, are significantly higher, with costs in the order of 1.6 per cent of national income per degree of warming. The principal reason for this is a very high assessment of sea level rise damages. By augmenting sea level rise costs by a factor 2.7 to account for storm surges, the study may overestimate damages. On the other hand, their assessment of non-sea-level-rise impacts appears to understate true damages, with an overall beneficial outcome in these categories.

Box 2.4
MONETARY $2 \times CO_2$ DAMAGE IN DIFFERENT WORLD REGIONS

	Fankhauser (1995) bn$	%GDP[1]	Tol (1994) bn$	%GDP[1]
● European Union	63.6	1.4		
● United States	61.0	1.3		
● Other OECD	55.9	1.4		
● OECD			74.2	1.5
● OECD Europe			56.5	1.3
● OECD Pacific			59.0	2.8
Total OECD	*180.5*	*1.3*	*189.5*	*1.6*
● E. Europe/Former USSR	18.2	0.7[2]	−7.9	−0.3
● Centrally planned Asia	16.7[3]	4.7[3]	18.0	5.2
● South and South East Asia			53.5	8.6
● Africa			30.3	8.7
● Latin America			31.0	4.3
● Middle East			1.3	4.1
Total Non-OECD	*89.1*	*1.6*	*126.2*	*2.7*
World	*269.6*	*1.4*	*315.7*	*1.9*

1 Note that the GDP base may differ between the studies
2 Former Soviet Union only
3 China only

Sources: as shown.

Regional differences can be substantial, as is exemplified by the estimates for developing regions and the former USSR. For the former Soviet Union damage could be as low as 0.7 per cent of GNP or even negative (i.e. climate change is beneficial). The negative figure by Tol mainly stems from large beneficial impacts in the agricultural sector. In the Fankhauser study, on the other hand, possible beneficial yield impacts are more than offset by the adverse impact of increased world prices on food imports. The region will also suffer from particularly high health and air pollution costs. The extremely high estimate for the Asian regions and Africa, on the other hand, are predominantly due to the severe life/morbidity impacts. As explained above, both the quantitative assessment and the underlying value-of-life estimates are very volatile, and the probability range of total damage is particularly wide for these regions.

Damage is likely to be more severe in developing countries, compared to developed countries as is shown by the estimates. Box 2.4 reports damages in non-OECD countries of about 1.6–2.7 per cent of GDP, some 50 per cent higher than the OECD average. The main causes for this high estimate are health impacts and the high portion of natural habitats and wetlands found in developing countries. Although the data for the non-OECD estimates are significantly weaker, they provide a clear indication that global warming will have its worst impacts in the developing world, with a damage of probably at least 2 per cent of GNP for $2 \times CO_2$.

In general, the estimates show a relatively narrow band for central damage calculations for the United States, and for developed countries in general. It is important to recognize, however, that this field of estimates is probably biased toward convergence. The reason is that the underlying sources of many of the estimates are the same. The convergence tends to become extrapolated to other regions, too, considering that several of the international estimates are obtained by extrapolation of the US estimates. The similarity of the estimates should therefore not necessarily be interpreted as evidence of their robustness. There remains a substantial degree of uncertainty in the estimates. Nevertheless the relative ranking of regions appears to be reasonably robust, with the most severe impacts to be expected in Asia and Africa, and northern and developed regions suffering less.

DAMAGE PER TONNE OF GREENHOUSE GAS EMISSIONS

Later chapters will make use of global warming damage estimates expressed in a different way. If we have some idea of total damage then it can be related back to the damage done by one tonne of carbon (or methane or nitrous oxide) emitted now and cumulating in the atmosphere over time. Box 2.5 summarizes the available estimates. The most sophisticated of these estimates are those by Fankhauser. We therefore note a damage estimate of around $20 per tonne of carbon, a figure we shall return to.

THE SECONDARY BENEFITS OF WARMING ABATEMENT STRATEGIES

The benefits of greenhouse gas abatement will not be limited to reduced climate change costs alone, but are likely to spill over to other sectors. This is a further reason why greenhouse damage is different to the benefits of greenhouse gas abatement. For example, if abatement

Box 2.5
THE SOCIAL COSTS OF CO_2 EMISSIONS (current value (1990)$/tC)

Study	Type	1991–2000	2001–2010	2011–2020	2021–2030
Nordhaus (1991a,b)	MC	◄─────── 7.3 ───────► (0.3–65.9)			
Ayres and Walter (1991)	MC	◄─────── 30–35 ───────►			
Nordhaus (1994)	CBA				
-certainty/best guess		5.3	6.8	8.6	10.0
-uncertainty/ expected value		12.0	18.0	26.5	n.a.
Cline (1992)	CBA	5.8–124	7.6–154	9.8–186	11.8–221
Peck and Teisburg (1992)	CBA	10–12	12–14	14–18	18–22
Fankhauser (1994b)	MC	20.3 (6.2–45.2)	22.8 (7.4–52.9)	25.3 (8.3–58.4)	27.8 (9.2–64.2)
Maddison (1994)	CBA /MC	5.9–6.1	8.1–8.4	11.1–11.5	14.7–15.2

Note: MC = marginal social cost study
      CBA = shadow value in a cost-benefit study
      Figures in brackets denote 90% confidence intervals

Sources: as indicated.

were brought about by an environmental tax (e.g. a carbon tax), the resulting revenues could in principle be used to lower other, distortionary taxes, such as those on labour. This could lower the welfare costs of governmental revenue raising – the so-called double dividend of carbon abatement. Efforts to halt deforestation in order to reduce the emission of CO_2 will contribute to the conservation of the world's biological diversity. Other ancillary benefits could occur in the form of local and regional air quality improvements, a reduction in traffic-related externalities like accidents or congestion, and the reduced risk of tanker accidents and oil spills. These problems are tied to global warming in that they are caused by largely the same activities, in particular the consumption of fossil fuels. Because no economic CO_2-removal technologies currently exist, attempts to limit CO_2 emissions will by and large concentrate on reducing the use of fossil fuels. A reduction in CO_2 emissions will therefore also reduce other environmental problems related to fuel combustion. These effects are called the *secondary benefits* of carbon abatement.

The secondary benefits from air quality improvements may be quite large. Various studies suggest that the average secondary benefits vary widely, from about $2 per tonne of carbon abated to over $500/tC. In absolute terms secondary benefits offset about 30–50 per cent of the initial abatement costs in the case of Norway (Alfsen et al., 1993) and over 100 per cent in the UK (Barker, 1993).

It is important to underline the different character of secondary benefits compared to their primary (warming damage avoidance) counterpart. Most critically, secondary benefits do not depend on climate variables but arise only in connection with greenhouse gas abatement. They occur locally or regionally and do not share the global public good character of greenhouse damages. The question of secondary benefits from carbon abatement should also be distinguished from the more comprehensive issue of the optimal abatement mix with respect to all pollutants. The secondary benefit argument is characterized by an implicit primacy of the greenhouse problem, in that improvements in other areas are seen as welcome side-effects of a global warming policy, but are not considered or sought in their own right. This is not necessarily the ideal way to proceed. Strictly, each pollutant should be taxed in proportion to the environmental damage it causes. If there are interdependencies between them, as is the case with global warming and air pollution, these would have to be reflected in the relative tax rates. The currently considered abatement strategies may then no longer constitute the optimal approaches. Once secondary benefits are taken into account, location will also matter. Unlike greenhouse gases, for other air pollutants it matters where they are emitted. Emission reduction measures should therefore be concentrated to those places where the joint benefit of reducing all emissions is highest.

CONCLUSIONS

Climate change is occurring, but why it is occurring is not known for certain. There is a concerted body of evidence to suggest that it may be occurring because of the release of greenhouse gases, mainly but not exclusively from the burning of fossil fuels. Estimates of damage suggest that global warming could result in significant economic damage, especially for many poorer countries. More recent evidence suggests that while the average rate of warming may not be quite as high as previously thought, the variability in that damage could be much higher. Clearly, if the scientific evidence is uncertain, the proper policy approach is to proceed cautiously. If there are 'win-win' options, options that cost little or nothing, it will pay to undertake them. There will then be 'no regrets' if the science of global warming eventually turns out not to be correct. Similarly, some action will be justified simply as an 'insurance policy' in the same way as insurance premia are paid to insure against uncertain events. And further measures could be justified if, as there appears to be, there are significant secondary benefits from the policies that control greenhouse gas emissions. All this adds up to a very positive policy on global warming despite the scientific uncertainty.

But some people want even stronger action. They tend to adopt a 'sustainability' approach whereby some ecological limit on the rate (and level) of warming has to be honoured. At one extreme there are those who argue for this limit regardless of cost. Others would say that it should be pursued so long as the cost is 'acceptable' – the 'safe minimum standards' approach. Certainly, it is difficult to understand any viewpoint that declares cost to be irrelevant. This is how some people argue, however, because they feel it is a moral duty to future generations not to impair their environment. The problem with such a view is that it is absolute: it fails to acknowledge that, once we go beyond the 'win-win' solutions, all policy involves a cost, and hence all policy involves a trade-off. Costs and trade-offs mean that somebody loses – cost is not 'mere money'. And if someone loses, their own 'right' to wellbeing is infringed. Of course, if global warming really is about catastrophe it is perfectly possible to argue that the two conflicting rights are not of equal status: future existence may be being traded against small changes in human wellbeing now. But that makes it an issue of the science, i.e. what we really can expect by way of damages. As yet, no one can be sure.

Chapter 3

The ozone layer

OZONE

The ozone layer is a near perfect example of a global public good. Its existence is essential for many life support systems to function. Ozone occurs at two levels in the atmosphere: in the stratosphere about 15–50 kilometres above the ground, and in the troposphere, the lower part of the atmosphere up to 15 kilometres above the ground. Ozone is a naturally occurring gas, and in the stratosphere it is concentrated into 'the ozone layer' which is like a thick belt around the Earth. This concentration of ozone protects the earth from ultraviolet (UV) radiation from the sun, taking out 90 per cent of the UV rays. Ozone concentrated at the lower atmospheric level, the troposphere, however tends to be harmful to health and vegetation and is involved in the general process of 'acid rain' formation. While tropospheric ozone formation is natural, it can be enhanced by the interaction of nitrogen oxides (NOx), oxygen (O) and volatile organic compounds (VOCs). Accordingly, high ozone levels in the troposphere are bad, high concentrations in the stratosphere are good. This chapter is concerned with stratospheric ozone.

CFCS AND THE DEPLETION OF THE OZONE LAYER

Regular measurements have been made of the ozone layer. Measurements taken at Arosa, Switzerland since 1926 reveal that up to about 1970 nothing much happens – the 'average' change is zero: the layer was getting neither thicker nor thinner. But after 1970 there was marked downturn: the ozone layer had begun to 'thin' so that the ozone layer would let through more UV radiation. While some extra sunlight on the Earth might seem attractive, added UV radiation poses all kinds of problems, as we will see shortly. (Strictly, it is one form of UV radiation – UV-B – which is relevant).

It was not until the early 1970s that scientists began to investigate the relationship between certain chemicals and the depletion of the ozone layer. Two Californian scientists, Mario Molina and Sherwood Roland focused on 'chlorofluorocarbons', or CFCs for short, as possible culprits. Normally, most chemicals break down or become dissipated when released into the environment, but CFCs manage to maintain their chemical stability. Moreover, they 'travel' upwards into the atmosphere where the effect of solar radiation does break them down but, in the process, releases large quantities of chlorine. It was already known that chlorine could set off a chain reaction which could destroy ozone molecules at a rapid rate. Moreover, being stable, the CFCs could stay in the atmosphere a long time, continuing to damage the ozone layer long after they had been released on Earth. In 1986 a major report was released under the auspices of the World Meteorological Office and the United Nations Environment Programme. This report confirmed the view that CFCs stayed in the atmosphere and damaged the ozone layer through the release of chlorine. It predicted a general trend of depletion worldwide, higher seasonal variations in depletion (i.e. the layer would deplete more in certain seasons), and variations in depletion in certain latitudes. The same report implicated CFCs in the greenhouse warming effects as well, although that science has changed in recent years (see Chapter 2). At roughly the same time British scientists made a dramatic discovery in the Antarctic. They estimated that ozone levels between September and November above the Antarctic had fallen by 50 per cent in 1986 compared to the 1960s. The resulting 'hole' was huge, about the size of the land area of the United States. The 'hole' tended to mend itself after this period of depletion, and then reappeared again in later years. Subsequent investigations revealed a similar 'hole' over the Arctic, and thinning over the northern hemisphere, and even the tropics.

CFCs had been introduced in the 1930s as a 'wonder gas'. CFCs are stable, non-flammable, non-toxic and non-corrosive. Unsurprisingly, they found a great many uses. Box 3.1 shows the uses of CFCs, which include refrigeration, aerosol propellants, foam manufacture, solvents and so on. Output and use have been going down since 1986 because, after the scientists' discovery of the link between CFCs and ozone layer depletion, the world acted quickly to control their use. In 1985 the Vienna Convention for the protection of the Ozone Layer was adopted, and in 1987 25 countries adopted the Montreal Protocol on Substances that Deplete the Ozone Layer. The Montreal Protocol came into force on January 1 1989. As scientific knowledge increased, however, the Montreal Protocol had quickly to be revised and made more strict. Box 3.2 outlines the main developments in the international agreements.

Box 3.1
THE PRODUCTION AND USES OF CHLOROFLUOROCARBONS

(a) World output of CFCs

Product	1986 (000 tonnes)	1991 (000 tonnes)	1991 output (as % of 1986)
CFC-11	415	263	63
CFC-12	441	259	59
CFC-113	241	143	59
CFC-114	18	5	30
CFC-115	13	11	85
Total	*1128*	*681*	*60*

(b) Structure of uses of CFCs

Application	Percentage of 1986 use	Reduction by 1991 since 1986 (%)
Propellants	28	58
Cleaning	21	41
Foam blowing	26	35
Refrigerants	23	7
Other	2	—
Total	*100*	*40*

Source: *Montreal Protocol, 1991 Assessment: Report of the Technology and Economic Assessment Panel*, United Nations Environment Programme, Nairobi, December 1991.

THE DAMAGE FROM OZONE LAYER DEPLETION

Why does increased UV radiation matter?

Human health effects

The most-popularized concern has been the effect of additional radiation on sunburn and skin cancer. Skins cancers can be of two kinds: carcinoma and melanoma. Melanomas (cancers of the pigment cells) can be fatal, and all forms of skins cancer are on the increase. How far the increase is due to changes in personal behaviour (the fashion for being 'tanned') and how far to increased UV radiation

Box 3.2
DEVELOPMENT OF THE MONTREAL PROTOCOL

Measure taken	Target for developed world	Target for developing world
Montreal Protocol 1987–1989	Reduce production and consumption of CFCs by 50% of 1986 levels by 1998 Freeze production and consumption of halons at 1986 levels	10-year grace period allowed before reaching the CFC target Provision of substitute technology to compensate for going without CFCs
London Meeting of the Protocol Parties June 1990	Reduce production and consumption of CFCs and halons by 50% of 1986 levels by 1995 Reduce production and consumption of CFCs by 85% of 1986 levels by 1997 Phase out consumption of CFCs and halons by 2000 Cut consumption of carbon tetrachloride by 85% by 1995, phase out by 2000 Cut consumption of 1,1,1 trichloroethane by 30% by 1995, 70% by 2000 and phase out by 2005	
Actions in 1992	USA CFC production to be stopped by 1995	

through ozone layer depletion is not certain, but one estimate has suggested that if nothing was done to reduce ozone layer depletion, skin cancer deaths for the population alive today or born by the year 2075 in the USA could be around 3 million. A rough rule of thumb is that a 1 per cent reduction in ozone produces a 1–2 per cent increase in

UV radiation and a 3–4 per cent increase in non-melanoma skin cancers.

Other health effects are less certain. There is some evidence that UV radiation can damage the human immune system, increasing the incidence of infectious diseases and reducing the effectiveness of vaccination programmes. The link to increased cataracts is more direct and a 1 per cent reduction in ozone could give rise to an extra 100,000 to 150,000 cases worldwide.

Ecosystem effects

Perhaps more disturbing than health effects – many of them are avoidable through behavioural change such as increased personal protection against the sun's rays – are the potential ecosystem effects. A major impact is on the single-celled algae – phytoplankton, which produce around half the world's biomass each year and 'fix' (absorb) a large proportion of the world's CO_2 in the oceans. UV radiation affects the phytoplankton by interfering with the process of photosynthesis and it also damages DNA, and hence growth and reproduction. The algae are eaten by krill which are in turn the food of larger ocean species, including the whale, and fish. Some research already suggests that the Antarctic 'hole' is reducing phytoplankton productivity by up to 12 per cent. One study suggests that a 16 per cent reduction in ozone concentration could result in a 5 per cent reduction in primary biomass production and a 6–9 per cent reduction in fish stocks. The science is still uncertain, and it is known that there are some natural defence mechanisms whereby some phytoplankton screen out some of the radiation. These species might end up expanding to compensate for the loss of others, but the effects of complex food chains are still uncertain.

The same potential effects apply to land-based ecosystems since increased UV radiation appears to be correlated with lower photosynthetic activity and reduced growth in vegetation. The impact on crops could therefore be significant.

THE COSTS AND BENEFITS OF CFC CONTROL

Faced with the formidable scientific evidence, the world's governments acted quickly with respect to ozone layer depletion. In little more than ten years from the discovery of the CFC–ozone link, the Montreal Protocol was in place. But the speed with which the Protocol will itself have an effect on ozone layer depletion should not be exaggerated. Box 3.2 shows the effect on concentrations of chlorine if CFC emissions are halted in 1995, 2000, or 2005. To get back to the level of concentration of 1975 (around 1.5–2.0 parts per billion by volume (ppbv)) will take until the end of the next century. This suggests an important point – sometimes it is simply too late to restore situations. This is especially so where pollutants are cumulative, i.e. where they have a long residence time in the environment, as CFCs do.

Apart from the dramatic evidence on ozone layer depletion, there is one other important reason for early international action on CFCs. Basically, they are not very expensive to replace. The cost of compensating the developing world to go without CFC use will be perhaps $2 billion between 1990 and 2010, which is fairly trivial compared to the annual flow of official aid of $45 billion.

The objective of getting back to some original starting point is not, of course, sanctioned by cost-benefit approaches (unless that just happens to be the outcome). This is why adopting certain rules of thumb relating to 'restoring' the environment is not necessarily consistent with the standard economic approach to environmental problems, although such rules may well be consistent with the idea of 'sustainability' and 'constant capital' – see *Blueprint for a Green Economy* (Pearce *et al.*, 1989). Thus, achieving 1.5–2.0 ppbv of chlorine is analogous to a 'sustainability' criterion, but we do not know if it would be sanctioned by a comparison of costs and benefits.

There is in fact only one cost-benefit analysis of CFC control and

---

Box 3.3
COSTS AND BENEFITS OF CFC CONTROL IN THE USA

The table below shows that the costs to the USA of reducing CFC emissions by 80 per cent were estimated to be some US $22 billion, but the health and environmental benefits were estimated to be a staggering $3500 billion (or $3.5 trillion). The evaluation of health benefits assumed that a 'value of a statistical life' (often misleadingly called 'the value of human life') is $3 million.

	No control	Cut of 80% in emissions ($ billion 1985)
Costs: 1989–2075, discounted at 2%	0	22
Health and environmental benefits	0	3553
Net benefit	*0*	*3531*

Source: US Environmental Protection Agency, *Regulatory Impact Analysis – Protection of Stratospheric Ozone*, Vol. 1, US EPA, Washington DC, 1988.

this was prepared as a 'Regulatory Impact Analysis' by the United States Environmental Protection Agency. Box 3.3 sets out the essential findings of that study but it is important to note that it relates to an evaluation of the *original* Montreal Protocol, i.e. unamended by the later agreements to make the controls more strict. The cost-benefit study shows that there were overwhelmingly substantial benefits to the USA from undertaking the controls formulated in the Montreal Protocol, even if all benefits could not be measured. Recall that perhaps 3 million deaths could be avoided from controlling CFCs. If each 'statistical life' is valued at $3 million, then the economic value of the saved lives alone would be $9 million million (or $9 trillion). Even allowing for the effect of 'discounting' – whereby future lives saved are assumed not to be as valuable as current lives saved – the effect is to make the benefits of CFC control absolutely enormous. This shows up in the net benefit calculation in Box 3.3.

Chapter 4

Biological diversity

WHAT IS BIOLOGICAL DIVERSITY?

The term 'biological diversity', commonly shortened to 'biodiversity', is used to describe the number, variety and variability of living organisms. Strictly interpreted, the term 'diversity' relates only to the variety of biological entities. The term 'biological resources' is better reserved for the quantity of biological entities. In practice, the two concepts tend to be merged in discussions of the conservation of biological resources. Reductions in biodiversity include all those changes that have to do with reducing or simplifying biological heterogeneity, from individuals to regions. Biodiversity may be described in terms of genes, species, and ecosystems, corresponding to three fundamental levels of biological organisation.

Genetic diversity

Genetic diversity is the total genetic information contained in the genes of individuals of plants, animals and micro-organisms. Each species is the repository of an immense amount of genetic information. The number of genes range from about 1000 in bacteria, up to 400,000 or more in many flowering plants. Each species is made up of many organisms, and virtually no two members of the same species are genetically identical. This means for example that even if an endangered species is saved from extinction, it will probably have lost much of its internal diversity. When the populations are allowed to expand again, they will be more genetically uniform than their ancestral populations. For example, the bison herds of today are biologically not the same in terms of their genetic diversity, as the bison herds of the early eighteenth century.

Species diversity

Species are regarded as populations within which 'gene flow' occurs under natural conditions. Thus, within a species, all normal individuals are capable of breeding with the other individuals of the opposite sex belonging to the same species, or at least they are capable of being genetically linked with them through chains of other breeding individuals. By definition, members of one species do not breed freely with members of other species. Although this definition works well for many animal and plant species, it is more difficult to delineate species in populations where hybridisation, or self-fertilisation or parthenogenesis occur. Arbitrary divisions must be made, and this is an area where scientists often disagree.

The true number of species on Earth is not known, even to the nearest order of magnitude. Wilson (1988) estimates that the absolute number of species falls between 5 and 30 million, although some scientists have put forward even higher estimates, up to 50 million. At present approximately 1.4–1.8 million living species of all kinds of organisms have been described. The best-catalogued groups include vertebrates and flowering plants, with other groups relatively under-researched, for example, lichens, bacteria, fungi and roundworms. Likewise, some habitats are better researched than others, and coral reefs, deep ocean floor and tropical soils are not well studied. This lack of knowledge has considerable implications for policy towards biodiversity conservation.

The single most obvious pattern in the global distribution of species is that overall species richness increases with decreasing latitude. Not only does this apply as a general rule, it also holds within the great majority of higher taxa, at order level or higher. However, this overall pattern masks a large number of minor trends. Species richness in particular taxonomic groups, or in particular habitats, may show no significant latitudinal variation, or may actually decrease with decreasing latitudes. In addition, in terrestrial ecosystems, diversity generally decreases with increasing altitude. This phenomenon is most apparent at extremes of altitude, with the highest regions at all latitudes having very low species diversity (although these areas also tend to be of limited size, which may be one factor resulting in lower species numbers). In terms of marine systems, depth is the analogue of altitude in terrestrial systems and biodiversity tends to decrease with depth. Gradients and changes in species richness are also correlated to precipitation, nutrient levels, and salinity, as well as other climatic variations and available energy.

Ecosystem diversity

Ecosystem diversity relates to the variety of habitats, biotic communities and ecological processes in the biosphere as well as the diversity within ecosystems. Measuring ecosystem diversity is complex since there is no unique classification of ecosystems at the global level.

Diversity can be described at a number of different levels and scales. Functional diversity is the relative abundance of functionally different kinds of organisms. Community diversity is the number, sizes and spatial distribution of communities, and is sometimes referred to as patchiness. Landscape diversity is the diversity of scales of patchiness.

No simple relationship exists between the diversity of an ecosystem and ecological processes such as productivity, hydrology, and soil generation. Neither does diversity correlate neatly with ecosystem stability – its resistance to disturbance and its speed of recovery. There is no simple relationship within any ecosystem between a change in its diversity and the resulting change in the system's processes. For example, the loss of a species from a particular area or region may have little or no effect on net primary productivity if competitors take its place in the community. The converse may be true in other cases. For example, if herbivores such as zebra and wildebeest are removed from the African savannah, net primary productivity of the ecosystem decreases. Despite these anomalies, Reid and Miller (1989) suggest six general rules of ecosystem dynamics which link environmental changes, biodiversity and ecosystem processes:

1 The mix of species making up communities and ecosystems changes continually.
2 Species diversity increases as environmental heterogeneity or the patchiness of a habitat does, but increasing patchiness does not necessarily result in increased species richness.
3 Habitat patchiness influences not only the composition of species in an ecosystem, but also the interactions among species.
4 Periodic disturbances play an important role in creating the patchy environments that foster high species richness. They help to keep an array of habitat patches in various successional states.
5 Both size and isolation of habitat patches can influence species richness, as can the extent of the transition zones between habitats. These transitional zones, or 'ecotones', support species which would not occur in continuous habitats. In temperate zones, ecotones are often more species-rich than continuous habitats, although the reverse may be true in tropical forests.
6 Certain species have disproportionate influences on the characteristics of an ecosystem. These include *keystone species*, whose loss would transform or undermine the ecological processes or fundamentally change the species composition of the community.

THE LOSS OF BIODIVERSITY

Speciation and extinction are natural processes. Traditionally, from the Darwinian perspective, extinction is the fate of species which lose in the struggle for survival. Taken to its logical conclusion, this view implies that extinction is a constructive process, eliminating obsolete species. However, it is now widely recognized that this is not the case due to the fact that human intervention distorts the natural process. Many extinctions are non-constructive, and a species' ultimate demise is not a reflection on its 'goodness' as a biological organism.

No precise estimate of the numbers of species being lost can be made, simply because the number which are present is not known. The vast majority of species are not monitored. However, there is no doubt that extinction is proceeding faster than it did before the turn of the nineteenth century. It seems likely that major episodes of species extinction have occurred throughout the past 250 million years at average intervals of approximately 26 million years. According to Wilson (1988) the current reduction of diversity seems likely to approach that of the great natural catastrophes at the end of the Palaeozoic and Mesozoic eras, the most extreme in the last 65 million years. Various estimates of the rate of loss are shown below.

Estimate of species loss	Global loss per decade (%)	Method of estimation
1 million species, 1975–2000	4	extrapolation of past exponentially increasing trend (Myers, 1979)
15–20% of species, 1980–2000	8–11	species-area curves (Lovejoy, 1980)
25% of species, 1985–2015	9	loss of half species in area likely to be deforested by 2015 (Raven, 1988)
2–13% of species, 1990–2015	1–5	species area curves (Reid, 1992)

Most of these estimates are based on estimates of loss of habitat. The procedure estimates potential losses of species based on extrapolation of rates of habitat destruction and calculation of associated extinctions using species area curves. This is based on principles of island biogeography and recognizes a relationship between the number of species present and the area of a given habitat (MacArthur and Wilson, 1967). There are a number of problems associated with the use of this rather over-simplified equation for calculation of extinction, and it seems likely that the figures calculated in this way may be under-estimates of the expected extinction rate.

WHY IS BIODIVERSITY IMPORTANT?
THE CONCEPT OF TOTAL ECONOMIC VALUE

Economists approach the issue of measuring importance in a parti-cular way. The essence of their approach is that importance is measured by people's preferences. In turn, preferences are 'measured' by looking at the individual's *willingness to pay* (WTP) for something. Economic value is then measured by the summation of many indivi-duals' willingness to pay for it. So, economic valuation in the envir-onment context is about 'measuring the preferences' of people for an environmental good (biodiversity) or against an environmental 'bad' (loss of biodiversity). Valuation is therefore of preferences held by people. The valuation process is *anthropocentric*. The resulting valua-tions are in money terms because of the way in which preference revelation is sought – i.e. by asking what people are willing to pay, or by inferring their WTP through other means. Moreover, the use of money as the measuring rod permits the comparison that is required between 'environmental values' and 'development values'. The latter are expressed in money terms, either in a dollar amount or an economic rate of return. Using other units to measure environmental values would not permit the comparison with the economic values that conservation has to compete with, i.e. the market value of economic development.

The language of economic valuation is often misleading. Studies speak of 'valuing the environment' or 'pricing the environment'. Similarly, changes in the environment affect health so it is necessary to find some valuations of changes in health status, the ultimate change, of course, being the cessation of life itself. It is commonplace to find references to 'the value of life'. Economists are apt to speak of 'the environment as commodity' which leaves them open – perhaps justi-fiably – to charges that this is all the environment is worth. All these terminologies generate an unfortunate image as to what the activity of economic valuation involves. What is being valued is not 'the envir-onment' or 'life', but people's preferences for changes in the state of their environment, and their preferences for changes in the level of risk to their lives. There is no dispute that people have preferences for and against environmental change. There is no dispute that people are willing to pay to prevent or secure change: donations to conservation societies alone demonstrate this. The problem arises when this WTP is taken as 'the' value of the environmental change. Many people believe that there are *intrinsic values* in environmental assets. They are of value in themselves and are not 'of' human beings, values that exist not just because individual human beings have preferences for them. There is no reason to reject the idea of intrinsic values because the idea of measuring preferences is adopted. What is being assessed are two different things: the value of preferences of people for or against environmental change (economic values) and the value that intrinsically resides 'in' environmental assets (intrinsic values). Nonetheless, there are problems with basing policy on intrinsic values, an issue discussed shortly.

Economic valuation is essentially about discovering the demand curve for environmental goods and services: the values of human beings for the environment. This is another way of talking about finding willingness to pay. (Strictly, the demand curve traces out the willingness to pay for extra (or 'marginal') amounts of something. So the demand curve is a 'marginal willingness to pay' schedule.) The use of money as the measuring rod is a convenience: it happens to be one of the limited number of ways in which people express preferences, i.e. through their willingness to pay. The practical problem with economic valuation is one of deriving credible estimates of that value in contexts where there are either no apparent markets or very imperfect markets.

Many of the biological assets that people generally feel are very important are in the developing world. Notable examples include the tropical rain forests, ecologically precious wetlands and mountain regions, and many of the world's endangered species. If conservation and the sustainable use of resources can be shown to be of economic value, then the dialogue of developer and conservationist may be viewed differently, not as one of necessary opposites, but of potential complements or alternative land uses that compete on an equal footing. The remaining stage rests on finding ways for the developing world to capture or appropriate the conservation benefits. If environmentalists in rich countries perceive value in conserving a rain forest in a poor country, this is of little consequence to the poor country unless there is a potential cash flow or technology transfer to be obtained. Economic valuation is therefore a two-part process in which it is necessary to demonstrate and measure the economic value of environmental assets – what we will call the *demonstration process*, and to find ways to capture the value – the *appropriation process*.

Total economic value

The economic value of environmental assets can be broken down into a set of component parts. This can be illustrated in the context of decisions about alternative land uses for a tropical forest, but the example can be generalized. Tropical forests are very rich repositories of biological diversity and the loss of such forests is perhaps the major threat to the world's biodiversity.

According to a benefit-cost rule, decisions to 'convert' a tropical forest, for say agricultural development, would have to be justified by showing that the net benefits from agriculture exceed the net benefits from 'conservation'. Conservation could have two dimensions: preservation which would be formally equivalent to outright non-use of the resource, and conservation which would involve limited uses of the forest consistent with retention of natural forest. The definitions are necessarily imprecise. Some people would argue, for example, that 'ecotourism' is not consistent with sustainable conservation, others that it may be. Accepting the lack of precise lines of differentiation, the benefit–cost rule would be to convert the forest land only if the development benefits minus the development costs are greater than the benefits of conservation minus the costs of conservation.

Typically, the benefits and costs accruing to the converted land use can be fairly readily calculated because there are attendant cash flows. Timber production, for example, tends to be for commercial markets and market prices are observable. Conservation benefits, on the other hand, are a mix of associated cash flows and 'non-market' benefits. This fact imparts two biases. The first is that the components with associated cash flows are made to appear more 'real' than those without such cash flows. There is 'misplaced concreteness': decisions are likely to be biased in favour of the development option because conservation benefits are not readily calculable. The second bias follows from the first. Unless incentives are devised whereby the non-market benefits are 'internalized' into the land use choice mechanism, conservation benefits will automatically be downgraded. Those who stand to gain from, say, timber extraction or agricultural clearance cannot consume the non-marketed benefits. This 'asymmetry of values' imparts a considerable bias in favour of the land use conversion option. These non-market benefits also have two spatial dimensions: benefits *within* the nation that possesses the resource, and benefits to other nations. Thus, the benefits of the tropical forest in nation A include such things as the watershed protection functions that forest may have. The benefits to country B of A's forest includes the contribution that the forest makes to global climate stability, and the benefits reflected in B's willingness to pay to conserve the forest habitat because of its biodiversity. These different spatial benefits may be referred to as *domestic* (or 'host country') benefits, and *global* benefits respectively.

Biodiversity conservation has a *total economic value*. Total economic value (TEV) for a tropical forest is explained in Box 4.1. TEV comprises use and non-use values. Conservation is consistent with some sustainable uses of the forest, including sustainable timber harvesting. *Direct use values* are fairly straightforward in concept but are not necessarily easy to measure in economic terms. Thus minor forest products output (nuts, rattan, latex etc.) should be measurable from market and survey data, but the value of medicinal plants for the world at large is more difficult to measure, although estimates exist.

Indirect use values correspond to the ecologist's concept of 'ecological functions'. A tropical forest might help protect watersheds, for example, so that removing forest cover may result in water pollution, siltation, floods and droughts, depending on the alternative use to which the forest land is put. Similarly, tropical forests 'store' carbon

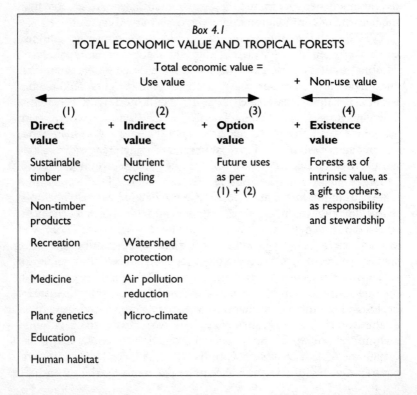

Box 4.1
TOTAL ECONOMIC VALUE AND TROPICAL FORESTS

Total economic value =
Use value   +   Non-use value

(1) **Direct value**	+	(2) **Indirect value**	+	(3) **Option value**	+	(4) **Existence value**
Sustainable timber		Nutrient cycling		Future uses as per (1) + (2)		Forests as of intrinsic value, as a gift to others, as responsibility and stewardship
Non-timber products						
Recreation		Watershed protection				
Medicine		Air pollution reduction				
Plant genetics		Micro-climate				
Education						
Human habitat						

dioxide. When they are burned for clearance much of the stored CO_2 is released into the atmosphere, contributing to greenhouse gas atmospheric warming. Tropical forests also store many species which in turn may have a wide range of ecological functions.

Option values relate to the amount that individuals would be willing to pay to conserve a tropical forest for possible future use. That is, no use is made of it now but use may be made of it in the future. Option value is thus like an insurance premium to ensure the supply of something the availability of which would otherwise be uncertain. While there can be no presumption that option value is positive, it is likely to be so in the context where the resource is in demand for its environmental qualities and its supply is threatened by deforestation. The significance of genetic diversity is often highlighted with reference to global agriculture and food security. This stresses the reliance of the majority of the world's human population on a small number of staple food species, which in turn rely on supply of genes from their wild relatives to supply new characteristics, for example to improve resistance to pests and diseases. Reductions in diversity threaten this process, making the risks of 'homogenization' significant, risks that may ultimately cause major food supply losses. Economists describe the process of increasing security against such losses as the 'portfolio effect': it is no different to saving financial assets by spreading holdings across different types of asset. One of the signs of the dangers of reducing diversity is the fact that, while average crops yields in the world have generally risen, their variability has also increased, i.e. the extent to which there are fluctuations around the average. Much of this variability appears to be due to the fact that the same crop is grown in different regions, often using the same cultivation techniques. An adverse effect on the crop in region A therefore tends to show up also in area B. Maintaining diversity can therefore be seen as a form of insurance against the dangers inherent in the variability that seems to come with reducing diversity. Such insurance measures may be at the expense of average yields, but they are consistent with sustainability. One implication of this insurance argument is that there should at least be a concerted effort to conserve the species most closely linked to existing species on which human beings depend for their food sources.

Existence value relates to valuations of the environmental asset unrelated either to current or optional use. Its intuitive basis is easy to understand because a great many people reveal their willingness to pay for the existence of environmental assets through wildlife and other environmental charities but without taking part in the direct use of the wildlife through recreation. To some extent, this willingness to pay may represent 'vicarious' consumption, i.e. consumption of wildlife videos and TV programmes, but studies suggest that this is a weak explanation for existence value. Empirical measures of existence value, obtained through questionnaire approaches (the contingent valuation method), suggest that existence value can be a substantial component of total economic value. This finding is even more pronounced where the asset is unique, suggesting high potential existence values for unique ecosystems. Some analysts like to add *bequest value* as a separate category of economic value. Others regard it as part of existence value. In empirical terms it would be hard to differentiate them.

Total economic value can be expressed as:

$$\text{TEV} = \text{direct use value} + \text{indirect use value} + \text{option value} + \text{existence value}$$

How useful this classification is in practice is debated. Most contingent valuation studies distinguish use values from 'non-use' values, but do not attempt to break down the component parts of non-use value (or 'passive use' value, as the recent literature calls it). Others deny that existence value is relevant to economic valuation since it may be representing 'counter-preferential' values, values based on moral concern, obligation, duty, altruism, etc. But if we take the purpose of measurement to be one of demonstrating economic value, however it is motivated, many of these problems disappear. Nonetheless, it is as well to be aware that the underlying principles and procedures for economic valuation are still debated.

MEASURING TOTAL ECONOMIC VALUE

A significant amount of research has built up on the actual size of total economic value, much of it in the tropical forest context. This research has estimated both use and non-use values. Since the previous discussion suggested that the non-use values may be very important, empirical estimates of non-use values are explained a little further here.

Non-use values

Recall that non-use values relate to positive willingness to pay even if the individual expressing the valuation makes no use of the resource and has no intention of making use of it. There is a presumption, which needs to be tested however, that non-use values for biological diversity will be highest when expressed by individuals in rich countries. In the tropical forest context, then, we seek rich people's willingness to pay to conserve tropical forests. 'Global valuations' of this kind are still few and far between. Box 4.2 assembles the results of some CVMs in several countries. These report willingness to pay for species and habitat conservation in the respondents' own country. These studies remain controversial. In the context of tropical forests and biological diversity this controversy has some justification. In particular, 'embedding' – the problem of valuing a specific asset rather than the general context of which the asset is part – is bound to be a major problem for assets that are remote from respondents or jointly produced with other assets (e.g. species within prized habitats). While we cannot say that similar kinds of expressed values will arise for

---

Box 4.2
PREFERENCE VALUATIONS FOR ENDANGERED SPECIES AND HABITATS
($US 1990 p.a. per person)

Species

Norway:	brown bear, wolf and wolverine	15.0
USA:	bald eagle	12.4
	emerald shiner	4.5
	grizzly bear	18.5
	bighorn sheep	8.6
	whooping crane	1.2
	blue whale	9.3
	bottlenose dolphin	7.0
	California sea otter	8.1
	northern elephant seal	8.1
	humpback whales[1]	40–48 (without information)
		49–64 (with information)

Other habitat

USA:	Grand Canyon (visibility)	27.0
	Colorado wilderness	9.3–21.2
Australia:	Nadgee Nature Reserve NSW	28.1
	Kakadu Conservation Zone NT[2]	40.0 (minor damage)
		93.0 (major damage)
UK:	nature reserves[3]	40.0 ('experts' only)
Norway:	conservation of rivers against hydroelectric development	59.0–107.0

1 Respondents divided into two groups, one of which was given video information.
2 Two scenarios of mining development damage were given to respondents.
3 Survey of informed individuals only.

Source: Pearce, 1993.

protection of biodiversity in other countries, even a benchmark figure of, say, $10 p.a. for the rich countries of Europe and North America would produce a fund of $4 billion p.a., around four times the mooted size of the fund that will be available to the Global Environment Facility in its operational phase as the financial mechanism under the two Rio Conventions and its continuing role in capturing global values from the international waters context, and perhaps 10 times what the Fund will have available for helping with biodiversity conservation under the Rio Convention. Clearly, a focal point for biodiversity conservation must be the conservation of tropical forests.

Box 4.3 looks at possible *implicit* prices in debt-for-nature swaps.

Box 4.3
IMPLICIT GLOBAL WILLINGNESS TO PAY IN DEBT-FOR-NATURE SWAPS

Country	Date	Payment (1990$)	Area (mha)	WTP/ha (1990$)	Notes
Bolivia	8/87	112,000	12.00	0.01	1
Ecuador	12/87	354,000⎫	22.00	0.06	2
	4/89	1,068,750⎭			
Costa Rica:					
	2/88	918,000	1.15	0.80	3
	7/88	5,000,000			
4 parks	1/89	784,000			
	4/89	3,500,000	0.81	4.32	4
La Amistad	3/90	1,953,473	1.40	1.40	5
Monteverde	1/91	360,000	0.014	25.70	6
Dominican R.	3/90	116,400			
Guatemala	10/91	75,000			
Jamaica	11/91	300,000			
Philippines	1/89	200,000⎫	9.86	0.06	7
	8/90	438,750⎭			
	2/92	5,000,000			
Madagascar	7/89	950,000⎫	0.47	2.95	8
	8/90	445,891⎭			
	1/91	59,377			9
Mexico	2/91	180,000			
Nigeria	7/91	64,788			
Zambia	8/89	454,000			10
Poland	1/90	11,500	unrelated to area purchase		
Nigeria	1989	1,060,000	1.84	0.58	11

Source: Pearce and Moran, 1994

Notes
A discount rate of 6 per cent is used, together with a time horizon of ten years. The sum of discount factors for ten years is then 7.36.

1   The Beni 'park' is 334,000 acres and the surrounding buffer zones are some 3.7 million acres, making 1.63 million *hectares* in all (1 hectare = 2.47 acres). 1.63 × 7.36 = 12 million hectares in present value terms.

2   Covers 6 areas: Cayembe Coca Reserve at 403,000 ha; Cotacachi-Cayapas at 204,000 ha; Sangay National park at 370,000 ha; Podocarpus National park at 146,280 ha; Cuyabeno Wildlife Reserve at 254,760 ha; Yasuni National Park – no area stated; Galapagos National park at 691,2000 ha; Pasochoa near Quito at 800 ha. The total without Yasuni is therefore 2.07 m.ha. Inspection of maps suggests that Yasuni is about three times the area of Sangay, say 1 m.ha. This would make the grand total some 3 m.ha. The present value of this over ten years is then 22 m.ha. This is more than twice the comparable figure quoted in Ruitenbeek (1992).

3   Covers Corvocado at 41,788 ha; Guanacaste at 110,000 ha; Monteverde Cloud forest at 3,600 ha, to give 156,600 ha in all, or a present value of land area of 1.15 m. ha. Initially, $5.4 million at face value, purchased for $912,000, revalued here to 1990 prices.

4   Guanacaste at 110,000 ha, to give a present value of 0.81 m.ha.

5   La Amistad at 190,000 ha, to give a present value of 1.4 m.ha.

6   Monteverde Cloud Forest at 2023 ha × 7.36 = 14,900 ha.

7   Area 'protected' is 5753 ha of St Paul Subterranean River National Park, and 1.33 m ha of El Nido National Marine Park. This gives a present value of land of 9.86 m.ha.

8   Focus on Adringitra and Marojejy reserves at 31,160 ha and 60,150 ha respectively. This gives a present value of 474,000 ha.

9   Covers 4 reserve areas: Zahamena, Midongy-Sud, Manongarivo and Namoroko.

10 Covers Kafue Flats and Bangweulu wetlands.

11 Oban park, protecting 250,000 ha or 1.84 m. ha in present value terms. See Ruitenbeek (1992).

Debt-for-nature swaps involve an organisation, often a conservation organisation in a rich country, buying up some of the foreign debt of an indebted developing country. This can be done by buying the debt, which is often very heavily discounted relative to its face value, in secondary debt markets. The debt is then offered back to the developing country in return for an agreement to conserve some environmental asset, e.g. a tropical forest. There are many variants of debt-for-nature swaps, but many involve conversion of the foreign debt from being denominated in hard foreign currency, to domestic currency. The proceeds of this domestic currency asset are then allocated to a local conservation agency or NGO. There is a sense then in which debt-for-nature swaps 'reveal' the rich nations' willingness to pay for conservation in developing countries. How far the procedure of estimating implicit prices of this kind is open to doubt, although it has been used by some writers – see Ruitenbeek (1992) and Pearce and Moran (1994). Numerous debt-for-nature swaps have been agreed.

Box 4.3 sets out the available information and computes the implicit prices. It is not possible to be precise with respect to the implicit prices since the swaps tend to cover not just protected areas but education and training as well. Moreover, each hectare of land does not secure the same degree of 'protection' and the same area may be covered by different swaps. We have also arbitrarily chosen a ten-year horizon in order to compute present values whereas the swaps in practice have variable levels of annual commitment.

Ignoring the outlier (Monteverde Cloud Forest, Costa Rica) the range of implicit values is from around $0.01 to just over $4 per hectare. Ruitenbeek (1992) secures a range of some $0.18 to $11 per hectare (ignoring Monteverde) but he has several different areas for some of the swaps and he also computes a present value of outlays for the swaps. But either range is very small compared to the opportunity costs of protected land, although if these implicit prices mean anything they are capturing only part of the rich world's existence values for these assets. That is, the values reflect only part of the total economic value.

Finding a benchmark from such an analysis is hazardous but something of the order of $5/ha may be appropriate. If so, these implicit existence values will not save the tropical forests. On the other hand, debt-for-nature swaps clearly involve many 'free riders' since the good in question is a pure public good and the payment mechanism is confined to a limited group (see the discussion in Chapter 1). Looked at another way, $5 per ha p.a. for saving say 25 per cent of the world's remaining closed tropical forests would amount to a fund of 780m ha × $5 × 0.25 = $1 billion p.a.

Inter-country valuation exercises are few. Kramer *et al.* (1994) reports average WTP of US citizens for protection of an additional 5 per cent of the world's tropical forests. One-off payments amounted to $29–51 per US household, or $2.6–4.6 billion. If this WTP was extended to all OECD households, and ignoring income differences, a broad order of magnitude would be a one-off payment of $11–23 billion. Annuitized, this would be, say, $1.1–2.3 billion p.a.

All these 'global' estimates are very crude, heroic even, but it is interesting to note that the hypothetical payments are not wildly divergent:

Valuation method	$ billion per year
Implied WTP (GEF)	$0.4
Implied WTP (DfN)	$1.0
Like assets approach	$4.0
Global CVM	$1.1–2.3

The disturbing feature of the valuations from the conservationist standpoint is that the world has effectively decided on its *actual* WTP for biodiversity conservation through the Global Environment Facility, and that actual WTP is markedly lower than the hypothetical WTP of the other estimates.

Carbon storage

All forests store carbon so that, if cleared for agriculture there will be a release of carbon dioxide which will contribute to the accelerated greenhouse effect and hence global warming. In order to derive a value for the 'carbon credit' that should be ascribed to a tropical forest, we need to know (a) the net carbon released when forests are converted to other uses, and (b) the economic value of one tonne of carbon released to the atmosphere.

Carbon will be released at different rates according to the method of clearance and subsequent land use. With burning there will be an immediate release of CO_2 into the atmosphere, and some of the remaining carbon will be locked in ash and charcoal which is resistant to decay. The slash not converted by fire into CO_2 or charcoal and ash decays over time, releasing most of its carbon to the atmosphere within 10–20 years. Studies of tropical forests indicate that significant amounts of cleared vegetation become lumber, slash, charcoal and ash. The proportion differs for closed and open forests; the smaller stature and drier climate of open forests result in the combustion of higher proportion of the vegetation.

If tropical forested land is converted to pasture or permanent agriculture, then the amount of carbon stored in secondary vegetation is equivalent to the carbon content of the biomass of crops planted, or the grass grown on the pasture. If a secondary forest is allowed to grow, then carbon will accumulate, and maximum biomass density is attained after a relatively short time.

Box 4.4 illustrates the net carbon storage effects of land use conversion from tropical forests; closed primary, closed secondary, or open forests; to shifting cultivation, permanent agriculture, or pasture.

Box 4.4
CHANGES IN CARBON WITH LAND USE CONVERSION (tC/ha)

	Original carbon	Shifting agriculture	Permanent agriculture	Pasture
Original carbon		79	63	63
Closed primary	283	−204	−220	−220
Closed secondary	194	−106	−152	−122
Open forest	115	−36	−52	−52

Shifting agriculture represents carbon in biomass and soils in second year of shifting cultivation cycle.

Source: Brown and Pearce (1994)

The negative figures represent emissions of carbon; for example, conversion from closed primary forest to shifting agriculture results in a net loss of 194tC/ha. The greatest loss of carbon involves change of land use from primary closed forest to permanent agriculture. These figures represent the once and for all change that will occur in carbon storage as a result of the various land use conversions.

The data suggest that, allowing for the carbon fixed by subsequent land uses, carbon released from deforestation of secondary and primary tropical forest is of the order of 100–200 tonnes of carbon per hectare.

The carbon released from burning tropical forests contributes to global warming, and we now have several estimates of the minimum economic damage done by global warming, leaving aside catastrophic events. Recent work suggests a 'central' value of $20 of damage for every tonne of carbon released (Fankhauser and Pearce, 1994). Applying this figure to the data in Box 4.4, we can conclude that converting an open forest to agriculture or pasture would result in global warming damage of, say, $600–1000 per hectare; conversion of closed secondary forest would cause damage of $2000–3000 per hectare; and conversion of primary forest to agriculture would give rise to damage of about $4000–4400 per hectare. Note that these estimates allow for carbon fixation in the subsequent land use.

How do these estimates relate to the development benefits of land use conversion? We can illustrate with respect to the Amazon region of Brazil. Schneider (1992) reports upper bound values of $300 per hectare for land in Rondonia, although much land exchanges hands for even less than this. The figures suggest carbon credit values 2–15 times the price of land in Rondonia. These 'carbon credits' also compare favourably with the value of forest land for timber in, say Indonesia, where estimates are of the order of $1000–2000 per hectare. All this suggests the scope for a global bargain. The land is worth $300 per hectare to the forest colonist but several times this to the world at large. If the North can transfer a sum of money greater than $300 but less than the damage cost from global warming, there are mutual gains to be obtained.

Note that if the transfers did take place at, say, $500 per hectare, then the cost per tonne of carbon reduced is of the order of $5/tC ($500/100 tC/ha). These unit costs compare favourably with those to be achieved by carbon emission reduction policies through fossil fuel conversion. Avoiding deforestation becomes a legitimate and potentially important means of reducing global warming rates.

Box 4.5 brings together some of the studies that have attempted to compare local and global benefits. They are necessarily incomplete, but they still suggest that global values, especially carbon storage, dominate local values. Non-timber products could be important, however.

The economic valuation of forest functions is still in its infancy. Notable weaknesses in the current state of knowledge include, above all, our limited idea of global non-use values. But even on the basis of what we have, some lessons are beginning to emerge. The dominant of these is that global values may well dominate local values. If true, the implication is that imaginative schemes for international transfers will be needed to supplement (a) the correction of local market failures, and (b) domestic distortionary policies which contribute to deforestation. A further, more hazardous, implication is that reliance on some of the global and local use values, such as the potential for pharmaceutical plants, to justify conservation, could be misplaced. Those values may not be large enough to correct the unbalanced playing field between conservation and development. If the focus does shift to global values – which is the focus of the Global Environment Facility – then there is at least one major risk and at least one challenge.

The risk is that the threat of global warming will disappear as the science of global warming improves. If that risk is removed, that can only be good news for the global community and even better news for those countries at particular risk from, e.g. sea level rise. But it will be bad news for the tropical forests since the evidence suggests that global carbon store values are of enormous importance for the tropical forests. Ironically, the good news, if it comes, is offset by the bad news for forests.

Box 4.5
COMPARING LOCAL AND GLOBAL CONSERVATION VALUES (US$/ha)

	Mexico (Pearce *et al.* 1993)	Costa Rica (World Bank, 1992b) (carbon values adjusted)	Indonesia (World Bank, 1993) (carbon values adjusted)	Malaysia (World Bank, 1991)	Peninsular Malaysia (Kumari, 1994)
Timber	–	1240	1000–2000	4075	1024
Non-timber products	775	–	38–125	325–1238	96–487
Carbon storage	650–3400	3046	1827–3654	1015–2709	2449
Pharmaceutical	1–90	2	–	–	1–103
Ecotourism/ recreation	8	209	–	–	13–35
Watershed protection	<1	–	–	–	–
Option value	80	–	–	–	–
Non-use value	15	–	–	–	–

Notes and Sources: adapted from Kumari (1994) but with additional material and some changed conversions. All values are present values at 8 per cent discount rate, but carbon values are at 3 per cent discount rate. Uniform damage estimates of $20.3tC have been used (Fankhauser and Pearce, 1994), so that original carbon damage estimates in the World Bank studies have been re-estimated.

IS TOTAL ECONOMIC VALUE REALLY TOTAL?

It is tempting to think that economists have captured all there is to know about economic value in the concept of TEV. But this is obviously not correct. Economists are not claiming to have captured all values, only economic values. The issue of *intrinsic values* remains. Second, many ecologists say that total economic value is still not the whole economic story. There are some underlying functions of ecological systems which are prior to the ecological functions that we have been discussing (watershed protection etc.). Turner (1992) calls them 'primary values'. They are essentially the system characteristics upon which all ecological functions are contingent. There cannot be a watershed protection function but for the underlying value of the system as a whole. There is, in some sense, a 'glue' that holds everything together and that glue has economic value. If this is true, then there is a total value to an ecosystem or ecological process which exceeds the sum of the values of the individual functions.

The discussion suggests three reasons why biological diversity is important. The first reason is based on the concept of economic value. If biodiversity is economically important we would expect this to show up in *expressed willingness to pay for its conservation*. The evidence suggests that this is indeed the case. The second reason is that economic value measurement will understate 'true' economic value because of the probable failure to measure *primary life support functions*. This kind of economic value is difficult to observe because it is unlikely to be recognized until some disastrous event has happened: landslides consequent upon deforestation, loss of fishing grounds due to pollution, and so on. The third reason is that economic value does not capture – nor is it designed to capture – *intrinsic value*. What can be said about intrinsic values?

First, through existence value it may well be that some measures of individuals' preferences will capture at least part of what is being called intrinsic value. This will be so if the people expressing values for the environmental change in question themselves possess some concept of the intrinsic value of things. They may then be partly valuing 'on behalf' of the environment as an entity in itself.

Second, even if intrinsic values are thought to be wholly separate from economic values because they are not values 'of' human beings, but of and 'in' the environmental assets themselves, there are problems in using intrinsic value arguments to save biological diversity. The problem that arises is that intrinsic value is difficult to relate to real-world choices. On one view, for example, it translates to environmental assets having a 'right' to exist. On this rights-based approach, non-human biota, and sometimes even non-sentient things, should be conserved regardless of the costs associated with conservation. This contrasts with the approach discussed above which is based on 'trade-offs' between cost and conservation. Conservation is pursued up to some point where the costs of conservation are thought to be 'too high'. There are divergent views as to how this trade-off is to be made. In particular, there are those who favour a balancing of economically valued costs and benefits, and there are those who favour leaving the trade-off to the political system. This categorization is not meant to be all-encompassing.

One of the problems with this values debate is that much of the discussion takes place quite independently of the real-world context of environmental change. Whilst abstract discussion and 'philosophizing' must always be central to scientific advance, its divorce from the context of actual choice risks making it of limited relevance in the policy arena. To see this, consider the question of why the loss of environmental assets indicated above has been so substantial and so fast. As Chapter 5 will show, the major cause of such losses has been land conversion, i.e. the conversion of land from uses in which biological diversity could remain relatively abundant, to uses where biodiversity is lost. The most common land conversion is to agriculture. The cost of conservation is therefore the loss of the stream of benefits to the agriculturist, i.e. his or her income. Without question, a great deal of land conversion can be shown to create no net financial gain when proper accounting methods are employed, but a lot of it does. Unless there is an appreciation of the driving forces for this land conversion, conservation stands no chance of succeeding. Population growth and poor government policies that encourage land conversion do much to explain those driving forces But if the cost of conservation is someone's income and wealth, and if that person is often (though by no means always) already poor, the 'conservation at all costs' approach, as typified by a rigid rights approach, implies no recognition of rights to a livelihood for the poor. In other words, rights approaches can easily be elitist and in conflict with other, equally 'reasonable' human rights. Much of the popularity of the rights approach arises from an understandable sense of frustration with the fact that trade-off approaches do involve 'acceptance' of some environmental loss. But it also has its foundations in a formidable lack of appreciation of what 'cost' actually means, a perception fostered by the view that cost is 'just money', as if money is unrepresentative of human wellbeing.

The unreality of the rights approach does not mean that rights are irrelevant. Environmental rights are clearly not absolute. They are relative to other rights and their superiority would require some meta-ethical principle which, of course, many 'deep ecologists' espouse. The argument here is that the deep ecological view fails to acknowledge the reality of rights conflicts because it fails to identify just what moral absolutism entails in the real world.

But if the rights-based approach has huge problems of impracticality and inconsistency, the economic approach is not without its problems either.

Relying on human preferences

The economic approach operates with human preferences. Humans are often poorly informed about the environment and the result of this poor information is that they will make choices which they may later regret, or which impose costs on others. There is indeed a problem here but it is far from being as serious as the critics make out.

First, no one would argue that valuation is appropriate in all cases and all circumstances. If that were true, then society would not override human preferences for drugs, alcohol and tobacco, or even for education (or the lack of it). Rather the presumption should be that economic valuation is the relevant approach unless there are good reasons for supposing otherwise. One of those reasons, as is widely recognized, is that the environmental asset in question is significantly 'distant' from individuals' familiarity and experience (Freeman, 1986; Vatn and Bromley, 1994). While this qualification applies to stated preference techniques, such as contingent valuation, it is far from clear that it applies to other procedures involving dose-response functions – see below. Information is also important for valuing market goods as well. Where information is deficient, for example with infrequent purchases such as housing, information markets emerge. To some extent, contingent valuation functions in this way – it supplies information to the respondent. In that respect it could be held to be superior to inferred valuations from behaviour in other markets, such as travel expenditures. This suggests that economic valuation will function more successfully the better the information. But lack of information is not an argument for rejecting WTP approaches. It is an argument for better information.

Second, information is often available for environmental goods and is no worse than it is for other goods and services for which preferences are allowed to determine resource allocation.

Third, where information is sparse, it can be supplied, as it often is in contingent valuation studies for example.

Fourth, some economic valuation techniques quite explicitly adopt 'expert' assessments in determining the quantity of the environmental attribute to be valued. The most widely used valuation technique for example is that based on estimating dose-response functions and then using market or quasi-market prices to value the effect. The dose-response function itself is not determined by human assessment: it is determined by scientific evidence linking, say, doses of pollution to health effects etc. But the basic distinction between a preference-based approach and an 'expert assessment' approach is that the actual values of the outcomes, whether they are states of human health or improved landscapes, reflect the values of those affected by the change in the state of nature. The role of experts is confined to conveying information. The 'lack of information' critique arises in part from over-concentration on techniques that appear to exclude the role of expert assessment.

A more basic criticism is that human wellbeing as interpreted in economics is not relevant at all, i.e. social decisions should not be based on economic wellbeing:

The question we must ask is whether 'welfare' has anything to do with happiness, well-being, or any goal that appeals to common sense, morality, law or culture.

(Sagoff, 1993)

This is a curious view even in a rich-world context. In a poor-world context it looks decidedly obscure. It argues that 'quality' of desires is more important than 'desires' per se. The danger in such a view is that it quickly becomes elitist. A declares B's preferences to be of 'low quality' and therefore inadmissible. A knows better and best. Yet the appropriate strategy in a world where quality of desires matters is education and persuasion. It cannot be the disenfranchisement of the illiterate and the non-aesthetes because they do not qualify as having the 'right' desires.

The environment as 'public good'

Chapter 1 discussed the fact that much environmental conservation could well be a public good. This means that its provision for any one person entails its provision for everyone else ('joint supply') and that it will generally be difficult to exclude others by some pricing mechanism (non-exclusion). In this respect, clean air has similarities with defence and public information. But this difference is not a reason for ignoring public preferences for the provision of environmental assets: it is an argument for being very careful to account for the pitfalls in finding out what those preferences are. This is exactly what economic valuation techniques are concerned with, and notably so in respect of the so-called 'free rider' problem in which people allegedly understate their preferences for such goods. There is in fact not much evidence for such 'strategic bias' in economic valuation, but even if there were it would be an argument for improving techniques to avoid it, not for ignoring preferences altogether.

Standards as social agreements

Another criticism of valuation is that it simply is not needed as a separate exercise. Society 'agrees' a set of environmental standards. The cost of achieving those standards is then society's valuation of the standard. It is of course possible to devise a social decision-making model in which the decisions made do reflect some sort of consensus of preferences of those affected. In such cases, the marginal cost of meeting the resulting standard might be thought to be an implicit social valuation of the standard. But how that implicit valuation is interpreted is important. The cost of achieving the standard is not an explicit social valuation of the standard. If it was, then all standards would have benefit-cost ratios of one or above. This is because the benefit of achieving the standard must be at least equal to the cost of achieving it since the latter is used to measure the former. From this it follows that all standards must be for the best. There can be no mistakes and hence no need ever to revisit a standard to see if it is justified or not. Whatever is, is for the best. Worse, standards cannot be informed by preferences – they simply emerge. Moreover, if all standards reflected accurate public preferences, there would never be a need for *ex post* assessment of those standards. Yet this is part of the elaborate process of checks and balances built into any democratic system.

Errors in willingness-to-pay estimates

Various arguments have been advanced as to why WTP estimates are error-prone. The first is that sufferers of pollution may not correctly perceive the effects of pollution. But as noted above, this criticism assumes all kinds of falsehoods: (a) that the aim is to 'value everything'; (b) that one cannot inform people before seeking their WTP; (c) that the valuation method itself cannot elicit the 'hidden' effects, whereas, as noted above, dose-response approaches explicitly do this. More insidious is the implication that since people do not know the full effects of something, they cannot be allowed to express preferences for or against that outcome. Decision-making by experts is one alternative and 'political' decision-making another. Yet expert decision-making accounts for a fair number of modern environmental hazards from nuclear waste to CFCs, whilst decision-making by politicians assumes a model of information and decision-making that is at least no better than that for 'uninformed' citizens.

The problem of future generations

Critics of economic valuation are on stronger ground when they argue that the preferences elicited are those of one generation – here and now – and not of future generations. However, even this criticism is far from fatal. It assumes, for example, that generations do not overlap whereas, in practice, they conspicuously do. Overlapping generations produce preference functions in which the interests of future generations are included. One can argue about the weights to be attached to those preferences, but it is absurd to suppose that future preferences count for nothing in WTP measures. Moreover, the issue of weighting reduces to an issue of discounting. Otherwise, if all future generations' preferences were to count equally, generations for thousands of years to come would have to be accommodated. But that is neither feasible nor necessary. There are legitimate disagreements on the 'proper' discount rate, but they do not invalidate using WTP as a measure of economic value.

Citizen versus individual preferences

Another widely countenanced criticism of WTP is that it records individualistic preferences, whereas what matters for social policy are preferences expressed by the individual as citizen, 'citizen's preferences' (Sagoff, 1993). Arguably, citizen's preferences are best elicited in different contexts to those in which WTP is measured. But there are several problems with this view. When asked for my WTP, or when my WTP is inferred from surrogate market behaviour, the motivations for WTP are not easily uncovered. My WTP for an environmental asset may reflect my concern about the asset because I use it, because I want my children to use it, because I want it to exist and have no intention of using it, because I think it is 'right' that it exists, and so on. There is nothing in WTP approaches *per se* that requires the expressed valuation to reflect one particular motive – any or all motives may be present. As it happens, some attempts have been made to uncover motivation for preferences for environmental assets. This is how the differentiation between use and non-use values has come about, the latter relating to WTP unassociated with any use of the asset or intention to use it. WTP for non-use may well capture so-called 'ethical' preferences, as discussed above. The essential point is that the contrast between citizen and individualistic preferences may be valid, but it has no implications in terms of the validity of WTP measures. The presumption that moral judgements and 'commitment' somehow render WTP illicit can only be relevant if commitment and morality cannot enter into expressions of preference. They are tautologically counter-preferential in the sense of being inconsistent with the preferences that would be expressed if commitment did not exist. But that is quite different to saying they cannot be indicated by WTP, as 'commitment payments' to conservation organisations testify.

However, this defence is open to one further criticism. If any kind of motive is consistent with WTP, and if revealed choice is the manifestation of preference, how can I tell if someone really prefers what they say they prefer? This is Sagoff's criticism (Sagoff, 1993), but it again seems to rest on a basic illogicality. If we knew what people's 'true' preferences were, it would not be necessary to infer those preferences by looking at choices as the revelation of those preferences. In other words, the criticism implies some world of 'true' preferences, perhaps even distinguished by motive, against which recorded, inferred or stated preferences can be measured. But the inference or statement is all that we have. There is nothing else, and to criticize observations of choice as a means of inferring value is to set up not just an arbitrary benchmark, but a non-observable one.

CONCLUSIONS

The world's 'stock' of biological diversity is clearly threatened. How far that matters depends on what value we attach to the conservation of diversity. Many people argue that the species and ecosystems exhibiting this diversity have intrinsic value and a right to exist independently of the values that humans may express for their conservation. This chapter suggests that while this may be true, the practical relevance of such rights in a real-world context is limited. Where conservation can be demonstrated to involve no trade-offs, the so-called 'win-win' situations, then of course no problem arises. But conservation invariably does involve someone losing, particularly given the main proximate cause of biodiversity loss, namely land conversion. In short, there are trade-offs because there are costs and benefits. Some calculus is needed for expressing those trade-offs, for balancing costs and benefits. That need not be an economic calculus. It could be left to the political system and ultimately, of course, it is the political system that decides. The issue is how those political decisions should be informed. The economic calculus of costs and benefits offers a powerful instrument for recording preferences and aggregating them.

PART II

Explaining resource degradation

◆

Chapter 5

The failure of economic systems

INTRODUCTION

Environmental economics teaches that the causes of many environmental problems lie in the working, or rather the mis-working, of the economic system at the local, national and international level. Basically, economic systems 'fail'. The extent of this failure is measured by the difference between the level of human wellbeing that *could* be achieved and the level that actually is achieved. At the practical level, what could be achieved is a matter of political feasibility. Many sources of economic failure have little to do with the environment, but two in particular do affect the environment in significant ways. The first arises from the fact that environmental goods and services often have no market. These 'missing markets' mean that the environment is treated as if it is a free resource. This is the essence of the open access argument introduced in Chapter 1. If there was ownership of the resource in some form, then the owners would recognize the limited nature of the resource and introduce restrictions on use, including charges for use. The effect of non-ownership is to make the price implicitly being charged zero. And when something is free it is subject to over-use and abuse. This was the main message of *Blueprint for a Green Economy* (Pearce et al., 1989).

The situation is the same with global resources. Indeed, it is far more likely to be the case that global resources are abused because ownership is more complex. It requires, first, that many nations come together and acknowledge the limited nature of the resource, and, second, that they agree on rules for restricted use. Getting nations to agree on these issues is more difficult than getting individuals within a nation to agree. Nations have governments. The world does not have a world government.

In addition to missing markets, economic failure arises because governments intervene in existing markets. This they do often for the most laudable of motives: to protect the poor, improve agricultural output and so on. Sometimes the motives are less responsible and include the protection of specific interest groups, repaying political favours, corruption and sheer greed. Not all intervention is bad for the environment. Environmental regulations are themselves interventions in the workings of the market-place. The issue cannot therefore be one of extensive regulation versus no regulation. It is one of the right balance. One of the interesting discoveries of environmental economics has been that interventions which invariably have no internal *economic justification* also tend to damage the environment. Governments therefore 'fail' as well as markets, and government failure is often a 'double baddy' – it is good for neither the economy nor the environment.

This chapter investigates the sources of economic failure. We do this in the context of biodiversity loss, but the story is a general one.

THE CONVERSION OF LAND

Most loss of biological resources comes about because of land conversion, i.e. a change in use from, say, forest or wetland to agriculture, urban developments, dams, roads and industry. The rate of conversion is illustrated in Box 5.1. There it can be seen that cropland and pasture are increasing at the expense of forested land and, in Asia, 'other' land which includes wetlands and uncultivated land generally. More detail is shown on rates of deforestation. Clearly, what matters is that we understand why the process of land conversion is occurring.

Box 5.1
LAND CONVERSION AND DEFORESTATION

(a) Land conversions 1979/81–1991 (million hectares)

	Cropland	Pasture	Forest	Other	Total
Africa	+9	+8	−26	+11	+1
N. and C. America	−2	+4	+2	−4	0
S. America	+13	+21	−42	+11	+3
Asia	+6	+66	−26	−43	+3
Europe	−2	−3	+1	+4	0

Sums of rows and sums of columns should add to zero, but rounding and data imperfections produce small errors, especially for Asia and South America. The forest column suggests annual loss rates of about 9 million ha p.a., significantly less than the loss rates shown below.

(b) Tropical forest loss

Rates of tropical deforestation in the 1980s
(million hectares p.a.)

	Closed forest			Total forest	
	Late 1970s[1]	Mid-1980s[2]	Late 1980s[3]	1980s	Late 1980s[4]
Number of countries	34				90
S. America	2.7	3.3	6.7	6.8	6.2
C. America and Caribbean	1.0	1.1	1.0	1.6	1.2
Africa	1.0	1.3	1.6	5.0	4.1
Asia	1.8	1.8	4.3	3.6 ⎫	
				⎬	3.9
Oceania	–	–	0.4	– ⎭	
Totals	6.5	14.9	13.9	17.0	15.4
Adjusted total[5]	n.a.	15.3	14.2	–	–
Forest remaining (%)	0.6	n.a.	1.8	0.9	0.9
Assuming forest area (m.ha)			780	1910	1756

Notes and sources

1 Late 1970s data for the 34 countries covered in Myers (see below) from Food and Agriculture Organisation, *Tropical Forest Resources*, Rome 1981.

2 Various years to 1986, taken from World Resources Institute, *World Resources 1992–1993*, Oxford University press, Oxford, 1992, Table 19.1. In turn, the estimates are based on FAO sources, including an update for some countries of the 1981 estimates, and some individual sources. Note that the estimates cover closed forests only.

3 N. Myers, *Deforestation Rates in Tropical Forests and Their Climatic Implications*, Friends of the Earth, London, December 1989. Myers' estimates cover 34 countries accounting for 97.3 per cent of the extent of tropical forest in 1989.

4 Food and Agriculture Organisation, Rome. 1993 estimates.

5 Myers estimates that 40 other countries with small tropical forests suffered deforestation rates totalling 0.36 million ha p.a. in 1989. We have 'grossed up' the World Resources Institute figures by the same factor (14.22/13.86) to ensure comparability.

A GENERAL THEORY OF ECONOMIC FAILURE

[This section may be omitted without loss of continuity, but readers are advised to try and follow it as it encapsulates much of the economic theory of resource degradation generally].

Figure 5.1 summarizes the essence of a theory of economic failure as it affects the environment. The diagram is shown for the context of biodiversity loss, but it is equally applicable to other forms of environmental degradation. The horizontal axis shows the rate of land conversion (left to right) and its functional inverse, the level of biodiversity (increasing from right to left). The land being converted could be wetland being drained for agriculture, tropical forests being cleared for crops or livestock, coastal land being reclaimed, and so on. The curves require some explanation.

$M\pi$ is a marginal private benefit (marginal profit) function showing that marginal profits decline as more land is converted. Marginal here means 'extra', so $M\pi$ is a curve showing the extra profits that come from converting one more unit of land from, say, forest to agriculture. This curve falls as more land is converted due to rising conversion costs as the conversion frontier is spatially extended, and/or declining land productivity as land is developed. This seems to be a reasonable representation of reality since most of the world's land suitable for agriculture is already in use. 'New' land is therefore likely to be of lower productivity. How much land would be converted to agriculture or other developmental uses if the free market ruled? In Figure 5.1 the

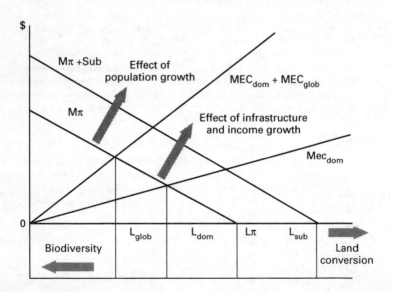

amount would be $L\pi$ because at that point the extra profit from land conversion is zero: it is not worth converting more land because this would involve making losses.

We can immediately illustrate two factors at work that will give rise to even more land conversion, and hence more biodiversity loss. The first is infrastructural developments – especially roads. These will lower conversion costs and raise profit margins, so that $M\pi$ shifts outward. As the curve shifts outwards in the direction of the arrows shown, so more land will be converted. A second factor that will move this curve outward is population growth: as populations grow so the demand for food will rise, and this will make converting the land to agriculture more profitable. Finally, as incomes grow there may also be pressure to increase land conversion. The effect of income growth is to raise agricultural prices making it more profitable to convert land. Figure 5.1 is therefore fairly static in concept, but we see immediately that some of the factors explaining land conversion can be illustrated in the diagram.

Land conversion imposes 'local' externalities, especially where the conversion is from tropical forest to agriculture. These costs are fairly well documented and consist of the deleterious effects of soil erosion, loss of local biodiversity and so on. In Figure 5.1 these are shown as MEC_{dom}. Again, the curve is shown in marginal terms, i.e. MEC_{dom} shows the extra damage being done because of the land conversion. How do these local damages affect the outcome? If free markets rule, the answer is that they are irrelevant because the individual converting the land has no incentive to take account of them. They are 'non-market' effects, costs borne by other people. But it is easy to see that, by ignoring these effects, the nation in question is not as well off as it would be if they were taken into account. This national wellbeing can be measured by the areas under each curve. (Areas under marginal curves give us the total value of the cost or benefit.) The largest net area, i.e. the area under $M\pi$ minus the area under MEC_{dom}, is achieved at L_{dom}, which involves less land conversion (and hence more biodiversity) than at $L\pi$. If everyone's wellbeing is taken into account, some measure is needed to 'correct' the external effect and reduce the amount of land conversion. Ways in which this can be achieved are considered in Part III.

But there are other externalities involved, since individuals outside the national territory suffer some of the consequences of deforestation: scientific knowledge is lost, as is any 'existence' or 'passive use' value. To the local externality, then, must be added a rest-of-the-world externality or MEC_{glob}. The total externality is therefore $MEC_{dom} + MEC_{glob}$, and the 'global optimum' is L_{glob}. To establish this, simply measure again the areas under the relevant curves. The maximum area under $M\pi$ minus the area under $MEC_{dom} + MEC_{glob}$ is at L_{glob}. If it is possible to 'capture' the global externality, then less land conversion takes place and more biodiversity is 'saved'. Chapter 4 already showed the potential for a bargain between rich and poor countries over carbon storage in forests. Such a bargain would therefore be an example of creating a market where none existed before.

Finally, land use is rarely left to market forces: government intervention is the rule not the exception. Such interventions often have deleterious environmental consequences due to the artificial encouragement of deforestation. The most widely studied interventions are subsidies to livestock, credit and land clearance generally, and the under-pricing and under-taxation of logging concessions – see Binswanger (1989), Schneider (1992), Repetto and Gillis (1988). (How far forest pricing *causes* accelerated deforestation through 'excessive' logging is disputed. Repetto and Gillis (1988) and Grut *et al.* (1991) argue that pricing and concession policies create 'rent seeking' activity, i.e. they attract those who seek out profitable opportunities for land conversion, whilst the exchanges between Hyde and Sedjo (1992, 1993) and Vincent (1993) suggest that raising forest taxation will do little for slowing rates of logging).

The result of such policies, which are explicit or implicit subsidies to land conversion, is to shift $M\pi$ outwards to $M\pi+\text{Sub}$, raising the level of land conversion that is 'optimal' from the point of view of the converter of land to L_{sub}. But L_{sub} is clearly further away still from the socially justified level of land conversion at L_{glob}.

The relevance of Figure 5.1, beyond being a didactic device, is that it shows that many forms of 'failure' can be present at one and the same time. Indeed, the forms of imperfection are:

$L - L_{sub}$ = intervention or government failure
$L_{dom} - L_{\pi}$ = local market failure
$L_{glob} - L_{dom}$ = global market failure or 'global appropriation failure'

and these failures may be summed to arrive at the total potential disparity between globally optimal and domestically optimal levels of land conversion.

Some people have argued that these failures represent a failure of 'orthodox' economics. This leads them to seek a 'new' or an 'alternative' economics, although quite what the tenets of this alternative approach are is not very clear. Certainly, economic failures reflect a failure of the way in which economic systems actually work, but that is quite different to saying that economics itself has failed. Economics fails only if it cannot explain environmental degradation comprehensively, and only if it cannot elicit from a causal analysis the measures needed to correct the failures. In practice, there are mechanisms for dealing with all the failures, as Part III shows. In fact, we have a very reasonable idea of why the 'wrong' amount of land conversion occurs, and how to correct it. All that is necessary is the extension of 'orthodox' economics to the global level. The issue is not the failure of orthodox economics, but the practical judgement as to which causes are most important.

LOCAL MARKET FAILURE

'Market failure' means that the interplay of market forces will not secure the economically correct balance of land conversion and land conservation. This is because those who convert the land do not have to compensate those who suffer the local consequences of that conversion – extra pollution and sedimentation of waters from deforestation, for example. The corrective solutions to this problem are well known – a tax on land conversion, zoning to restrict detrimental land uses, environmental standards, and so on. From this it follows that we cannot rely on market forces to save the world's environmental assets as long as those assets are dispensable because of market forces. Notice, however, that the measures needed to correct this market failure do not result in zero land conversion. In the economist's language there is an 'optimal' rate of loss. It is less than what happens now, but it is not zero. This perhaps helps in understanding one of the differences between those who argue on purely 'moral' grounds that environmental degradation is 'wrong' and those who argue that there are 'trade-offs', as discussed in Chapter 4. The moralists would not accept that there is a socially justified level of resource degradation, thus implicitly rejecting any rights to wellbeing of those who derive their wellbeing from the process of land conversion. For the moralist the 'optimum' in Figure 5.1 is at 0.

Panayotou (1993) provides a convenient listing of local market failures:

- ill-defined or non-existent property rights;
- missing markets;
- high transaction costs inhibiting trade in conservation benefits;
- publicness of conservation benefits;
- market imperfections such as monopoly;
- myopia and hence high discount rates;
- uncertainty and risk aversion; and
- irreversibility.

Assessing just how important these factors are is difficult.

Many authors cite *poor or perverse land tenure* as a factor in deforestation. Poor tenure by existing occupants of forest land helps to explain reduced resistance to rival claims from those who wish to clear land. Mahar and Schneider (1994) note that only 11 per cent of Brazilian Amazon land was titled in the early 1980s, creating an essentially 'open access' resource. Perverse land tenure applies when the colonizer has an incentive to clear because clearance is evidence of tenure. Countries where clearance is evidence of land tenure include Costa Rica, Honduras, Panama, Brazil, Ecuador. In Brazil, for example, the land settlement agency still determines the spatial extent of settlement rights by multiplying the cleared area by a factor of three (Mahar and Schneider, 1994). But few of the econometric studies surveyed in Brown and Pearce (1994) tested for land tenure as a factor explaining deforestation. Southgate *et al.*'s (1989) study of Ecuador suggests a strong influence of tenure insecurity on deforestation.

Missing or incomplete local markets are endemic to the tropical forest context. Tropical forests yield many products for which there *are* markets, but the resulting market prices tend to reflect only the opportunity cost of labour and capital, not the true rents of the forest land (Panayotou, 1993). In turn, the effective zero or negligible rents perceived in the market place owe much to the absence of property rights discussed above. Externalities also arise from deforestation, and trades or bargains to reduce them are scarce because of high transaction costs, poor information and the prevailing structure of interests and power. Thus, estuarial fishermen do not bargain with upstream forest colonizers to reduce the effects of sedimentation on fisheries. Yet we know these effects can be important. Hodgson and Dixon (1988) show that a ban on logging upstream of Bacuit Bay, Philippines would have reduced fishery losses from sedimentation by 50 per cent, and would have increased tourist revenues by a factor of four. In Ruitenbeek's study of the Korup rainforest in Cameroon (Ruitenbeek, 1992), over 50 per cent of the direct and indirect use values of the forest were accounted for by downstream fishery benefits. In contrast, and underlining the site-specificity of many of the local benefits, Kumari (1994) found negligible fishery effects in moving from unsustainable to sustainable logging practices in the Selangor forest swamps in Peninsular Malaysia.

Public goods are also endemic to tropical forests. Public goods consist of non-excludable and jointly provided goods and services. Notable local public goods – those where the domain of value is limited to the relevant nation – include watershed protection, micro-climate, and biological diversity. Few of these have been the subject of economic valuation exercises. Pearce *et al.* (1993) estimate only modest watershed benefits from forest conservation in Mexico relative to other values.

Monopolistic markets may well work to the advantage of conservation if the monopoly relates, say, to mineral deposits in the forest area: restrictions on output to maximize profits may well reduce forest destruction compared to the competitive alternative. While Panayotou (1993) cites monopolized informal rural credit markets as a factor working *against* conservation, the effect may well be ambiguous. If smaller farmers cannot secure access to credit at non-inflated prices this may well reduce the incentive to invest in existing land areas compared to the alternative of colonizing new land. Exclusion from normal credit markets easily arises if ownership is a precondition of collateral for credit, as is often the case in agricultural areas (Pearce and Warford, 1993). But cheap credit has also been implicated in deforestation in the Amazon areas, controlled interest rates being an effective subsidy to land clearance. Econometric studies of deforestation have largely ignored credit markets as a factor in explaining deforestation.

Surprisingly little is known about the actual *discount rates* that forest zone farmers exhibit. The effect of a high discount rate is to discriminate against the future because future gains are reduced in value. Cuesta *et al.* (1994) estimate that 80 per cent of farmers in Costa Rica have discount rates in the range 16–21 per cent in real terms. While social discount rates can be of the order of 10 per cent in developing countries, if per capita real consumption growth rates are high, the Costa Rica estimates suggest that private rates may well be at least twice the social rate. Moreover risk and uncertainty arising from insecure land and resource tenure are excluded in the Cuesta *et al.* study because the farmers in question owned their land. Even at these 'tenure-risk-free' discount rates, Cuesta *et al.* conclude that optimal soil conservation measures will not be undertaken without a conservation subsidy.

Overall, the evidence for local market failure is strong. How strong it is relative to other forms of failure remains an issue of judgement.

GOVERNMENT FAILURE

Figure 5.1 showed a second explanation for resource loss: 'intervention failure' or 'government failure' – the deliberate intervention by governments in the working of market forces. The examples are, by now, well known (Pearce and Warford, 1993) and include the subsidies to forest conversion for livestock in Brazil up to the end of the 1980s; the failure to tax logging companies sufficiently, giving them an incentive to expand their activities even further; the encouragement of inefficient domestic wood-processing industries, effectively raising the ratio of logs, and hence deforestation, to wood product, and so on. What intervention does is to distort the competitive playing field. Governments effectively subsidize the rate of return to land conversion, tilting the economic balance against conservation.

Box 5.2 assembles some information on the scale of the distortions that governments introduce. Such distortions are widespread. The general rule in developing countries is for agriculture to be taxed not subsidized, but significant subsidies exist in several major tropical forest countries such as Brazil and Mexico. By comparison, OECD countries are actually worse at subsidizing agriculture. In 1992 OECD

Box 5.2
ECONOMIC DISTORTIONS TO LAND CONVERSION

(a) Agricultural producer subsidies[1]

Mexico	mid-1980s	+53%
Brazil	mid-1980s	+10%
S. Korea	mid-1980s	+55%
S.S.A.	mid-1980s	+9%
OECD	1992	+44%

(b) Timber stumpage fees as percentage of replacement costs[2]

Ethiopia	late 1980s	+23%
Kenya	late 1980s	+14%
Ivory Coast	late 1980s	+13%
Sudan	late 1980s	+4%
Senegal	late 1980s	+2%
Niger	late 1980s	+1%

(c) Timber charges as percentage of total rents

Indonesia	early 1980s	+33%
Philippines	early 1980s	+11%

1 Producer subsidies are measured by the 'Producer Subsidy Equivalent' (PSE) which is defined as the value of all transfers to the agricultural sector in the form of price support to farmers, any direct payments to farmers and any reductions in agricultural input costs through subsidies. These payments are shown here as a percentage of the total value of agricultural production valued at domestic prices.
2 A stumpage fee is the rate charged to logging companies for standing timber. It is expressed here as a percentage of the cost of reforesting (b) and as a percentage of total rents (c).

Sources: Agricultural PSEs: Moreddu et al., 1990; OECD, 1993; stumpage fees: World Bank, 1992; and Repetto and Gillis, 1988.

subsidies exceeded $180 billion (OECD, 1993). These subsidies work in two ways. Subsidies in developing countries will tend to encourage extensification of agriculture into forested area. Subsidies in the developed world make it impossible for the developing world to compete properly on international markets, locking them into primitive agricultural practices. While the removal of OECD country subsidies would appear to be a recipe for expanding land conversion in the developing world to capture the larger market, the demands of a rich overseas market are more likely to result in agricultural intensification and hence reduced pressure on forested land. Box 5.2 also shows that many developing countries fail to tax logging companies adequately, thus generating larger 'rents' for loggers. The larger rents have two effects: they attract more loggers and they encourage existing loggers to expand their concessions and, indeed, to do both by persuading the host countries to give them concessions. Persuasion involves the whole menu of usual mechanisms, including corruption.

GLOBAL APPROPRIATION FAILURE

The final economic failure arises because some of the people who suffer a loss of wellbeing from resource degradation are in different countries. Indeed, in the tropical forest case, many people in many different countries suffer a loss because of tropical deforestation. That loss of wellbeing may simply be a feeling of loss that such beautiful diverse systems as tropical forests are being destroyed, or it may be that there is a scientific interest in what we can learn from such ecosystems. Motives will vary, as the discussion of 'existence value' in Chapter 4 made clear. Chapter 4 also offered some tentative evidence on the scale of this 'global value' and showed that it could be substantial. If so, the failure of the global economic system to establish markets in that value becomes a major factor in explaining resource degradation. Some 'global markets' do exist, as the discussion of debt-for-nature swaps showed. Part III will discuss other ways in which global markets are emerging to appropriate global value.

Chapter 6

International trade and the environment

INTRODUCTION

In recent years some environmentalists have argued that the prevailing international trading system accounts for a significant part of global resource degradation. That system, they argue, is characterized by continuing and extensive protection measures, such as quotas and tariffs on imports, but is being 'liberalized' by various international agreements, especially the various 'trade rounds' under the General Agreement on Tariffs and Trade (the GATT), now superseded by the World Trade Organisation (WTO). It is the liberalization of trade that they object to because they argue that freer trade encourages economic growth which in turn damages the environment. Additionally, free trade encourages countries to specialize in the production of various commodities which may then travel many thousands of miles to their destination, e.g. vegetables and flowers for the European market but grown in east and south African countries, thus using up resources. A more 'self-sufficient' mode of trade would avoid these costs. Finally, the trading system is argued to be biased against the developing countries who have to export their natural resources to markets where resource prices tend to decline through time. To secure a given amount of foreign exchange income, then, the developing counties have to export even more, further reducing their resource base.

This chapter examines these views. Unquestionably, there are environmental problems inherent in the existing trading system. But there is also extensive confusion in the environmentalist critique of freer trade.

THE ISSUES

The basic issues in the environment – trade debate are:

● Free trade is alleged to 'cause' environmental degradation: hence liberalization of trade should be attenuated for environmental reasons. An example might be the trade in tropical hardwoods.

- Protection of domestic markets is said to cause environmental degradation: hence trade liberalization favours the environment. An example might be the Common Agricultural Policy. (This is clearly inconsistent with the point above.)
- It is argued that trade liberalization needs to be attenuated when environmental degradation arises from trade:
  - through imported polluting products (damage is done in the importing country) (the 'uni-directional externality' case);
  - through the *process* of production in the exporting country which may incur damages to the exporting country and the importing country (the 'common property' or 'mutual externality' case).
- It is argued that high environmental standards in an importing country are 'non-tariff barriers' designed to protect the domestic market against potential imports that fail to meet those standards. Hence, all countries should harmonize environmental standards. Since richer countries tend to have higher environmental standards, this is frequently seen as an argument for lowering standards to permit development in poorer countries. On the other hand, countries with low environmental standards might be thought of as giving implicit subsidies to their exports ('ecological dumping') since the costs of environmental degradation are not part of the prices of those exported products. This tends to be an argument for raising environmental standards in poor countries.
- It is argued that other environmental policy instruments, e.g. environmental taxes or subsidies, also distort trade.
- Some international agreements retain trade discrimination as a weapon of compliance. That discrimination is thought by some to be contrary to the principles of the GATT, and hence, presumably, of the new WTO. If so, and if GATT/WTO takes precedence then there are formidable implications for the design and effectiveness of international agreements.

Since the General Agreement on Tariffs and Trade (GATT) and the new WTO have as their aim the mitigation of the forces that give rise to protectionism, all the above issues are relevant to the design of the world trading system and hence to the possibility of its 'reform'. The implications are considered to be (according to the point of view) that:

- a free trade system may result in environmental degradation by refusing to allow environmentally motivated trade restrictions;
- trade restrictions as weapons of compliance for international agreements might be abandoned in the name of free trade.

The GATT was devised at a time when environmental awareness and concern was low. It seems reasonable therefore to take a fresh look at the trade–environment nexus in the context of growing environmental concern. It needs to be stressed that GATT/WTO is not a supra-national authority. It is not independent of governments. It establishes fundamental rules of trade in goods and provides a mechanism for lowering tariffs and some other barriers to trade. As such, the new WTO cannot offer views about environmental goals any more than the old GATT could. It can at best interpret actions by member countries in light of the existing pattern of rights and obligations in the GATT treaty. But the current environmentalist critique of free trade is actually about changing the balance of rights and obligations, i.e. it is about changing the rules of trade.

THE BENEFITS OF FREE TRADE

Free trade tends to be a 'good thing', not as an end in itself but as a means of securing improvements in world living standards. Some efforts have been made to quantify the gains from trade, or, to look at it from another way, the costs of protection. While many studies find such costs run at up to 1 per cent of GNP annually for as long as the protection lasts, there are good reasons for supposing that these estimates understate true losses. This is because the studies are often carried out in a 'partial equilibrium' framework (i.e. they do not account for all the various interactions) and identify immediate production and consumption losses only; and they ignore other forms of inefficiency.

The production loss from protection arises because domestic producers can, with a tariff, produce at costs of production above the true world price. Consumption losses arise because consumers consume less at the new price inclusive of the tariff. Together, these losses comprise what is known as the 'deadweight' loss from protection. However, changes in the prices and quantities of the protected good will affect other prices and quantities in the economy. To obtain an overall estimate of the gains and losses to the economy as a whole it is necessary to engage in 'general equilibrium' modelling, i.e. to simulate all the various interactions. Some general equilibrium studies suggest that protection may cost as much as 5 per cent of GNP (Grais *et al.*, 1986), others that the costs may be less (Shoven and Whalley, 1984).

There are, however, other costs from protection. Protection may encourage slacker management of costs, resulting in 'X-inefficiency', i.e. higher costs of production than are necessary; it may encourage monopoly which has further losses because of output restrictions; and it may encourage 'rent-seeking' and 'directly unproductive profit' seeking (DUP). Rent-seeking arises because import restrictions make the traded commodity relatively scarce and hence give rise to rents. Rent-seekers then spend resources trying to capture these rents, e.g. through lobbying activity. DUP embraces all activities which are unproductive but which secure profit, and would include pressure to create restrictions on trade in order to generate rent which is then captured by rent-seeking. Some estimates of DUP (for India and Turkey) indicate that they may be as high as 7–15 per cent of GNP (World Bank, 1987).

Given the potentially large gains to be obtained from free trade, adopting restrictions on trade for environmental purposes is a policy that needs to be approached with caution. Most importantly, all other approaches to reducing environmental damage should be exhausted before trade policy measures are contemplated. Of course, this view will not appeal to those who believe economic growth itself should be abandoned.

FREE TRADE AND ENVIRONMENTAL DEGRADATION

The gains from trade are not without their costs to the environment. There are several ways in which the environment might suffer from liberalization of trade.

First, free trade tends to increase economic activity and this will tend to mean more materials and energy being 'dragged through' the economic system to feed the expanded economic activity (the materials balance principle). This is the 'growth effect' of trade liberalization. Such an increase is likely but not necessary since it depends on what happens to the technical coefficients between economic activity and inputs. If energy inputs per unit of economic activity decline over time, as they have done in industrialized countries, then an expansion of output need not increase energy consumption. But economic expansion is also likely to involve land use changes which threaten natural environments. Previous 'green sites' will be converted to housing and factories, roads and other developments. The EC single market, for example, has been predicted to involve a potential worsening of environmental quality in the EC. As an example, transfrontier lorry traffic is predicted to grow by 30–50 per cent because of the internal market.

Second, free trade may result in industrial and agricultural reorganization to capture the economies of scale from larger markets. This might involve larger productive units – factories which are aesthetically unpleasing, and farms which remove hedgerows and use intensive agricultural techniques.

Third, free international trade neglects the environment in the same way that domestic free markets fail to account for environmental losses. In other words, trade liberalization can be expected to increase market failure.

Fourth, and offsetting the previous effects to some extent, freer trade will involve the removal of subsidy systems since subsidies are barriers to free trade. Where those subsidies take the form of price support, over-production will tend to be reduced and this may benefit the environment. The Common Agricultural Policy is a case in point, depending on what the land use change will be as the CAP support system is reduced over time.

Trade liberalization may also lead to increased specialization. Countries with significant endowments of natural resources will therefore tend to use more of them; those with lower endowments will use less. If the latter countries begin with low environmental standards, the effects of reduced usage will be environmentally beneficial. Other positive impacts on the environment may also arise. Freer trade expands the consumption possibility set, thus raising incomes and hence the demand for environmental goods. Governments may then respond by raising environmental standards.

Overall, then, trade liberalization is likely to give rise to negative environmental externalities, but also to some environmental gains. But the policy implication of a negative association between freer trade and environmental degradation is not that freer trade should be halted. What matters is the adoption of the most cost-effective policies to optimize the externality. Restricting trade is unlikely to be the most efficient way of controlling the problem, especially where trade retaliation may occur. The losses can best be minimized by firm *domestic* environmental policy design to uncouple the environmental impacts from economic activity. This firm environmental policy may itself have international trade effects (see later). The 'first' best approach to correcting externalities is to tackle them directly through implementation of the polluter pays principle (PPP), not through restrictions on the level of trade. Where the PPP is itself not feasible (e.g. if the exporter is a poor developing country), it is likely to be preferable to engage in cooperative policies, e.g. making clean technology transfers, assisting with clean-up policies etc., rather than adopting import restrictions.

Nonetheless, some environmentalists have argued that Article VI of GATT should be amended so as to recognize ecological dumping as an illicit subsidy to traded products. Put another way, a long-term objective should be that all environmental costs should be internalized in product prices, and trade liberalization should be pursued after that price adjustment has occurred. From a developing country standpoint such a proposal would amount to protectionism by the North. It also raises the difficulty of determining whose standards determine the degree of internalization. In an ideal world, externalities might be well defined and measurable, providing a standard by which to determine the optimal environmental standard. Deviations from this optimum would then define the extent of 'ecological dumping'. In practice, environmental standards vary significantly and it is not clear how an environmentally reformed trading system could determine the extent of implicit subsidy.

More extreme environmentalists focus on the environmental losses associated with free trade and actually argue explicitly for 'green protectionism'. These arguments tend to be allied with views about the desirability of some form of self-sufficiency in which exports and imports are balanced (Hines, 1990). The arguments tend to be superficial, however, revealing little recognition of the welfare-improving potential of freer trade, or any understanding of the efficient design of environmental policy.

PROTECTION AND ENVIRONMENTAL DEGRADATION

Just as freer trade may in fact worsen environmental degradation if the 'right' domestic policies are not pursued, so protection may worsen the environment as well. In terms of the domestic environment, protection may result in over-intensive use of the land (e.g. the CAP), and similar effects may occur if protection is given to exporting countries. Thus, the arrangement whereby the EC gives favoured treatment to Botswana beef exports is widely thought to be partly responsible for over-grazing and desertification in Botswana.

Since the gains from protection tend to be confined to specific groups within the importing or exporting country, and since protection is itself a distortion away from welfare-maximizing policies, the option of arguing that other policies to control the effects of protection are preferable to free trade appears not to be open.

THE GATT AND THE ENVIRONMENT

It is useful to look at the GATT in order to establish its approach to environmental issues. The World Trade Organisation may, of course, be designed specifically to account for environmental concerns, but inspection of the existing GATT is helpful in seeing what the problems might be for any new agreement. Since the environment was not an international issue at the time GATT was signed (1947), as much depends on interpretation as on the actual clauses. In turn, interpretation depends on judgement and on the deliberations of the disputes panels in cases that can be regarded as 'environmental'.

The essence of the GATT approach to environment can be summarized as follows:

Free trade principles

- All domestic policies with trade effects are subject to two basic principles: most-favoured nation (MFN) – Article I – and 'national treatment' (NT) – Article III. Under MFN any trade advantage conferred by one country on another country must automatically be extended to all other GATT contracting parties. National treatment requires that all contracting nations treat imported goods in the same way as 'like or competing' domestic goods. Thus, it should not be possible to tax an import if the same domestic good is exempted from the tax.
- Under Article II any protection should be based on 'bound tariffs', i.e. maximum tariffs for goods listed in an annex. In turn, these bound tariffs should decline through time through the successive GATT 'rounds' of negotiations.
- Article XI forbids the use of quantitative restrictions, e.g. quotas.
- Article XVI deals with subsidies which are, by and large, tolerated if they do not harm the export interests of other nations. There is a separate Subsidies Code (Agreement on Interpretation and Application of Articles VI, XVI and XXIII) to which not all GATT members have been signatories.

Exceptions to free trade

- Exceptions to the general free trade requirements can be made for severe balance of payments problems (Articles XII and XVIII); national security (Article XXI) and severe industrial impacts (Article XIX). Environmental exceptions come under Article XX which, in turn, sets out general exceptions to GATT principles. Article XX(b) allows exceptions for measures 'necessary to protect human, animal or plant life or health', while XX(g) specifies measures 'relating to the conservation of exhaustible natural resources if such measures are made effective in conjunction with restrictions on domestic production or consumption'.

These clauses do not specify the location of the resources to be protected or conserved. In principle, therefore, they could relate to resources outside the country taking the restrictive action. However, it seems difficult to construe XX(g) in this way since the reference to similar treatment of domestic resources tends to imply that the threatened resources are themselves domestic. XX(b) could perhaps be more generally interpreted. As we shall see, some GATT dispute resolutions have made it clear that 'extra-territorial' conservation – i.e. conservation of resources outside national boundaries – is not a legitimate concern of GATT.

It is also important to note that all Article XX exceptions are subject to a general requirement that any restriction should not 'constitute a means of arbitrary or unjustifiable discrimination between countries where the same conditions prevail, or [act as] a disguised restriction on international trade'.

The Agreement on Technical Barriers to Trade (TBT) – The Standards Code – does deal explicitly with environmental standards. In principle, standards should not create unnecessary obstacles to trade, and countries can seek resolution of disputes that may arise. To date, however, no formal resolutions of disputes have been made.

While XX(b) can be interpreted to apply to environmentally induced restrictions, this was not its origin which was primarily to cover quarantine and health cases. In a reformed system Article XX(b) is one of the clauses requiring clarification. Article XX(g) has as its most obvious interpretation that discrimination against imports is justified if domestic environmental standards are not met by the import. But the scope of the clause is largely untested. Again, if there is to be reform, Article XX(g) needs clarification.

Examples of ambiguity in the two clauses are:

- The reference to 'exhaustible' resources in XX(g) is ambiguous. All resources are exhaustible, even renewable ones if they are not managed sustainably. It is unclear if GATT ever considered the distinction between renewable and non-renewable resources, with both categories being potentially exhaustible.
- The meaning of 'health' in XX(b) – e.g. it appears to include the health risks from voluntarily consumed goods (the case of US cigarettes subject to an import ban in Thailand on health grounds – see below) but no test has been made on, e.g. impact on aesthetics.
- The location of the environmental damage relevant to an exception is unclear, although it appears to refer to the environment of the importing country.
- XX(b) requires that the measures undertaken are 'necessary' for protection of health but the meaning of 'necessary' is unclear (e.g.

does 'necessary' mean there is no other choice or that the trade restriction is the most suitable measure?).

- The nature of a measure 'related to' conservation in XX(g) is also unclear. The implication is that conservation per se need not be the prime concern provided the restrictive measure is in some way related to conservation. Indonesia's ban on the export of whole logs was primarily intended to capture the value-added of domestic processing, not to conserve forests (indeed, through inefficient processing, deforestation has probably been accelerated). Yet Indonesia has used Article XX in its defence of the ban. The argument for using XX(g) is weak since Indonesia has not instituted measures to conserve forests domestically and it has not restricted domestic production or consumption, as Article XX(g) requires.
- The exact status of social objectives, such as health protection, in connection with the objective of free trade is open to question. The Thai tobacco imports case tends to suggest that objectives other than free trade have equal or greater status, with the Panel declaring that Article XX clearly allowed parties to give priority to human health over trade liberalization. The requirement that the exceptions in Article XX should not be used to discriminate arbitrarily or unjustifiably may be taken to elevate free trade above other considerations. And whether environment has the same status as health in terms of defending restrictions remains unclear.

Overall, then, the GATT treats any environmental case for restrictions as an exception to be dealt with either under Article XX or through the Standards Code. Moreover, this presumption in favour of free trade is reinforced by the dispute settlement procedures which require that any Panel first look for the incompatibility of the restriction with GATT rules, and second, where there is potential compatibility, at compatibility with Article XX. That is, there is a presumption that a trade restriction is wrong, and the burden of proof rests with the defender of that restriction. Nonetheless, there is sufficient ambiguity in Article XX and elsewhere in GATT for confusion to arise and for inconsistent rulings to be made on exceptions.

Interestingly, Article XX began life as Article 45 of the Havana Charter which was to have set up the International Trade Organization (ITO) which, in turn, was to be the third cornerstone of the post-war reconstruction of the world economy, along with the World Bank and International Monetary Fund. The ITO was stillborn due to the United States' refusal to ratify the Charter. But the original Clause 45 included an additional exception to the free most favoured nation presumption. This covered measures:

> taken in pursuance of any intergovernmental agreement which relates solely to the conservation of fisheries resources, migratory birds or wild animals and which is subject to the requirement of paragraph 1(d) of Article 70.

ENVIRONMENTAL DISPUTES UNDER GATT

Commentators dispute the number of environmental cases that have come before the GATT Disputes Panel. At the most, five cases had an 'environmental' component raised under Articles XX(b) and XX(g). Only two cases are discussed here: the Mexican tuna fish case, and the Thai cigarette case. The latter, though not an environmental case strictly, is included in order to illustrate XX(b).

Mexican tuna exports to the USA, 1988–91

Purse-seine netting involves the use of large nets which are circled round a school of fish by a motorboat which then attaches its end of the net to the fishing vessel. A cable at the base of the net is then drawn in to form a 'purse' which is then closed from the top to capture all the fish. In the Eastern Tropical Pacific Ocean (ETP) it has been observed that dolphins and schools of fish tend to exist in association and fish are frequently located by observing and chasing dolphins. Use of purse-seine nets therefore results in the capture of dolphins along with the fish.

In 1988 the USA amended its 1972 Marine Mammal Protection Act (MMPA) to restrict imports of fish and fish products which have been caught with technology that results in ocean mammal losses in excess of US standards. Special provisions of the Act forbid imports of yellowfin tuna harvested with purse-seine nets in the ETP unless the Secretary for Commerce finds that the harvesting procedure results in catch rates of mammals equal to the average rate for US vessels, or that the government in question has a regulatory programme similar to that of the USA. The MMPA authorizes some mammal takes by US fishermen in the ETP. The import restriction impacted heavily on Mexico.

Mexico appealed to GATT on the grounds, among others, that the measure was inconsistent with Article XI forbidding quantitative restrictions; was inconsistent with Article XIII because it imposed discrimination for a specific geographical region; and that the national treatment clause is breached since the average kill rate for dolphins is known only at the end of the season and Mexico would not therefore know until then whether it could sell tuna to the USA.

The USA argued that the MMPA was an internal regulation and that the import restriction was part of the internal regulation, consistent with Article III:4; and that, even if the measures were not consistent with Article III, they were covered by Articles XX(b) and XX(g). The measures were designed to protect an exhaustible resource, and no alternative means existed for the USA to protect dolphins in the ETP. In response, Mexico argued that Article XX could not be read to apply to measures with effects outside the territory of the nation taking the measures. There was, in other words, no 'extraterritoriality' whereby one nation could take action to conserve resources in another nation. For GATT to be so extended would be a breach of international law. Taken to a logical conclusion, it could result in one nation restricting beef imports to avoid killing cows abroad. The US argued that nations could prohibit imports in order to protect the lives of humans or animals outside its jurisdiction: Article XX(g) did not specify the location of the resource in question. Furthermore, the Convention on International Trade in Endangered Species (CITES) did exactly that. Moreover, dolphins were an exhaustible resource even though the yellowfin tuna was not endangered (i.e. it was exhaustible not exhausted). Mexico argued that the concept of exhaustibility did not apply to renewable resources and hence could not relate to living things.

The Panel ruled in favour of Mexico. First, it ruled that MMPA did not regulate the sale of the product, but rather the process of manufacture (the mode of harvesting in this case). Hence the import prohibition could not be regarded as part of an internal regulation. Article III:4 obliges the USA to afford Mexico treatment no less favourable than that accorded to US tuna, regardless of whether the method of catch involves dolphin takes similar to those of the US catches. Second, the Panel observed that Article XX could be invoked only under a narrow interpretation: the burden of proof had to be with the nation seeking exceptions since Article XX runs counter to the general spirit of GATT. Third, the Panel observed that Article XX(b) did not clearly state whether the resource being protected could be outside the jurisdiction of the nation taking the action. Nonetheless, inspection of the drafting history of XX(b) indicates that the drafters intended it to apply only to the jurisdiction of the country taking the action. Moreover:

The Panel considered that if the broad interpretation of Article XX(b) suggested by the United States were accepted, each contracting party could unilaterally determine the life or health protection policies from which other contracting parties could not deviate without jeopardizing their rights under the General Agreement.

(GATT, 1991a, para 5.27)

Fourth, the Panel gave a similar interpretation concerning the intended territoriality of XX(g). Moreover, a measure gaining acceptance under XX(g) must be primarily aimed at conservation. But this was not possible in this case because the conformity with US standards required the Mexican authorities to know the average take of dolphins achieved by the US fishermen during the same period of time. This produced 'unpredictable conditions'. Finally, the Panel ruled that the restriction was not necessary as other means were open to the USA, including that of seeking an international agreement.

The Mexican tuna case is perhaps the only 'truly environmental' case to have come before a Disputes Panel of GATT. The issues were:

● whether the restriction was primarily for conservation or industrial protection;
● whether the restriction was 'necessary for' conservation;
● whether Article XX(g) extends to processes (methods of catch in this case) as opposed to products;
● whether quantity restrictions are allowable.

The Panel's ruling that XX(g) does not allow restrictions which protect natural resources outside the jurisdiction of the country making the restriction raises an interesting economic issue. Although from an economic point of view the US can be argued to have suffered an externality (through the impact on concern for wildlife, regardless of where it is), GATT effectively ruled that the externality has to be 'territorial'. Moreover, the Panel reaffirmed its previous ruling that restrictions cannot be justified if they relate to the process of production rather than the product itself: i.e. only consumption externalities are relevant – production externalities are not.

In 1992, the European Community and The Netherlands (on behalf of the Netherlands Antilles) asked the GATT Disputes Panel to rule on the same issue: they were in dispute with the USA which had restricted imports of tuna. The Panel reported in June 1994 and found that the US restrictions embodied in the US Marine Mammal Protection Act were contrary to Articles III and XI. As far as Article XX was concerned, the Panel reached a similar decision to the first tuna case but for a different reason. Whereas in the Mexican case, the consequence of extending jurisdiction to another sovereign state was thought unacceptable because it would effectively limit the GATT to relations between nations with identical regulations, in the second case the Panel concluded that extra-jurisdictional application of domestic laws was not precluded by Article XX(b). This was because XX(b) does not specify the location of the living things; because other provisions in the GATT do have extra-jurisdictional coverage; and because states can regulate the behaviour of their own nationals outside their own territory. Nonetheless, the US action was not consistent with the GATT because it was not 'necessary'. This was because the measures in question would force other countries to take measures to change their own policies in order to comply with the US embargo. This is inconsistent with the GATT. The Panel took a similar view with respect to XX(g), i.e. that extraterritoriality was not the issue but that the measure would force other countries to change their policies.

Did the GATT change its mind on the extra-jurisdictional point between the two cases? Rowbotham (1994) argues that it did not: in arguing that XX(b) did not specify the location of the resources in question, the second case reaffirmed what was known, but left open, in the first case. But it is possible to take another view and argue that the first tuna case effectively did, on balance, preclude restrictive actions if they were extra-territorial, the view taken above. If so, the second tuna panel may have added to the confusion over when it is and is not legitimate to restrict trade on environmental grounds.

The Thai cigarette case, 1990

Whilst not an obviously 'environmental' case, this case illustrates XX(b). Under its Tobacco Act of 1966 Thailand restricted imports of cigarettes and imposed a higher tax rate on imports on the few occasions when they were allowed. Sales of cigarettes in Thailand are controlled by the Thai Tobacco Monopoly. The United States requested the Disputes Panel to rule on the Thai action on the grounds that it was contrary to Article XI of the General Agreement; was not an exception under XI:2(c) which allows exceptions for fisheries and agricultural products if their restriction is necessary to enforce measures to restrict the production of a like domestic product; and were not allowable under XX(b) because the restrictions were not necessary to the protection of public health, i.e. controlling the consumption of cigarettes did not require an import ban. Thailand argued that cigarettes were an agricultural product within the meaning of XI:2(c) and that import restrictions were necessary in order to control production of domestic tobacco leaf; that XX(b) also justified the restriction because the chemical and other additives in US cigarettes made them a risk to public health; and that the tax treatment was not higher for US cigarettes. The US countered that there were no comparable domestic industry restrictions, hence 'national treatment' was at stake. There was no effective government policy to restrict the quantities of Thai cigarettes produced and consumed, although various Cabinet-level resolutions existed.

The World Health Organization (WHO) became involved at the Panel's request. WHO indicated that Thai tobacco was harder to smoke than Western cigarettes so that the availability of US cigarettes could encourage some people to smoke. There was a decline in per capita consumption of cigarettes in Thailand and this was due to laws prohibiting tobacco advertising, sponsorship, and to an educational programme which included forceful health warnings on packets. The Thai public health system could not counteract the marketing might of the US tobacco multinationals. The WHO representatives also suggested that relaxation of state controls and the opening up of cigarette markets typically resulted in increased smoking. They also suggested that tax measures were very effective as means of controlling consumption.

The Panel ruled against Thailand. The absence of import licences over a long period of time was, they said, inconsistent with Article XI:1. Article XI:2(c) did not provide an escape because cigarettes and leaf tobacco were not 'like products'. The Panel acknowledged that Article XX allowed contracting parties to elevate human health above trade liberalization. But the Thai measure was not 'necessary' within the terms of XX(b) because other measures could be taken that were 'GATT consistent', e.g. bans on advertising etc. The Panel repeated the statement of a previous Panel to the effect that:

> a contracting party cannot justify a measure inconsistent with other GATT provisions as 'necessary' in terms of Article XX(d) if an alternative measure which it could reasonably be expected to employ and which is not inconsistent with other GATT provisions is available to it.

> (GATT, 1989)

The Panel considered that further control over advertising and control of prices through taxation were available to Thailand.

Lessons from the disputes

These case studies could be taken to suggest that GATT would not, despite the exceptions indicated in Article XX, permit the use of trade restrictions to further environmental objectives. However, the cases in question have not been judged to have environmental objectives as their main concern, i.e. they have been judged to be protectionist first and conservationist only second. It is not clear, therefore, what would have happened if a measure that had a small degree of domestic economic benefit and a significant conservation benefit had been brought to GATT's attention. One problem is that most environmental measures will have some incidental 'protectionist' element, whether it is a domestic environmental standard or a restriction on imported logs. Deciding when protection or conservation is the *primary* motive could be very difficult. For that reason alone, there is a case for seeking clarification of Article XX at least. Moreover, as several commentators have pointed out, the GATT panellists were not environmental experts.

Another reason for seeking clarification in the future is that it is not clear what would happen if there was an appeal against trade sanctions allowed under international agreements, e.g. the Montreal Protocol. Some commentators fear that the sanctions weapon would have to be removed from all such agreements. But there are significant differences between the essentially bilateral trade restrictions so far tested under GATT and the restrictions that would come into play under an international agreement. These are: (a) the restrictions in the latter case would be collectively enforced, i.e. enforced by more than one country on a defaulter; and (b) the primacy of the environmental objective in the international agreement ought to be clear.

Nonetheless, GATT offered no guidance on these possibilities and the future WTO needs to ensure that these issues are clarified.

A third concern arises from the presumption that the gains from trade exceed the losses from environmental damage that may be associated with the trade. This is an empirical issue which has never been tested. Essentially, it would become an exercise in comparing the welfare gains from liberalized trade with the welfare losses in both the exporting and importing countries from any associated environmental degradation wherever it occurs.

The final cause for concern is GATT's distinction between environmental damage arising from the product and the method of production. In economic terms there is a 'legitimate' externality in either case, so that the distinction appears to be an artificial one. We might make a distinction between damage and externality (welfare loss). The damage may be caused in the exporting country (deforestation say) but the welfare loss may be suffered in the importing country because of that country's disapproval of the deforestation. The next section investigates this issue in more detail.

JUSTIFYING TRADE RESTRICTIONS:
THE UNI-DIRECTIONAL EXTERNALITY CASE

A uni-directional externality arises when the exporter of a good imposes an environmental cost on the importer of the good. There are two possibilities:

(a) the externality arises when the good is consumed in the importing country;
(b) the externality arises when the good is produced in the exporting country.

Examples of (a) tend to arise when the import fails to meet domestic environmental standards. Suppose, for example, that the importer has set standards for the recyclability of a product, and that imports fail to meet that standard. Then, if the import is allowed in, it could be argued that it has imposed an externality on the importing country because of the inability of the importer to recycle the product. The importer might then seek to impose a trade restriction on the non-recyclable import on environmental grounds. Other examples include the US 1989 temporary ban on the import of all Chilean fruit because of health scares arising from a case linked to Chilean grapes; and the EC 1989 ban on US beef containing growth hormones.

Examples of (b) include the hardwood trade where, even if the exporting country considers that there is no externality to itself, the importing country deems that the resulting deforestation is unacceptable. The externality arises from the damage done by the process or the product in the exporting country causes a welfare loss in the importing country. As noted in the discussion of the GATT disputes, GATT is clear in its intention of ruling out any externality arising from production. Only consumption (product) externalities are relevant.

Consumption externalities

Type (a) cases have been tested within the EC. Outside the environmental context, the creme de cassis case, where Germany attempted to ban French imports of this drink on the grounds that its alcohol content did not meet German standards, went to the European Court of Justice in 1979. The Court rejected Germany's case. The presumption was then that this kind of 'standards-induced' consumption externality was not sufficient cause to justify the trade restriction. In the environmental context, Denmark secured the very opposite judgement against the Commission itself when the Court ruled that its ban on the import of non-returnable beverage containers was justified on environmental grounds.

How do the rules of the GATT apply to such consumption externalities?

1 It would be necessary to demonstrate damage and externality, i.e. that the effects are sizeable. The relevance of a health risk as the nature of the externality has been established, but the relevance of environmental externalities unrelated to health is still unclear.
2 Any restriction – whether a quantitative one, a tax or a subsidy – must be shown to be 'necessary' (XX(b)) or 'relating to' (XX(g)), i.e. that the restricting country could not achieve the externality reduction some other way. The Thai tobacco case, for example, concluded that Thailand had legitimate concerns with health but that it had weapons available to it other than a trade ban, e.g. information campaigns.
3 If the restriction differentiates between sources of the import, that differentiation must not be arbitrary or unjustified.

From this it follows that GATT's interpretation would be that a consumption externality is *prima facie* a legitimate reason for a restriction under Article XX, provided there is evidence of the externality, provided the trade restriction is 'efficient' in some sense, and provided the restriction is uniformly applied.

Is this interpretation consistent with economic analysis? By and large it is since the GATT rules could be interpreted to suggest that trade restrictions should only be used if their net welfare gains are positive and are secured at least cost. The two problems are:

1 Cost-efficiency may not be a relevant interpretation of GATT's 'necessary to' restriction: the GATT rules may require that a more costly measure be taken if it is available. From an economic standpoint, the relevant comparison would be in terms of net gains and losses in welfare.
2 The requirement for 'non-discrimination' could actually be economically inefficient since it would be optimal under the polluter pays principle to discriminate between imports according to damage done (e.g. a tax should be damage-related).

Production externalities

Externalities that arise in the process of production are likely to be the most important challenge to future trade liberalization. An obvious example would be internationally transported acid rain. But the production externality is much wider than such direct impacts. In the logging–deforestation case, for example, the externality may be distributed between exporter and importer. The exporter may suffer because clear-felling increases soil erosion, and sedimentation of water systems, reducing water productivity (e.g. reduced fish catches). The importer may suffer because of concern over the loss of biological diversity (loss of use, option and existence value). The issues arising are whether the importer can justify an import restriction on the grounds of the externality suffered by the importer's population, and/ or the externality suffered in the exporting country. The uni-directional case is best served by concentrating on the former type of externality. Austria and The Netherlands already have import bans on tropical timber that is produced unsustainably. The latter type of externality is not irrelevant, however, since, although one would typically argue that it is best dealt with by domestic policies in the exporting country, a number of cases arise in which the importer could be said to be acting on behalf of minority or persecuted groups (e.g. Amazon Indians).

GATT seems clear that externalities arising from production as opposed to consumption are not relevant: i.e. they would not be allowed as an exception. In economic terms, however, there is no difference between the nature of the externality. Both consumption and production externalities generate welfare losses in the importing country. The differentiation between the types of externality can only therefore arise from some notion of property rights, i.e. that no importing nation has a right to interfere with the production tech-nology of another country. This is the principle underlying the 'extra-territoriality' ruling in the Mexican tuna case, but which appeared to be modified in the later tuna case.

GATT appears not to allow the production externality case in principle. It is not therefore an issue of whether trade restrictions are the most efficient way of reducing the externality. In most cases they certainly will not be. What is at fault is the domestic policies of the exporting nations. But if a process of political persuasion fails to alter those policies, should importing nations be able to discriminate against products from countries producing, say, acid rain? If the 'necessary for' principle is invoked, the importing nation would have to demon-strate that all other reasonable measures had been taken. But the problem is worse than this since it is not clear, if an exception was allowed, which product could be the subject of the restriction. Acid rain comes from power generation and electricity is 'embodied' in virtually all products. If the electricity is itself not traded, then the trade restriction cannot be against the product that is directly produced by the polluting technology. It would have to be against other products and that raises all kinds of concerns about blanket import restrictions.

Thus, while there appears to be no intrinsic difference between production and consumption externalities, there are formidable problems of allowing exceptions for production externalities. It is not clear where the process would end.

JUSTIFYING TRADE RESTRICTIONS: THE MUTUAL EXTERNALITY CASE

Mutual externalities arise when the pollution from an exporting nation affects a common resource – the ozone layer, the atmosphere, the oceans. Typically, controlling such externalities requires an international agreement and such agreements may use trade sanctions as a weapon for mutual compliance, i.e. to prevent 'free rider' behaviour. In GATT terms the issue becomes one of determining the necessity of such measures. Reinstein (1991) suggests that the need for trade restrictions arises not just from the need to secure agreement for environmental purposes, but because the agreement imposes costs on participating parties which non-participating parties avoid. Thus, participants may bear some competitive disadvantage. In those circumstances only collectively enforced trade restrictions will produce the desired result.

Under the Montreal Protocol on protection of the ozone layer, Article 4 controls trade in CFCs between signatories and non-signatories and trade in CFC-containing products. It includes the threat of trade bans on products made with CFCs but not actually containing them – a clear example of a production externality. As Reinstein notes, if implemented, this would affect all trade in electronic equipment since CFCs are widely used to clean semiconductor chips. GATT-compatibility was extensively discussed at the time of the Protocol, and the negotiators felt there was consistency between the Protocol and the GATT's Article XX because of the headnote to Article XX which states that the exceptions are subject to:

> the requirement that such measures are not applied in a manner which would constitute a means of arbitrary or unjustifiable discrimination between countries where the same conditions prevail, or a disguised restriction on international trade.

The argument was that conditions in the non-signatory countries were different to those of the signatory countries, and hence the justification for trade restrictions was consistent with Article XX.

As noted above, the role of collective discrimination against non-signatories or defaulters might be used to distinguish trade restrictions in international agreements from other restrictions. Combined with the 'same conditions prevail' requirement in Article XX, and the view that restrictions would be more readily demonstrated to be 'necessary' in such cases, this suggests that trade restrictions under international agreements would be GATT-compatible generally. However, this is far from guaranteed and, once again, some clarification would be valuable.

TRADE LIBERALIZATION AND ENVIRONMENTAL POLICY

Environmental policy is secured through: standards, taxes, and subsidies. How compatible are these with the GATT or any new liberalized trade system? Standards and taxes are compatible with the Polluter Pays Principle (PPP). Subsidies are not unless they are a transitional measure or are linked to taxes (e.g. deposit-refund systems). GATT has a Code on Subsidies and Standards but has no explicit guidelines on taxes. Thus the PPP and GATT are potentially compatible. The main source of incompatibility lies in the consumption and production externality distinction. PPP is wholly consistent with taxing a production externality, and an import tax may therefore fulfil that function. As we have seen, GATT does not appear to consider that production externalities qualify for exceptions under GATT.

Standards

Domestic environmental standards can clearly be barriers to trade. While domestic industries face higher costs from the standards, so do their competitors if imports are treated in the same way. GATT has an Agreement on Technical Barriers to Trade, the Standards Code (1979) which 38 contracting parties have so far accepted. This permits environmental standards to be established provided they do not act as trade distortions where the same conditions prevail.

The Code recommends the use of internationally agreed standards, i.e. it supports the idea of harmonized standards. Stricter standards can be justified, however, i.e. countries can enact higher standards domestically than in other countries. It is legitimate to set standards higher than international standards in order to protect human, animal or plant life and the environment. The Standards Code therefore makes explicit reference to the environment, whereas Article XX does not. But the Code does not define the term 'environment'. Generally, although not explicit, lower standards than the international norm appear not to be allowed, but this is not clear. Recent discussions have contemplated allowing lower than international standards where climatic, geographical or technological problems arise. Whether a country can insist on imports having the same standard as domestic products is not clear. The Code appears to discuss products only, although Article 14.25 mentions process and production methods. Most probably, as with the main Articles, production externalities are excluded from consideration since the standards in question must be shown to be 'necessary' and in keeping with 'scientific evidence'. Thus the EC claimed that the Code did not cover processes and production methods and hence its ban on hormone-fed beef from the USA was outside the scope of GATT. The US argued that GATT is relevant to processes. GATT has never resolved the issue.

Discussions in the Uruguay Round centred on the idea of 'proportionality' i.e. standards should be in proportion to the environmental objective. The Draft Technical Barriers to Trade agreement would extend the 1979 code to 'terminology, symbols, packaging, marking or labelling requirements as they apply to a product, processes or production method', i.e. embracing environmental standards. It is generally thought that this extension, combined with some other GATT decisions, will enable a satisfactory resolution of the products standards issue, but not production and process method (PPM) standards.

The Standards Code thus remains ambiguous most importantly in the area of (PPM) standards (i.e. our production externalities). Given the Mexican tuna fish case, it would be odd if the Standards Code were to be extended to PPM. But there is some discussion of this possibility. The Mexican tuna fish case raises all the issues of the nature of allowable standards. For example, if there was an internationally agreed standard on fishing technology for tuna – i.e. a standard related to a process – and Mexico did not sign up to it, would the US then be justified in its import ban? The tuna Panel appeared to entertain this possibility.

Since the interpretation of the Standards Code is open to much latitude it is difficult to assess its compatibility with economic principles. Certainly the presumption that international environmental standards should be harmonized is not consistent with economic analysis. Countries might very legitimately have different standards in order to reflect: (a) different tastes and preferences for environmental quality; and (b) different assimilative capacities. As with all the GATT issues, the problem is one of balancing the gains from trade against the imposition of externalities.

Taxes

Under GATT domestic taxes can be applied to imports of 'like products' so long as they are applied equally and are not designed for protection. The Superfund Tax case ruling also suggests that the pollution impact does not have to be domestically located for the import tax to be justified. The precise compatibility between this extraterritorial impact and the extraterritorial impacts in the Mexican tuna fish case is not clear.

In order to qualify as a tax which allows border tax adjustments, any tax must be 'borne by the product', i.e. must be in the nature of an excise tax or an input tax where the input is embodied in the product. The idea is that such taxes directly cause consumer prices to be raised. Imports are not therefore at a competitive disadvantage if such taxes are then placed on imports. Other taxes like income taxes are excluded, as is a tax on fuel inputs because such a tax is a tax on the process not the product. Such taxes could be absorbed by the product without domestic prices rising. If then applied to import prices, imports would be at a competitive disadvantage, contrary to the principles of GATT. Thus, indirect taxes are allowed to be extended to imports, but 'process' taxes are not.

The implications of this rule for environmental taxes seem to be that only a pollution tax levied on the pollution content of the product would qualify for extension to imports. Even then PPP would allow discrimination between different imports according to their environmental damage effects, whereas Article I of GATT precludes this form of discrimination because there must be no discrimination between 'like products'. Put another way, it is not currently possible to argue that products are not 'alike' because of their differing pollution profiles. We may note also that GATT offers no definition of what constitutes a 'like product'. Case-by-case approaches have so far been used. If it is not allowed to discriminate against 'like products' then one approach is to argue that discrimination against polluting products is justified because they are not alike precisely because they have different pollution impacts. Most commentators seem to feel this is an unlikely scenario.

GATT appears to be in conformity with pollution taxes which, in turn, can be shown to be efficient. However, the continuing distinction between product and process makes the compatibility limited, as does the precluding of product taxes differentiated by environmental impact.

Subsidies

Subsidies are typically frowned upon under the Polluter Pays Principle. Until the recent Uruguay Round, GATT was ambivalent on subsidies. The main factor bringing them to the fore has been the US insistence that agricultural subsidies in Europe constitute unfair competition. The US argued that such subsidies justify countervailing duties (CVDs). One immediate problem is what constitutes a subsidy. Many argue that the absence of environmental regulations constitutes a subsidy to exports no different from financial subsidies actually transferred.

Under GATT export subsidies which result in lower export prices for manufactured goods than on the domestic market are prohibited. However, this test of a subsidy tends not to embrace production subsidies. Subsidies on primary products have typically not been addressed by GATT in other than vague language, whilst agricultural subsidies have generally been outside GATT since a waiver to the USA in 1955. Where a subsidy is proscribed, GATT rules allow countervailing duties no greater than the amount of the subsidy if there is a 'material' threat to the domestic industry.

The Subsidies Code attempts to codify what is and what is not allowed, but only some 30 countries (out of 90 contracting to GATT) have signed it. Export subsidies outside agriculture are technically prohibited, but not for developing country exports. Agricultural export subsidies are supposed to be limited so as to avoid a 'more than equitable share of world export trade' – a generally vague requirement. There is a general call for other subsidies not to be used to the detriment of other countries, but developing country subsidies are generally excluded from even this requirement.

By and large, then, environmental subsidies would appear to be allowable under the old GATT rules. The Uruguay Round considered some more precise text in which subsidies to adapt existing facilities to new environmental standards would qualify as GATT-compatible, as would R&D subsidies to even stricter environmental technology. As it stands at the moment, the argument that lack of standards constitutes a subsidy could be valid in GATT terms, i.e. it could constitute grounds for countervailing action. Such an interpretation of a subsidy could have dramatic implications for the developing countries where environmental regulations are often minimal and where the cost of adopting such standards could be significant. Equally, however, no such test of an implicit subsidy has been made and authorities differ as to the likelihood of success. It would, for example, require there to be an affirmative duty to protect the environment in the first place. Clearly, there is a need for extensive clarification.

DO ENVIRONMENTAL REGULATIONS INHIBIT COMPETITIVENESS?

One major argument for the international harmonization of environmental standards is that variable standards will encourage (a) loss of competitiveness in the regulating country and (b) the migration of industry to countries with the lowest standards. The relevance to GATT is limited since GATT does not concern itself with rules relating to the behaviour of multinational companies nor with an individual country's competitiveness. The relevance to environmental policy is stronger because threats of re-location are widely used by industrial lobbies against stricter environmental standards. The issue is linked to the more general one of whether firms lose competitive advantage due to environmental regulations.

Loss of competitiveness

Dean (1991) surveys the competitiveness literature and concludes that the impacts of past and existing environmental regulations on competitiveness is very small. This is because:

- regulatory abatement costs are a small proportion of total costs and thus not significant;
- output losses are small; and
- trade impacts are small.

Walter (1973, 1982) found that abatement costs in US export industries were only 1.75 per cent on average, compared to 1.5 per cent for US imports. Yezer and Philipson (1974) found output reductions due to environmental regulations (ERs) amounted to less than 1 per cent. Mutti and Richardson (1976) found ERs gave rise to 1 per cent price increases and 1.5 per cent output reductions. Robinson (1988) finds similarly small changes in US trade as a result of ER costs. Tobey (1990) calculates US ER costs at under 1.85 per cent of total costs for 40 industries, and from 1.85 to 2.89 per cent for 24 industries and shows that there is no statistically significant difference between exports of 'strictly regulated' and 'leniently regulated' firms.

Slade (1991) conducted a different experiment. She asks what would happen to resource production, consumption and revenue if the 'South' adopted the same environmental standards as the 'North' (i.e. spends as much on abatement as the North – represented in the model by the USA), whilst the North increases its environmental expenditures to achieve even stricter standards. The usefulness of this model is that it encapsulates the major concern of the developing world that it will have to comply with stricter standards in the developed world, thus reducing its competitiveness. The results relate to ferrous and non-ferrous metals and to energy. They suggest that the impacts are very small: prices change on average by 1.5 per cent, and quantities by 0.8 per cent. Compared to the market fluctuations for these commodities the changes are trivial. Moreover, export revenues actually increase most for the low income countries, are still positive for the medium income countries and are negative for high income countries. In other words, the implicit environmental 'tax' is progressive. Low (1991) offers a similar analysis for Mexico by simulating the effects of US pollution abatement costs on Mexico's exports. US abatement costs comprise around 0.5 per cent of total industrial costs, with the highest level being 3 per cent and nearly all industries being below 1 per cent. Applying such a 'tax' to Mexico's exports in 1988 would result in a trade reduction of less than 2 per cent of Mexican exports. Birdsall and Wheeler (1991) also suggest that the openness of the Chilean economy has resulted in increased competition between domestic and multi-national companies. Since new technology tends to be cleaner and competition encourages adoption of new technology, the net effect is environmental improvement even beyond local standards.

Only Lucas et al.(1991) have found evidence of 'toxic displacement' whereby stricter OECD country environmental standards have resulted in the movement of high risk industries to developing countries. However, they note that 'pollution intensity' has grown fastest in the closed economies of the developing world rather than the open economies, suggesting that 'policy problems, rather than regulatory cost differences, may have been the main stimulus to toxic industrial migration'.

Overall, then, there is no evidence that industrial competitiveness has been affected by environmental regulation.

Pollution havens

The interest in pollution havens is primarily political and strategic. Since countries do vary in their environmental endowments and in preferences for environmental quality, it would be economically efficient if firms did actually move to locate in areas where laxer environmental standards genuinely reflected these different endowments and tastes (Low and Yeats, 1991). In practice, those who would suffer the externalities will tend to complain that they are being unfairly treated and that polluting technologies are being deliberately foisted on them.

As it happens there is very little evidence to suggest that firms move in response to variable environmental policies. The reasons include those given above under loss of competitiveness – i.e. the price and output impacts of controls are generally very small. Even where they are significant, however, relocating will only be profitable if the difference in actual and expected environmental costs is greater than other costs of relocation. Leonard (1984, 1991) has both surveyed the literature and carried out case studies. US overseas investment by manufacturing firms between 1970 and 1987 showed no responsiveness to domestic environmental legislation. In fact, investment was highest in industries with low pollution control costs. Some industries did come under pressure to move. These included manufacturers of toxic products who were unable to meet domestic standards – notably asbestos, arsenic trioxide, benzidine-based dyes, some pesticides and some carcinogenic chemicals. In a number of cases, however, the temporary relocation of industry or of sources of supply was halted when consumption fell within the USA. In some other cases – copper, zinc and lead processing – some international dispersion occurred, but the role of environmental regulation was limited since other factors relating to the requirement for processing in the country of origin and raw material availability were also present. Some chemical activities may also have moved, primarily because of workplace safety legislation, but other market factors were also at work. Leonard's main finding is that industrial flight cannot be identified for any industry facing expanding demand or with technological superiority: 'Technological innovation, use of new raw materials or substitute products, reclamation of waste materials, tighter process and quality controls, and other adaptations generally have proved better responses than flight for many firms' (Leonard, 1991).

Low and Yeats (1991) did find evidence that 'dirty' industries – defined as industries with the highest pollution control expenditures – have relocated to some extent. Between 1965 and 1988 they found that 3.5 per cent of dirty industries moved from industrial to non-industrial countries, mainly from North to South America. In 1988, however, 75 per cent of all dirty industries' trade was still in industrial countries. But how far even the 3.5 per cent shift was due to the cost burdens of environmental standards in industrial countries is doubtful. Other factors have been at work, including differential labour costs and the very stages of development: most dirty industries are basic industries which occupy a larger share of GNP in the early stages of development.

Overall, then, there is little evidence to support the 'pollution haven' hypothesis.

CONCLUSIONS ON TRADE AND THE ENVIRONMENT

The main findings of this chapter may be summarized as follows:

(a) Does free trade harm the environment?

Because free trade has as its prime purpose the expansion of output and consumption, it will contribute to environmental degradation by expanding the demands that are made on natural resources and on land. However, restricting trade for this reason would be wholly wrong since environmental impacts can be controlled by vigorous and well-targeted environmental policy. There is a strong role for market-based incentives in this context. These aim to 'decouple' economic activity and environmental impact. In other words, the prime focus of policy must be on correcting the sources of environmental degradation in the country of export. Using trade restrictions is a last resort when all other means to correct the damage have failed. There is an exception for international agreements (see below).

It is important to recognize, however, that free trade is not to be pursued at all costs. The environmental damage associated with expanded trade is a real cost that needs to be deducted from the (generally) large benefits of freer trade. There is no justification in free trade arguments for ignoring environmental costs. Environmental costs change the conditions under which free trade maximizes world human wellbeing.

(b) Does protection harm the environment?

Many forms of protection can harm the environment, as exemplified by the Common Agricultural Policy. Less obviously, harm can be done to the sustainable development of countries supplying imports under special agreements, as with beef from Botswana to the EC. There is evidence to implicate the special agreement between the EC and Botswana in range degradation in Botswana due to the incentive to over-stock cattle.

(c) How does trade-related environmental degradation arise?

Trade is linked to two forms of environmental damage. Damage can arise from the consumption of an imported product which gives rise to an environmental loss. Most usually such 'consumption externalities' are health-related, e.g. pesticides on imported fruit, treated products etc.

The second form of damage arises because of the production of the good in the exporting country. Tropical hardwood from unsustainable forestry, for example, imposes a cost on importing countries if the population of the importing country cares about deforestation (regardless of whether that population makes direct use of the forest). The same production process may also impose costs on the exporting country (e.g. loss of watershed functions due to soil erosion from deforestation). While these latter costs are the legitimate concern of the exporting country, importers may also feel concerned if, for example, minority groups suffer (e.g. forest-dwelling tribes).

The important point to note is that while consumption externalities have as their point of damage the importing country, many 'production externalities' will impose damage that is physically outside the importing countries. This raises the issue of the 'right' of importing countries to use trade restrictions to convey or impose their concern on countries who possess the resources in question.

A further category of damage arises from transboundary pollution, e.g. acid rain. Here the damage is physically located in the 'importing' country but caused by activity in the 'exporting' country. Trade restrictions as a weapon against the exporter are problematic since it may not be possible to target the product in question (e.g. electricity). GATT is generally consistent with environmentally motivated trade restrictions (under certain conditions – see below) on products, but is wholly inconsistent with generalized retaliation for an environmental harm done through some industrial process. Indeed, in terms of the distinction made above, GATT rules do not permit restrictions to be employed against processes or methods of production, only against products. In general, then, GATT does not acknowledge production externalities, only consumption externalities. This is confirmed by the recent ruling in the Mexican tuna fish case which found against the USA for prohibiting imports of Mexican tuna fish because of the loss of dolphins in the nets used. That is, GATT ruled against a production externality being relevant to trade restrictions. It also ruled against concern with extraterritorial physical impacts (the dolphin), although it appears that it is legitimate to employ an import tax against polluting goods if the same tax is applied domestically, regardless of the fact that the pollution from the imports may be physically outside the importing country.

If GATT was to be 'greened' to allow for production externalities it is clear that a massive potential would exist for countries to restrict trade on the grounds that they disapproved of the way other countries produce their products. From an economic perspective, however, such concerns, if legitimate, are no less real a cost than the damage done from consuming a polluted import.

Are trade restrictions justified on environmental grounds?

GATT accepts that the trade weapon can be used where a product generates an environmental cost in the importing country. From an economic standpoint such a cost arises if the import contains 'more pollution' than the domestic product, i.e. fails to meet the domestic environmental standard. GATT, however, is wary of allowing domestic standards to be used as a weapon to raise the cost of imports. To date, there is considerable ambiguity over the use of standards as trade weapons. GATT recommends the international harmonization of standards to ensure a 'level playing field'. Economic analysis suggests that harmonized standards are not economically efficient since countries vary in their environmental preferences and in their resource endowments. But even if harmonization is accepted as a general goal, it is not clear at what level harmonization should occur. Left to a political process, any country failing to meet an agreed standard could be accused of providing an implicit subsidy to their exports. This might be challenged under the Subsidies Code, although no case of this has yet occurred. There is a need to clarify just what constitutes a subsidy. Moreover, subsidies are typically not consistent with the polluter pays principle (PPP) of OECD.

Environmental taxes are, in principle, consistent with GATT. However, environmental taxes can be justified for processes as well as for products, whereas GATT is clear in opposing the extension to processes, although there are some debates about this. Moreover, environmental taxes ought, if they are to be efficient, to vary according to the pollution content of the import. But such a variable tax would be illicit under GATT since it must be non-discriminatory between 'like goods'. It can be argued that GATT needs clarification about the meaning of 'like goods' in the environmental context, i.e. that environmental characteristics should be used to distinguish goods. Once again, however, the prospect is one of virtually endless debate and dispute if this was to happen.

(e) GATT and international environmental agreements

There is an understandable concern that GATT's disallowance of trade restrictions except in strict circumstances could make compliance with international agreements more difficult. Such agreements might use trade restrictions as a weapon for compliance. Currently only 19 out of 170 international environment agreements make use of trade weapons to ensure compliance, but these include the Vienna Convention for the Protection of the Ozone Layer (1985); the

Montreal Protocol on Substances that Deplete the Ozone Layer (1987); the Basel Convention on the Control of Transboundary Movements of Hazardous Wastes and Their Disposal (1989), and the Convention on International Trade in Endangered Species (CITES) (UNCTAD, 1991). It would seem worthwhile establishing clear guidelines in GATT which separate out this context of trade restriction from all others. The distinguishing features would seem to be:

1 that the restrictions are explicitly to secure compliance with, or the working of, an international agreement;
2 that they are necessary to the agreement in that other compliance incentives are not likely to be available;
3 that the trade restrictions would be collectively enforced by the signatory countries; and
4 that the 'same conditions prevail' clause of GATT differentiates non-signatory countries from parties to the agreement (i.e. non – signatories face different conditions).

In respect of (iv), however, a contracting party to GATT who is not a contracting party to an environmental agreement might challenge trade restrictions imposed through the environmental agreement on the grounds that GATT members may not vary the rights of third parties.

A possible mechanism for bringing international agreements into GATT is via Article XX(h) which provides an exception for measures undertaken:

> in pursuance of obligations under any intergovernmental commodity agreement which conforms to criteria submitted to the Contracting Parties and not disapproved by them or which is itself so submitted and not disapproved.

It may therefore be the case that the extension of 'international commodity agreement' to 'international agreement' generally would provide the safeguard for the use of trade sanctions as weapons of compliance with such agreements. The option of using (XXh) in this way has been advocated by the German government and by the World Wide Fund for Nature. The Mexican tuna fish panel resolution also indicated that multilateral agreements were one of the options open for the USA to protect tuna outside its territory, suggesting that, if the Panel's rulings are adopted, that GATT is likely to approve of such agreements.

(f) Clarifying clause XX

Clause XX of GATT is the clause most in need of clarification under a new WTO from an environmental standpoint. The term 'environment' is not used, although it does appear in the Standards Code. Even a phrase like 'exhaustible resource' is unclear. Its original intent may have been to refer to non-renewable resources, but all resources are exhaustible in one sense or another. Clause XX(b) could be modified to include the phrase 'the environment', although the prior requirement (the 'chapeau') of the Article requires that all restrictions should be applied in a non-discriminatory way and must not be disguised protectionism.

(g) Overall features of GATT

The presumption in GATT is that the benefits of free trade exceed the environmental costs of free trade. But this is an empirical issue, and not an article of faith. GATT is on much stronger ground by insisting that trade restrictions are only justified when they are 'necessary' or 'related to' other objectives. Trade restrictions are generally unlikely to be the most efficient way of tackling environmental problems. But for compliance with international agreements they may well be the only way given the absence of world government. As such, international agreements warrant special and explicit attention.

The remaining observations are that: (i) the lack of clarity in the wording of GATT and the associated Codes may work to the detriment of both free trade and the environment, and (ii) the strict focus on product damage omits most of the important environmental costs being generated by the production of goods for world trade. In general, however, reforming GATT to take account of production externalities would almost certainly do more harm than good.

THE WORLD TRADE ORGANISATION

In 1994 the GATT of old became the WTO. The WTO takes on the 'old' GATT provisions but a measure of the success of the environmental critique of the GATT is the preamble to the WTO which states that:

> their relations in the field of trade and economic endeavour should be conducted with a view to ... ensuring ... a large and steadily growing volume of real income and effective demand, while allowing for the optimal use of the world's resources in accordance with the objective of sustainable development; seeking both to protect and preserve the environment and to enhance the means for doing so in a manner consistent with their respective needs and concerns at different levels of economic development.

This suggests that the *presumption* of free trade is modified in the WTO: sustainable development and environmental protection issues matter more. What happens with the WTO and how it will interpret this revised general obligation remains to be seen.

Chapter 7

Population and poverty

INTRODUCTION

Chapter 5 showed briefly how two pressures – population growth and economic growth – might fit into the general picture of economic failure as a cause of global environmental degradation. There it was suggested that both had the effect of making land conversion more profitable. Combined with the fact that conservation values are often exhibited outside the market, the 'playing field' between conservation and land conversion becomes severely biased in favour of conversion. Few experts dispute the role that population growth has in resource degradation, although it is sometimes thought to be 'politically incorrect' to argue such a case. There can never be a case for distorting the truth because of political sensitivities. Population growth is a major factor explaining resource degradation. Since the issue was addressed extensively in *Blueprint 2* we offer only the briefest discussion of the population–degradation link here.

Economic growth involves increases in real income levels. The argument that economic growth 'causes' resource degradation therefore sits a little uneasily with another widely advanced view that poverty, not economic growth, causes degradation. One of the links by which poverty is thought to influence resource use is indebtedness. The more indebted a country is the more it is likely to 'mine' its resources in an effort to secure foreign exchange to repay foreign debt.

Both the population and poverty hypotheses are capable of some empirical testing. This chapter looks briefly at the statistical tests so far carried out to test the relationships involved.

ECONOMETRIC TESTS

If poverty and population growth are linked to environmental degradation we would expect to be able to test for the relationship by statistical techniques. The kind of approach that could be used is multiple regression. In multiple regression, data on environmental degradation are regressed on factors thought to explain the degradation, e.g. population growth, population density, indebtedness, income, perhaps the price of agricultural products (since higher prices might encourage land conversion), and so on. There is indeed a modest literature that provides such tests but generally only in the context of deforestation. The reason for this narrow focus is that data on environmental degradation across many countries are very scarce. Deforestation data themselves are notoriously deficient, but the situation tends to be worse for many pollution variables simply because such data are not collected on a systematic basis. Box 7.1 brings the deforestation studies together in summary form.

The studies suggest, first, that there is no absolutely conclusive link between any of the selected variables and deforestation. However, cautious conclusions might be:

- The balance of evidence favours the hypothesis that population growth is a significant factor explaining deforestation.
- Population density is clearly linked to deforestation rates.
- Income growth is fairly clearly linked to rates of deforestation, suggesting that deforestation has more to do with growth of incomes than with poverty – a result that runs counter to the popular interpretations of the causes of environmental degradation.
- The evidence on the role of agricultural productivity change is finely balanced. One would expect growth in productivity to lessen the pressure on colonisation of forests, i.e. the coefficient of association should be negative. The two studies finding this association are for South America and Indonesia. The two studies finding the opposite association are for Thailand (Katila, 1992) and the Brazilian Amazon (Reis and Guzman, 1994).
- The link between indebtedness and deforestation is also unclear. Perrings (1992) finds a positive link for tropical moist forests but not for other forests. Kahn and McDonald find a positive link, but Capistrano and Kiker's models do not find such a link. Again, this ambivalence is at odds with the popular interpretations of the causes of environmental degradation.

In terms of the economic failure arguments of Chapter 5, however, it is worth noting that the econometric tests do not include factors that might be thought relevant: government intervention and global missing markets, for example. Moreover, few of the studies actually test for the factor that most economists would think is very important: the presence or absence of clearly defined property rights. The few studies that do include land tenure or some proxy for security of rights show that they are clearly very important.

Econometric studies of this kind are in their infancy and suffer many

Box 7.1
ECONOMETRIC STUDIES OF DEFORESTATION

A minus sign means that an increase in the variable leads to a decrease in deforestation. A plus sign means an increase leads to an increase in deforestation. Blank entries mean either not statistically significant or not tested for.

Deforestation significantly related to:	Rate of population growth	Population density	Income	Agricultural productivity	International indebtedness
Allen and Barnes, 1985	+				
Burgess, 1992		+	−		
Burgess, 1991	a) − b) −		+ +		+ +
Capistrano and Kiker, 1990	a) b) c)	+ (c)	+ + +		− −
Constantino and Ingram, 1990		+	−	−	
Kahn and McDonald, 1994	−				+
Katila, 1992		+		+	
Kummer and Sham, 1991	+				
Lugo, Schmidt and Brown, 1981	+				
Panayotou and Sungsuwan, 1994	+	−			
Palo, Mery and Salmi, 1987		+			
Perrings, 1992	a) + b) −	+ +	+		+
Reis and Guzman, 1994				+	
Rudel, 1994	+		+		
Shafik, 1994					
Southgate, 1994	+			−	
Southgate, Sierra and Brown, 1989	+				

Source: adapted from Brown and Pearce (1994).

data reliability problems. Nonetheless they offer a way of cutting through the popular preconceptions about the causes of environmental degradation. Invariably, what the popular explanations are doing is citing one or more causes that fit the political philosophy of those arguing the case. Even if it is imperfect, econometric testing is to be preferred as a scientific explanation of resource degradation.

ENVIRONMENTAL KUZNETS CURVES

A very similar approach to econometric testing is the 'environmental Kuznets curve'. Simon Kuznets was a famous economist and Nobel laureate who investigated the relationship between economic development and the distribution of income. He showed that, as economies develop, inequality gets worse but then better. Because of the resulting 'hump-back shape' of the curve (Box 7.2) curves showing a link between environmental quality and income have been labelled 'environmental' Kuznets curves. The idea is that, in the course of economic development, countries will experience adverse environmental quality and then improved quality. Notice that, if this is correct, it runs counter to the 'anti-growth' argument that economic growth – which is a constituent part of economic development – will always lead to a deterioration in environmental quality. It therefore seems worthwhile investigating whether environmental Kuznets curves exist, and, if they do, what they look like.

In a seminal paper, Grossman and Krueger (1991) examined the relationship between income growth and sulphur dioxide concentrations. They found that, indeed, SO_2 concentrations first rise with income and then, at around $5000 p.a. average per capita income, they fall. Why then doesn't the anti-growth view hold up? The answer is of course that per capita incomes are only one of the factors explaining the change in environmental quality over time. A simple way of seeing this is through an identity:

$$\underset{(a)}{\frac{\text{Emissions}}{\text{Area}}} = \underset{(b)}{\frac{\text{Emissions}}{\text{GNP}}} \times \underset{(c)}{\frac{\text{GNP}}{\text{Population}}} \times \underset{(d)}{\frac{\text{Population}}{\text{Area}}}$$

Expression (a) can be thought of as a measure of ambient quality; (b) is a measure of the 'efficiency of pollution' – a lower ratio implies less pollution per unit of economic activity; (c) is the standard measure of per capita income; and (d) is a measure of population density. Inspection of the identity shows that income per capita could be rising but emissions could be falling due to a reduction in emissions per unit of GNP. And that is exactly what has happened with sulphur dioxide

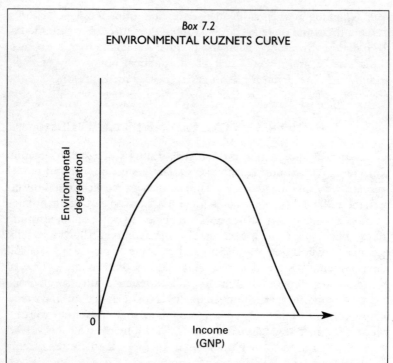

Box 7.2
ENVIRONMENTAL KUZNETS CURVE

The argument is that, as incomes grow, environmental degradation gets worse but then improves as preferences for environmental quality change and resources become available for pollution control.

pollution – the reduction in ratio (b) has outweighed the 'scale effect' in ratio (c). At least the identity shows the naivete of the anti-growth argument: the scale effect may indeed dominate, but it does not have to, especially as the ratio of emissions to GNP is controllable through direct policy measures. Indeed, other factors are at work. The *composition* of GNP may change as economies develop, away from heavy industry towards lighter, less polluting industry. This is also what has happened in advanced economies. Hence the identity above is itself simplistic. Many argue, for example, that pollution in the economies in transition will come down dramatically as economic development takes place there. This does not mean that environmental policies are unnecessary, but it does mean that structural change in the economy is something that needs to be forecast well if environmental policy is not to be wrongly targeted.

So, what happens to ambient environmental quality depends on a number of factors including:

- the scale effect: the effect of rising incomes;
- the composition effect: the effect of structural change in the GNP of the economy;
- the efficiency or technology effect: the ratio of emissions to GNP.

The environmental Kuznets curve has also been tested in the context of deforestation. Indeed, the studies listed in Box 7.1 can be thought of as sophisticated tests of the Kuznets curves. Cropper and Griffiths (1994) test the Kuznets curve for 64 countries for 29 years and conclude that Kuznets curves exist for Africa and Latin America. Shafik (1994) also finds a Kuznets curve for deforestation, but concludes that the evidence is weak – statistically speaking, income per capita has virtually no explanatory role in deforestation. Shafik also found that investment helped explain annual rates of deforestation, perhaps because investment places a higher burden on natural resources (consider the link between infrastructure development and deforestation discussed in Chapter 5). Less intuitively, Shafik found that high electricity prices were correlated with deforestation. This is counter-intuitive because high electricity prices might be thought to encourage other forms of energy use, including biomass energy from trees. Shafik found no link between the openness of the economy and deforestation, i.e. international trade policy appears unrelated to deforestation. A similar finding is reported for indebtedness.

What should we conclude from the studies of environmental Kuznets curves? First, environmental data on a cross-sectional and/or time series basis are notoriously difficult to assemble. As such, much of the uncertainty about the linkages may simply reflect the poor quality of the data. Second, if there are bell-shaped Kuznets curves, it cannot be concluded that the best thing to do is to leave the environment to the forces of economic development so that it eventually improves. For example, deforestation rates may eventually slow, but the forest area will be irretrievably reduced. We cannot say that what is lost is the amount of socially desirable losses. What happens is not necessarily what should happen. Third, curves for one environmental variable need not be the same for other variables. We know, for example, that there is no Kuznets curve for CO_2 emissions: they tend to rise consistently with income. Fourth, while the evidence is ambiguous, there is no ground for supposing that environmental degradation is made systematically worse by economic growth. There can be reversals and improvements in quality.

Chapter 8

'Overconsumption'

RESOURCE SCARCITY

Environmental economics teaches that a proximate cause of environ-mental degradation is 'excessive' use of raw materials and energy relative to the availability of resources. The term 'excessive' has no meaning unless it is related to some norm of acceptability. Resources might be being used 'excessively' because the rate of use will give rise to the exhaustion of the resource in some time period deemed to be too short for society to adjust to. Or exhaustion may not be a concern for the current generation's wellbeing, but is for the wellbeing of future generations. The resources in question may be materials (e.g. copper, bauxite, etc.) and energy (coal, oil, gas), or they may comprise the 'sinks' that receive waste from the economic system – e.g. the oceans, the atmosphere, the stratosphere, and so on. In the immediate post-second-world-war period and up to the early 1970s, there was concern that the world would 'run out' of certain materials and certain energy resources. It seems fair to say that few people express that concern now and certainly some of the dire predictions of 'eco-catastrophe' have not come true. This is for several reasons:

- the 'stock of resources' is itself a variable concept: new reserves are found, lower grades of resources become usable as technology improves;
- the ratio of materials and energy use to economic output tends to fall over time, i.e. we become more efficient in our use of resources;
- 'new' resources substitute for old ones, especially in the energy context where significant changes are occurring in the use of renewable energy technologies.

Some (though by no means all) economists argue that the economic system will 'take care' of resource scarcity because as resources become scarce so prices will rise, inducing the kinds of adjustment outlined above. This argument has its own problems, not least because it cannot provide assurance that the rate at which these processes of substitution and technological change will be such as to avoid economic disruption. Nonetheless, 'running out' of energy and materials no longer appears to be such a concern.

The picture is quite different when 'sink resources' and biological diversity are addressed. The Rio Conventions are in fact a sign of global recognition that these resources are scarce. The basic difference between resources such as the atmosphere, stratosphere, oceans and biological diversity and materials and energy resources is that the latter are traded in markets. The former are not. Hence we have no market signals to rely on to correct the growing scarcity. Moreover, since these resources have public good characteristics, as discussed in Chapter 1, we cannot be sure that even if we had markets they would produce the 'right amount' of waste sinks and biodiversity.

From these observations certain conclusions follow immediately:

- The issue for these public-good-type resources is one of creating markets, not of relying on, or modifying, existing markets to correct scarcity.
- Looking at economic indicators of scarcity, such as resource prices, is irrelevant, for there are no resource prices to observe. This explains why much of the economic literature on resource scarcity is, while interesting, irrelevant to practical concerns.
- We need to create indicators of global resource scarcity.
- We need to understand why these global resources are being depleted.

The final 'cause' we need to address is 'overconsumption'. This has become a popular issue for discussion and assessment in recent years. Unfortunately, it has also produced extensive confusion.

THE OVERCONSUMPTION HYPOTHESIS

The overconsumption hypothesis says that resource degradation comes about because people consume 'too many' resources. Moreover, if we inspect the data on who consumes the resources, we find that the richer countries are responsible for most of the materials and energy consumption in the world (Box 8.1). It follows that, since the rich world is responsible for much of the world's degradation, the rich world should (a) reduce its own consumption in order to reduce the burden it imposes on the world's resources, especially those resources that have public good characteristics, and (b) pay for the restoration of the world's environment. What is required the arguments goes, is 'sustainable consumption'. There is considerable force in the argument, but it needs to be handled carefully. The main problem is that it implies that there is only one 'cause' of environmental degradation –

Box 8.1
RESOURCE CONSUMPTION BY RICH AND POOR

Resource or product		Developed countries	Developing countries	Ratio, developed to developing
		(kg or m² per capita)		
Food:	cereals	717	247	2.9
	milk	320	39	8.2
	meat	61	11	5.5
Wood:	roundwood	388	339	1.1
	sawnwood	213	19	11.2
	paper			
Fertilizers		70	15	4.7
Cement		451	130	3.5
Iron/steel		469	36	13.0
Aluminium		16	1	16.0
Cars		0.28	0.01	28.0

Source: World Resources Institute, *World Resources Report 1994/5*, Oxford University Press, Oxford and New York.

---

consumption behaviour – whereas, as the previous chapters show, there are complex forces at work causing the problems. Being rich is not the only factor in environmental degradation. The poor can degrade their environments as well, as Chapter 7 shows.

Other problems arise because of the failure to define what is meant by 'consumption', so that 'reducing consumption' in the rich world means, to some, reducing incomes in the rich world. Moral concerns about the distribution of the world's wealth are also mixed up in the argument. While the moral concerns are wholly legitimate, some false conclusions have been derived as to the policy implications of an unfair world distribution of income.

The confusion has partly arisen because of the loose wording of chapter 4 of *Agenda 21* which speaks of 'sustainable consumption', 'sustainable consumption patterns', and 'lifestyle changes' without defining any of them. The waters are further muddied by reference to the 'optimisation of resource use' and the 'minimisation of waste' without reference to the meaning of optimization, or to any concept of cost. To shed some light on the problem we first need to distinguish between *consumption* and *the consumption of materials and energy, and the assimilative capacity of the environment to deal with waste.* Consumption involves the use of goods and services to meet current wants. The extent to which materials, energy and assimilative capacity – 'resources' as we have described them above – are used up in the act of consumption depends on the *ratio* of resource use to production and consumption. To take the simplest example, the amount of energy used to produce $1 of consumption – the energy intensity of consumption – is an example of such a ratio. The reason that the distinction is important is that consumption can rise while the ratio of resources to consumption can fall at the same time. The extent to which total resource use rises then depends on whether the ratio falls faster than the level of consumption rises.

For the most part, the thrust of *Agenda 21* is that the world needs to raise consumption whilst reducing resource use. Thus, paragraph 4.9 of chapter 4 of *Agenda 21* calls for consideration of 'how economies can grow and prosper while reducing the use of energy and materials and the production of harmful materials'. But some people have wrongly concluded that what is needed is a reduction in consumption. We need to understand why this is not just a misinterpretation, but a serious mistake which, if acted upon, would make the populations of the developing world significantly worse off.

First, reducing consumption can only come about either (a) by raising the fraction of income that is saved for future consumption (investment), or (b) by reducing incomes generally. The savings fraction is open to manipulation by governments through the taxation system or through control of the incentives to save (e.g. interest rates). Control of the overall long term rate of change of income in the economy ('economic growth') is not, by and large, under the control of governments, although there is undoubted scope for lowering economic growth over the short term through sheer mismanagement.

Would either path contribute to an improvement of the wellbeing of the developing world? If savings are increased, some of the increase could be diverted to foreign aid. That would be a transfer of income from North to South, and there are good reasons for supposing that such additional transfers are justified. If incomes are reduced in the North, this does nothing for the South, and is very likely to make them worse off. This is because the 'lost dollar' of consumption in the North does not magically reappear in the South. Not generating it in the North simply means it is not generated at all. Moreover, in so far as some of the consumption in the North spills over into demand for the products of the South, the South is worse off since it loses a market. Sacrificing economic growth, then, means making both the North and the South worse off – this can hardly be the intention of those who advocate 'sustainable consumption'.

In contrast, there are good reasons to reduce resource consumption everywhere by reducing the ratio of resource use to consumption. This will improve the global environment, whilst maintaining economic growth. But we again need to be clear that making those changes in the ratio will not automatically improve the wellbeing of the South. Suppose, for example, the North reduces its ratio of energy use to consumption, as it has done for a very long time in fact. Clearly, this conserves exhaustible energy resources for a longer period than would otherwise be the case. But one tonne of oil not consumed now by the North does not become one tonne of oil that can be consumed by the South. Simply making a resource available does not confer on anyone the power to consume it. That power only comes about through the generation of income, and that means economic growth. Put another way, then, if the North conserves one tonne of oil it does nothing for the economic growth prospects of the South. Of course, if the North's resource consumption falls significantly, resource *prices* could fall. This would benefit the South if the South imports the resources in question. But it will make the South worse off if they export the resource. Ironically, those who call for reductions in the North's consumption are invariably those who complain about low commodity prices on world markets. The two goals may well be inconsistent. Arguing that lower resource consumption in the North will, somehow, make 'ecological space' for the South is seen to be fallacious. Resources may be conserved but they do not in any realistic sense become more available to the South because of that.

The only exception to this rule is if we believe that the future growth prospects of the South are going to be constrained by the absence of resources. That is possible, but not very likely, at least as far as the *supply* of materials and energy is concerned. Growth prospects have far more to do with the pursuit of sensible domestic policies and careful development aid.

We need to find the legitimate sense in which conservation of resources by the North will help the South. It is increasingly apparent that the really scarce resources are not materials and energy, but the receiving capacities of our environments. These are damaged through the use of materials and energy, as exemplified by ozone layer depletion, global warming, ocean pollution etc. Since the world shares these global common resources, damage done by their consumption is shared by everyone, North and South alike, as Chapter 1 showed. Indeed, there is evidence to suggest that the South will suffer disproportionately more from some types of global environmental damage. Chapter 2 showed that the South is likely to suffer more than proportionately in respect of global warming damage, for example.

Finally, reducing resource consumption will of course reduce the environmental impacts in the North itself. Such improvements are unlikely to have a significant effect on the environments or real incomes of the South, but they clearly have their own justification. That is, it makes sense for the North to reduce resource use out of the North's own self-interest.

Agenda 21 speaks interchangeably of changing consumption and changing consumption *patterns*. (It also speaks illogically of 'very high consumption patterns'. A pattern cannot be high or low). But the two are quite different. Consumption can change without the pattern – the product composition of demand – changing, and the pattern can change without the overall level of consumption changing. If our interest is in reducing *resource* consumption, as we argued above it should be, then changing consumption patterns away from resource-intensive products to less resource-intensive products will help achieve the desired effect. From a policy standpoint, however, the kinds of measures that need to be adopted will be the same. They will be characterized by measures that penalize high resource-intensive activities and which therefore make other less resource-intensive activities more attractive.

Care needs to be taken when interpreting the loose wording of *Agenda 21*. If it is interpreted as an old-fashioned call for less *economic growth* in the North, then it is a mischievous and irresponsible interpretation. Sacrificing economic growth will do nothing to improve the wellbeing of the South. It is far more likely to make things worse. Of course, reducing economic growth could improve the natural environment, but it is easily seen that it is a heavy-handed and unnecessary weapon to achieve that objective. It hardly makes sense to make people poorer (even if reducing long-term growth rates was something that could be an object of policy – as noted above, it is far from clear that it has much to do with policy at all) to achieve a goal that can be achieved without making people poorer. Nor do we have any guarantee that reducing growth of consumption in the North would be any more 'sustainable' than current levels. By fostering unemployment and social unrest it could easily be less sustainable.

Making consumption sustainable involves far more complex policies than *Agenda 21* contemplates. It involves not just the 'decoupling' of consumption and resource consumption through the use of economic instruments such as environmental taxes, as advocated in *Blueprint 1*, but the re-investment of rents from the exploitation of natural resources, as advocated in *Blueprint 3*.

TACKLING OVERCONSUMPTION OF RESOURCES

Once the meaning of sustainable consumption is established, the task of addressing how it can be achieved becomes clearer. The role of any policy has to be to 'drive a wedge' between consumption and resource consumption. It so happens that economic instruments have superior attributes that make them more suitable for this task than conventional environmental policies based on 'command and control' approaches. An economic instrument operates by charging a price for the use of environmental resources. This price might be introduced as a direct tax – a carbon tax for example – or it might be introduced more indirectly through a tradeable pollution permit or resource quota. A resource quota, for example, operates by limiting the total amount of a resource that may be used to a set limit. Quotas up to that limit are then issued and resource users – fishermen, say – can bid for the quotas. The price of the quotas in the market place is then very similar to an environmental tax – it is the price to be paid for using up a scarce resource.

Such economic instruments work to achieve sustainable resource consumption in two ways. First, they encourage reductions in the ratio of resource use to product output. Second, because some of the cost is passed on to consumers, they encourage consumers to switch consumption from resource-intensive products to less resource-intensive products. In the language of *Agenda 21* they achieve both reduced materials consumption and changes in consumption patterns.

Note that one can use traditional environmental policy to 'drive a wedge' between resource consumption and consumption. Any environmental regulation, for example, makes the use of the environment more expensive. Regulations are not costless. So long as the regulations are obeyed, then we can also expect resource consumption to be reduced and consumption patterns to change.

While 'command and control' can help achieve the desired outcome of sustainable consumption, it is well known that economic instruments are a superior means of achieving this end, as *Blueprint 1* argued. Briefly, this superiority lies in:

● *Cost efficiency:* economic instruments tend to involve industry in much lower compliance costs than command and control instruments. This is because they give industry much greater flexibility in the means of compliance. For example, command and control often takes the form of technology-based standards ('best available technology' – BAT) which leaves industry no option as to how to comply. BAT is invariably the most expensive option (Tietenberg,

1991; Pearce and Brisson, 1994). Note that cost efficiency is not just a matter of resource allocation. Industry is more likely to resist high-cost environmental measures. Hence environmental objectives may be better achieved by persuading industry that economic instruments are to their advantage.

● *Dynamic incentives:* economic instruments contribute to the continuing search for better and better technology to reduce resource use. This is because the price incentive remains as long as pollution damage remains.

● *Revenue raising:* in recent years the role of environmental taxes as revenue raisers has become increasingly important. Economists have long argued that taxes on effort and enterprise are inefficient and act as a 'drag' on the economy. Indirect taxes – taxes on consumption – are much to be preferred. People can then decide whether to pay the tax or not by deciding whether to consume the product or not. Environmental taxes are indirect taxes and can serve two functions: making it easier to cut other distortionary taxes and helping to reduce resource consumption at the same time. More recently still, it is recognised that environmental taxes can serve a 'double function' of reducing resource consumption and helping to stimulate employment by using the revenues to reduce payroll taxes.

If economic instruments are so attractive, why are they not commonplace? The first thing to say is that they are more widespread than might perhaps be thought. Box 8.2 shows the range of instruments already in place in OECD countries. A large number of countries use economic instruments in one form or another. However, increases since 1987 have been fairly modest and they are concentrated in a few countries – basically Scandinavia and the USA. Why has there been such slow progress?

The reasons are several. First, there is a very long legacy of command and control measures, often dating back to the very first public health legislation. Changing a regulatory philosophy that has been in place often for more than a hundred years is not easy. There is a substantial in-built inertia to the system.

Second, industry is suspicious of economic instruments and does not trust government. A pollution tax introduced today becomes a general revenue-raising tax tomorrow. The way to resolve this problem is to introduce economic instruments so that they provide 'up front' incentives for industry to cooperate. To overcome the fear that environmental taxes will be used for general revenue-raising purposes, environmentalists would be well advised to begin thinking of using tax

Box 8.2
ECONOMIC INSTRUMENTS IN OECD COUNTRIES, 1992

	Emission charges	Product charges	Deposit refunds	Tradeable permits	Enforcement incentives
USA	5	6	4	4	2
Sweden	3	11	4	0	2
Canada	3	7	1	2	2
Denmark	3	10	2	0	0
Finland	3	10	2	0	0
Norway	4	8	3	0	0
Australia	5	1	3	1	2
Germany	5	3	2	1	0
Netherlands	5	4	2	0	0
Austria	3	4	3	0	0
Belgium	7	2	1	0	0
Portugal	4	3	3	0	0
France	5	2	0	0	0
Switzerland	3	2	1	0	0
Italy	3	2	0	0	0
Iceland	1	1	2	0	0
Japan	3	1	0	0	0
Ireland	2	1	0	0	0
Greece	0	2	1	0	0
Spain	3	0	0	0	0
UK	1	1	0	0	0
NZ	1	0	0	0	0
Turkey	0	0	1	0	0

Source: OECD, 1994.

Countries in **bold** have increased their use of economic instruments since 1987, the date of the last survey carried out by OECD.

revenues to provide industry with immediate benefits, e.g. through capital investment allowances.

Third, a further reason for distrust is that industry has a well-rehearsed lobby that understands the regulatory system in place. It knows who to lobby and how. It can, in the economist's language, 'capture' the regulators. Industry also knows where it is with a regulation: it can accommodate it and help mould the process. Dealing with environmental taxes and tradeable permits is more difficult. The source of the measure is invariably the Ministry of Finance, not the Environment Ministry. Regulatory capture is more complex under market-based instruments.

CONCLUSIONS

'Overconsumption' has quickly become a fashionable explanation for environmental degradation and a rallying cry for those who, rightly, argue for deeper, extended concern for the world's poor. Unfortunately, it has also generated a misleading literature.

First, one of the purposes of economic development is to make people better off in terms of their real incomes. There is no evidence that people wish to reduce or even just maintain their current level of real income. To argue, then, that the rich of the world are 'too rich' is to deny basic aspirations. There may be good arguments for doing this if there is no alternative, and if the reason for constraining incomes is itself superior to serving people's wants. Some advocates of sustainability might argue that sustainability is indeed such a superior objective. But even if this were true, it is then important to demonstrate that there is no alternative means to achieving the same end.

Second, even if curtailing the growth of real incomes was an objective of policy, it is not very clear how it would come about, or at what cost in social terms. Governments almost certainly do not control long-term growth rates, however much credit they may wish to take for economic growth. Reducing growth therefore becomes a matter of persuading people that what they want is less growth. There can be no problem with that, although there are few signs of it happening. While we wait, environments degrade.

Third, curtailing economic growth in the North does nothing to improve growth prospects in the South. It almost certainly makes the prospects for the South worse.

Fourth, what is needed is not 'growth control' but reductions in the use of materials and other resources. But that is achievable by making significant reductions in the 'environmental intensity' of economic activity. Chapter 7 shows that, historically, that is quite feasible in growing economies.

Fifth, 'overconsumption' – in the sense of high resource intensity – is the result of the wrong economic signals being present in the economy. As long as resources have low prices relative to the environmental costs involved in using them, excessive resource consumption will be encouraged. Overconsumption is not a fundamental cause of environmental degradation. Overconsumption is a symptom, a reflection of the kinds of economic failure discussed in Chapter 5. Correcting economic failures will correct overconsumption. The 'right' level of resource consumption is that which emerges when the true costs of resource use are embodied in the prices of products and materials. (But that was the message of *Blueprint 1*.)

PART III

Capturing global value

———— ◆ ————

Chapter 9

Global bargains

INTRODUCTION

Part I explained the nature of 'the global commons', resources which are threatened by human activity and on which we all depend in ways that require scientific analysis to explain. Part II was devoted to an understanding of why these resources are being degraded. Causal explanations are complex. Unquestionably, population growth is at the heart of much of the problem through the role that population growth plays in expanding the demand for activities which give rise to land and coastal zone conversion. While conventionally popular, other explanations are not real explanations of resource degradation, as with the 'overconsumption' hypothesis addressed in Chapter 8. Yet other explanations turn out to be more complex than the popular literature suggests, as with 'poverty' and 'indebtedness'. Much of the explanation lies with economic failure, the failure of local and global economic systems to 'internalize' the costs of environmental degradation. In the global context three elements of this economic failure stand out: market failure at the local and national level, the failure of governments to understand that their actions in various spheres have detrimental economic consequences, and the failure of global markets to function. Chapter 5 dealt with local market failure and government failure. It also showed how 'missing markets' in the global context also explain resource degradation. This chapter looks at how we can exploit the global missing markets phenomenon and create markets in global environmental goods.

SUSTAINABILITY AND GLOBAL VALUE

The previous chapters have argued that economics is well on the way to demonstrating the economic value of environmental assets. Chapter 5 used the tropical forest context to demonstrate global value and to hint at ways in which there might be 'global bargains' – bargains between those who act as the proximate agents of environmental destruction and those who derive economic benefit from conservation. While there are significant local conservation benefits, there is evidence to suggest that the global benefits dominate in the context of tropical forests. This latter proposition remains uncertain since (a) the science of global warming is not finalized, so that the carbon storage benefits of forests are probabilistic, and (b) investigations into global existence value have barely commenced. The former can only be resolved by waiting for the scientists. The latter requires a concerted research effort in economic valuation. This leaves the issue of appropriation: how are the economic values turned into cash, technology or commodity flows to make them 'real' to those who make land-use decisions in the tropical forests?

Pursuing the tropical forest example, the appropriation issue has first to be put into the context of sustainable land utilization. The essence of the land-use decision in tropical forests is that, in many cases, there exists a supply of open access land beyond the existing frontiers of cultivation. Provided this land is available, there is no 'land constraint' and the absence of this constraint provides a major incentive for 'nutrient mining' whereby the soil and biomass nutrient stock in the forest is treated as an exhaustible resource, not a renewable one. What this means is that the biomass of the forest becomes a nutrient to the soil when converted to ash by burning. Added to the often limited natural nutrient values of forest soils, the farmer effectively has a stock of nutrients which can be used up over time – often very short periods of time – before they are exhausted and the farmer moves on to a new plot. Southgate (1994) suggests that some Central and South American countries and the Caribbean have hit the land constraint, either because of natural barriers – Bolivia and Peru – or for other reasons – Uruguay, Costa Rica, Nicaragua, Honduras, El Salvador, Guatemala, Dominican Republic and Jamaica. In Haiti the extensive margin has actually gone beyond the 'zero rent' point, i.e. the point where no profit at all is derived from the extra land. Using a simple econometric model, Southgate shows that land conversion rates are less in those countries where the land constraint bites, and that increases in agricultural productivity substantially reduce the drive to extend the frontier. This offers one clue to policy design – increases in agricultural productivity may be the single most important measure for slowing the rate of deforestation in certain areas. If so, a good deal of rethinking is required with respect to conventional policy: saving biodiversity through forest protection policies not only does nothing to contain the drive to extend the frontier, it may actually exacerbate it. Similarly, the distinction between 'development' and 'environment' policies virtually disappears: some development policies become the most powerful means of protecting local and global environmental benefits. (None of this should be allowed to divert attention from 'management failure' as a factor in deforestation, i.e. inefficiency arising from poor forest management).

Box 9.1 illustrates the essential features of the forest sustainability argument. Profitability is shown on the vertical axis, and time on the horizontal axis. Forest clearance usually takes place through burning. The burn converts the major part of the nutrient stock, which is in the forest biomass, into ash which makes the nutrients available to the

---

Box 9.1
SUSTAINABILITY AND INTERNATIONAL COMPENSATION:
THE TROPICAL FOREST EXAMPLE

[This box may be omitted without loss of continuity]

The diagram shows how a forest colonizer might behave; $\pi 1$ and $\pi 2$ are profit curves for the farmer. On clearing the forest, profits are good as the initial stock of nutrient from the burning process is used to grow crops or ranch livestock. As the nutrients decline, however, profits decline until at time T1 they are exhausted. Even before they are exhausted, however, the farmer may move on to another plot of forest land since profits from that land may be higher (see $\pi 2$). As long as the forest is not near its 'extensive margin', i.e. the point where more land is simply not available, this process of continuous degradation is likely to carry on. These profit curves can be compared to the sustainable land use profits, shown as SS. The sustainable management options last longer but may offer lower profitability to the farmer. The difference in profits is shown as the shaded area. If the rest of the world benefits from forest conservation it will be prepared to pay some amount to the farmer. These amounts of 'global value' may well be in excess of the shaded area, in which case there is scope for a global bargain.

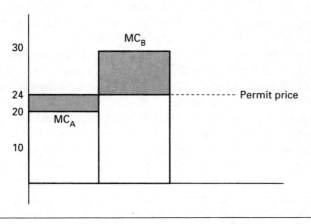

nutrient-deficient soil, clears pests and makes the land suitable for crops. But the nutrients are a stock resource, so that cropping reduces the stock over time and hence the productivity of the soil. This is shown by the strictly concave profit functions. Since there may be multiple users of the land the picture is complicated. Loggers may be there first, followed by crop farmers followed by ranchers (Schneider, 1992). For any single user the switchover point – the time at which the farmer moves on to new land – will be determined by a comparison of the profitability of staying on the existing piece of land and the profitability of moving to the new land. Transport and other costs are likely to rise the further the frontier moves out, so that $\pi2$ begins at a lower point of profitability than $\pi1$. T1 is then the switchover point. Since there are multiple users, the original land area may continue to be used beyond T1, although, as long as new land is available to other users as well, they too will move before total exhaustion is reached at T2. This means that some nutrients are left and regeneration is possible, albeit with a different diversity of biomass. The land is not 'dead' altogether, but its nutrient stock is potentially severely depleted.

However, if the second area is not available because the extensive margin has been reached, then there are incentives to invest in productivity-raising assets – soil conservation, for example. But since we are trying to explain deforestation, the focus is on regions where, after nutrient mining in one area, a new area is cleared. From the colonizer's standpoint, it is the (present) value of the succession of future profits that matters. Nothing is lost by reinterpreting the concave functions in Box 9.1 as discounted flows. These flows need to be compared to the 'sustainable' alternative, say agro-forestry with a focus on non-timber products and some internalization of the global externalities. For simplicity, we show this alternative as the gently declining line SS in the diagram in Box 9.1. The conservation issue is threefold in the case where no land constraint bites: (a) raising the height of SS in order to demonstrate that sustainable utilization may well be profitable in some cases; (b) raising the height of $\pi1$ to reduce the incentive to move to area 2; and (c) compensating the colonizer for the forgone profits shown as the shaded area in the diagram. Policy (a) is preferred if sustainable use alternatives are viable and the issue is one of information and demonstration. Policy (b) is preferred if sustainable use alternatives simply do not appear to be competitive. Policy (c) is preferred where (a) and (b) cannot, for any reason, be applied, i.e. both sustainable alternatives and on-site productivity improvements are not feasible. Policy (c) requires finding compensation mechanisms to enable colonists to capture the forgone profits shown as the shaded area. These compensation mechanisms are what comprise global bargains, i.e. payments in cash, kind or as some other form of benefit by those who secure gains in wellbeing from conservation to those who would otherwise behave, often quite rationally from their point of view, so as to destroy the environment asset in question. In short, securing sustainability through conservation requires that the losses from sustainable behaviour, as viewed by the resource user, should be compensated by the gainers.

MECHANISMS FOR VALUE CAPTURE

There are several ways in which global missing markets can be corrected through creating global environmental markets (GEMs). We distinguish between private and public ('official') ventures, and between those that are regulation-induced and those that are spontaneous market initiatives. Public regulation – induced activity arises because of international agreements, such as the Biodiversity and Climate Change Conventions. Box 9.2 sets out a schema.

Regulation-induced trades

The existence, or threatened existence, of regulations acts as a stimulus to trade.

Box 9.2
A SCHEMA FOR GLOBAL ENVIRONMENTAL MARKETS

	Regulation-induced	Spontaneous market
Public/official ventures	Examples: government-to-government measures under joint implementation provisions of the Rio treaties: Norway, Mexico, Poland, GEF.	Example: government involvement in market ventures: Swiss Green Export aid; debt-for-nature swaps.
Private sector ventures	Examples: carbon offsets against carbon taxes and externality adders.	Examples: purchase of exotic capital – Merck and Costa Rica.

Government–government trades

The first 'joint implementation' agreement has been agreed between Norway, Poland and Mexico, through the medium of the Global Environment Facility (GEF). The nature of joint implementation is set out in Chapter 12 but the essence of the concept is that country A secures a benefit by reducing emissions or undertaking conservation in country B. A's benefit is the 'credit' under some global environmental agreement for improving the environment, or it may be that A simply seeks a good global 'green image'. Under the agreement in question, Norway agrees to create additional financing (through the revenues from its own carbon tax) for GEF carbon-reducing projects in Mexico (energy-efficient lighting) and Poland (converting from coal-burning to natural gas) (Global Environment Facility, 1992). The US Environmental Defence Fund is understood to be developing a reforestation project in Russia. The US government announced the Forest for the Future Initiative (FFI) in January 1993 under which carbon offset agreements will be negotiated between the USA and several countries, including Mexico, Russia, Guatemala, Indonesia and Papua New Guinea. The aim is for the US Environmental Protection Agency to broker deals involving the private sector.

Private sector trades

The European Community's on-going flirtation with a carbon tax and other European legislation also provides an incentive to trade in this way, as does state regulation on pollution by electric utilities in the USA. While not strictly a private enterprise trade, in the Netherlands, the state electricity generating board (SEP) established a non-profit making enterprise in 1990. FACE (Forests Absorbing Carbon Dioxide Emissions) aims to sequester an amount of CO_2 equivalent to that emitted by one 600 MW power station. This is estimated to require some 150,000 hectares: 5000 ha in the Netherlands, 20,000 ha in central Europe and 125,000 ha in tropical countries. At the end of 1993 the actual area had risen to 180,000 ha with the additional area in tropical countries (Box 9.3).

In the US case the offset deals are currently not directly linked to legislation, but several have occurred which are clearly a mix of anticipation of regulation and 'global good citizenship' (Newcombe and de Lucia, 1993). These include the New England Power Company's investment in carbon sequestration in Sabah, Malaysia through the reduction of carbon waste from inefficient logging activities. The forest products enterprise is run by Innoprise. New England Power estimate that some 300,000 to 600,000 tonnes of carbon (C) will be offset at a cost of below \$2/tC. Rain Forest Alliance will

Box 9.3
PRIVATE SECTOR CARBON OFFSET DEALS

Company	Project	Other participants	Million tC sequestered or reduced	Total cost ($ million)	$ tC sequestered
AES	Agro-forestry Guatemala	US CARE Govt. of Guatemala	15–58 over 40 years	15	a) 0.5–2* b) 1–4 c) 9
AES	Nature reserve Paraguay	US Nature Conservancy FMB	13 over 30 years	6	a) 0.2 b) 0.45 c) < 1.5
AES	Secure land tenure, sustainable agriculture Bolivia, Peru, Ecuador	Other utilities giving consideration to deal	na	2	na
SEP	Reforestation:				
	Netherlands		0.9	20	b) 22.7
	Czech Rep.		3.1	30	b) 9.7
	Malaysia	Innoprise	6.3	15.7	b) 2.5
	Ecuador		9.7	17.3	b) 1.8
	Uganda		7.2	8.0	b) 1.1
	Indonesia		6.8	21.17	b) 3.2
Tenaska and others	Reforestation Russia	EPA, Trexler, Min. of Ecology, Russian Forest Service	0.5 over 25 years	0.5?	a) na b) 1 c) 1–2
Tenaska	Forest conservation in Costa Rica, and reforestation in Washington state	Other utilities giving consideration	na	5+	b) 43
PacifiCorp	Forestry, Oregon	Trexler	0.06 pa	0.1 pa	a) na b) na c) 15–30
PacifiCorp	Urban trees Utah	Trexler TreeUtah	?	0.1 pa	a) na b) na c) 15–30
New England PC	Forestry, Malaysia	Rain Forest Alliance, COPEC	0.1–0.15	0.45	a) na b) 3–4.5 c) na
New England PC	Methane recovery in Appalachians	na	na	na	na

| Wisconsin Electric Power Co; NIPSCO Industry; Edison Devpt Co. | Coal-to-gas conversion | Bynov Heating Plant, Decin, Czech Republic | 12,800 tpa? | 1.5 | b) 43 |

Source: Pearce (1994). CO_2 converted to C at 3.67:1. Dutch guilders converted to $US at 1.75 DG per $.

Notes: a) Assumes 10% discount rate applied to total cost to obtain an annuity which is then applied to carbon fixed per annum, assuming equal distribution of carbon sequestered over the time horizon indicated.
b) Assumes no discounting.
c) Cost per tC as reported in Dixon *et al.* (1993).

assist in monitoring the project. New England Power regard the Innoprise project as the first of a series aimed at assisting with the Corporation's plan to reduce CO_2 emissions by 45 per cent by the year 2000. PacifiCorp, an electric utility in Oregon, is considering reforestation projects and urban tree planting programmes in the US, and an international sequestration project (Dixon *et al.*, 1993). Two pilot projects have been announced: (a) a rural reforestation project in Southern Oregon which funds planting subject to a constraint of no harvesting for 45–65 years, at an estimated cost of around $5/tC; and (b) an urban tree programme in Salt Lake City, Utah at a provisionally estimated cost of $15–30/tC sequestered. Tenaska Corporation is considering sequestration projects in the Russian boreal forests. Ultimately, some 20,000 ha of forests may be created in the Saratov and Volgograd regions at a cost of $1–2/tC. Russian partners in the venture include the Russian Forest Service, the Ministry of Ecology and others. Tenaska is also planning reforestation projects in Washington state to complement a project in Costa Rica (see Box 9.3).

While these investments are aimed at CO_2 reduction, sequestration clearly has the potential for generating joint benefits, i.e. for saving biodiversity as well through the recreation of habitats. Much depends here on the nature of the offset. If the aim is CO_2 fixation alone, there will be a temptation to invest in fast-growing species which could be to the detriment of biodiversity. It is important therefore to extend the offset concept so that larger credits are given for investments which produce joint biodiversity–CO_2 reduction benefits.

The US Energy Policy Act of 1992 requires the Energy Information Administration to develop guidelines for the establishment of a database on greenhouse gas offsets, together with an offset 'bank'. The Keystone Center in the USA is also establishing an interchange of information with a number of electric utilities to explore the issues involved in the establishing offset deals.

Global good citizenship

Several offset deals appear to have been undertaken quite independently of legislation or anticipation of regulation. Applied Energy Services (AES) of Virginia has also undertaken sequestration investments in Guatemala (agroforestry) and Paraguay and is in the process of setting up another project in the Amazon basin. The Guatemala project is designed to offset emissions from a 1800 MW coal-fired power plant being built in Uncasville, Connecticut. The intermediary for the project is the World Resources Institute and in Guatemala the implementing agency is CARE. The project involves tree planting by some 40,000 farm families, soil conservation techniques, and biomass conservation through fire prevention measures etc. Carbon sequestration is estimated to be 15.5 million tons of carbon. The $15 million cost includes $2 million contribution from AES; $1.2 million from the Government of Guatemala; $1.8 million from CARE, with the balance coming in-kind from US AID and the Peace Corps. The motivations for involvement vary. AES's involvement relates to its concern not just to offset CO_2 emissions, but to achieve local development and environmental benefits the deal brings. Dixon *et al.* (1993) report the sequestration cost as $9/tC overall, but inspection of the data suggests it may be much less than this. $9/tC would be expensive for carbon sequestration alone, but there are other benefits from the scheme, including local economic benefits. In the Paraguay deal, AES has advanced money to the (US) Nature Conservancy for investment in some 57,000 ha of endangered tropical forest. The International Finance Corporation agreed to sell the land for $2m, well below the market price of $5–7m. AES expects to sequester some 13 million tC at around $1.5/tC to offset CO_2 emissions from the Barbers Point 180 MW coal-fired plant in Oahu, Hawaii. Local benefits include eco-tourism, scientific research, recreation, agroforestry and watershed protection. AES is also planning to offset emissions from a third power plant with support for indigenous peoples in Peru, Ecuador and Bolivia to secure title to their lands and to develop sustainable extractive activities.

Buying down private risk

Newcombe and de Lucia (1993) have drawn attention to another potentially very large private trade which has global environmental benefits. Investment by the private sector in the developing world is invariably constrained by risk factors such as exchange rate risks, repayment risks, political risks and so on. In so far as this investment benefits the global environment, as with, say, the development of natural gas to displace coal, the existence of the risks reduces the flow of investment and hence the global environmental benefits. But these risks might be shared ('bought down') by having an international agency, such as the Global Environment Facility, provide some funds or services which help reduce the risk. Given the scale of private investment flows, the potential here is enormous. Nor is there any reason why it should not benefit biodiversity, either indirectly as a joint benefit of other investments in, e.g., raising agricultural productivity and hence in reducing the pressure for land degradation, or directly through afforestation schemes.

'Exotic capital'

Financial transfers may take place without any regulatory 'push'. The consumer demand for green products has already resulted in companies deciding to invest in conservation either for direct profit or because of a mix of profit and conservation motives. The Body Shop is an illustration of the mixed motive, as is Merck's royalty deal with Costa Rica for pharmaceutical plants and Pro-Natura's expanding venture in marketing indigenous tropical forest products. There is, in other words, an incentive to purchase or lease 'exotic capital' in the same way as a company would buy or lease any other form of capital.

The deal between Merck & Co, the world's largest pharmaceutical company, and INBio (the National Biodiversity Institute of Costa Rica) is already well documented and studied (Gámez *et al.*, 1993; Sittenfield and Gámez, 1993; Blum, 1993). Under the agreement, INBio collects and processes plant, insect and soil samples in Costa Rica and supplies them to Merck for assessment. In return, Merck pays Costa Rica $1 million plus a share of any royalties should any successful drug be developed from the supplied material. The royalty agreement is reputed to be of the order of 1 per cent to 3 per cent and to be shared between INBio and the Costa Rican government. Patent rights to any successful drug would remain with Merck. Biodiversity is protected in two ways – by conferring commercial value of the biodiversity, and through the earmarking of some of the payments for the Ministry of Natural Resources.

How far is the Merck-INBio deal likely to be repeated? Several caveats are in order to offset some of the enthusiasm over this single deal. First, Costa Rica is in the vanguard of biodiversity conservation, as its strong record in debt-for-nature swaps shows. Second, Costa Rica has a strong scientific base and a considerable degree of political stability. Both of these characteristics need to be present and their combination is not typical of that many developing countries. Third, the economic value of such deals is minimal unless the royalties are actually paid and that will mean success in developing drugs from the relevant genetic material. The chances of such developments are small – perhaps one in one to ten thousand of plants species screened (Pearce and Moran, 1994). INBio has undertaken to supply 10,000 samples under the initial agreement. There is therefore a chance of one such drug being developed. But successful drugs could result in many hundreds of millions of dollars in revenues. Finally, there are two views on the extent to which deals of this kind could be given added impetus by the Biodiversity Convention. The Convention stresses the role of intellectual property rights in securing conservation and is sufficiently vaguely worded for there to be wide interpretation of its provisions. But it also appears to threaten stringent conditions concerning those rights and technology transfer and it remains to be seen how the relevant Protocols are worded. If so, parties to the Convention may find private deals being turned into overtly more political affairs with major constraints on what can be negotiated (Blum, 1993).

Other examples of direct deals on 'biodiversity prospecting' include California's Shaman Pharmaceuticals (Brazil and Argentina) and the UK's Biotics Ltd (general purchase and royalty deals), while Mexico and Indonesia are looking closely at the commercialization of biodiversity resources.

The demand for direct investment in conservation is not confined to the private sector. The demand for conservation by NGOs is revealed through debt-for-nature swaps, which are further examples of these exotic capital trades (for an overview see Pearce and Moran, 1994 and Deacon and Murphy, 1994).

Mixed private/public trades: resource franchise agreements

A great variety of trades involving both the public and private sectors is possible. For example consider the general area of resource franchise agreements (RFAs). The general principle of RFAs is that specific land uses in defined zones are restricted ('attenuated') in return for the payment of a premium. At one extreme, if all land uses other than outright preservation are forbidden, the premium equals the rental on the land that would arise in the 'best' developmental use. If some uses are restricted, the premium will tend to be equal to the differential rent between the unrestricted 'highest and best' use and the rental on the restricted use. The minimum supply price offered by colonizers and host governments will be this differential rent. The demand price will be determined by global willingness to pay for the benefits of attenuating land uses. This is the essence of the comparison made earlier between land prices and global warming damage estimates, for example. Payment of the premium would be, say, annual since an 'up front' payment could result in the host country reneging on the understanding after payment is received. To secure compliance, annual payments would be made in order that they can be suspended in the event of non-compliance.

Such trades are not without their problems. The example of carbon storage values in Chapter 4 compared land prices with the present value of global warming damage from a tonne of carbon dioxide. Two discount rates are embedded in this comparison: the farmer's and the world's. If payments have to be annual, the present values need to be annuitized. Since it is the farmer who has the property rights, his discount rate will dominate. The relevant comparison will be between annual willingness to pay and annual willingness to accept a premium. Another issue relates to the successional uses of land. The logger should effectively pay a price for land that reflects not just the logging value, but also a residual price of the land if it can be on-sold to ranchers or farmers. Markets need to work fairly well for the conservation and development values to be compared.

Several authors have suggested franchise-type agreements – Sedjo (1988); Panayotou (1994); Katzman and Cale (1990). Such development rights could become tradeable, just as joint implementation schemes could become open to subsequent bargains leading to a full emissions trading programme. The potential buyers could range from local conservation groups through to international conservation societies, corporations, governments and so on, with motives ranging from profiting from sustainable use through to scientific research and good citizenship images. Panayotou (1994) suggests that corporations in developed countries could be given credit for buying into such tradeable rights, e.g. through relaxations on domestic regulatory obligations. Measured against the status quo this obviously has the disadvantage of 'trading' environmental quality between developed and developing country economies, a problem that has brought criticism on joint implementation proposals already. Nonetheless, the approach could be utilized in the event of tighter developed country restrictions being contemplated.

CONCLUSIONS ON GLOBAL BARGAINS

The ways in which economics can help the global environment have hardly been tested. The potential for creating mutually beneficial bargains rests on a two-stage procedure of 'demonstration and capture' involving:

● demonstrating that substantial economic value resides in the protection of the global environment;
● showing how mutually profitable trades can emerge so as to capture that economic value.

None of this implies a diversion from policies aimed at correcting domestic market failures nor domestic intervention failures, nor management failure – the equivalent of 'X inefficiency' in forest management. Nor does it imply an exclusive focus on the developing world. The rich world has more than its fair share of gross distortions that destroy the rich world's remaining environmental assets. But the focus on developing countries is justified because (a) they possess many of the global resources, such as the tropical forests which, in turn, have such an array of ecological, and therefore economic, benefits for the world in general; and (b), a critical point, the corrective measures needed can stimulate economic development as well as conserving resources.

But there are clear risks in resting conservation arguments solely on the economic values of conservation. A balanced approach would stress the incidental conservation benefits of other policies aimed at correcting economic distortions. Indeed, those benefits may be huge. As far as tropical forests are concerned, while the evidence is still limited, what there is suggests that those who argue for the conservation of tropical forests on grounds of local economic value alone – e.g. non-timber products and sustainable timber benefits (Peters *et al.*, 1989) – may not have such a strong case. The initial enthusiasm that greeted claims of high-value sustainable forest use based on non-timber forest products (NTFPs) has waned somewhat in the face of (a) methodological doubts about such studies (e.g. Godoy and Lubowski, 1992; Southgate and Whitaker, 1994); (b) revised estimates of NTFP productivity; (c) wrong extrapolation from one forest type to another (Phillips, 1994; Godoy and Lubowski, 1992); and (d) doubts about the sustainability of NTFP exploitation itself (Peters *et al.*, 1989).

Some of the global use benefits may also not be large enough to outweigh the developmental benefits of forest clearance. Simpson *et al.* (1994) suggest that pharmaceutical values, for example, are modest. The value of the 'marginal species' is likely to be very low due to (a) the high number of species, and (b) the substitution possibilities. Translated into per hectare values, we may be speaking of only a few dollars. But two elements of global value stand out in the tropical forest context: carbon storage value of forests, and 'existence' value. This may well be several times the domestic value, and the issue then is how to capture that value through measures such as joint implementation and perhaps eventually a full greenhouse gas trading regime. But if global values are going to save the tropical forests and other 'global' environments there has to be an imaginative use of a wide range of instruments, from debt-for-nature swaps to tradeable development rights to joint implementation and private green image investments. The challenge remains: demonstrate and appropriate.

Chapter 10

The Global Environment Facility and the Rio Conventions

INTRODUCTION

The Montreal Protocol (MP) has as its financial mechanism the Multilateral Fund (the MF), out of which all agreed incremental costs are to be met on a grant financing (zero interest rate) basis. The MF is jointly managed by the World Bank, the United Nations Development Programme (UNDP), and the United Nations Environment Programme (UNEP). The interim financial mechanism of the two Rio Conventions is the Global Environment Facility (GEF) which is managed by the same three institutions. The GEF began life in 1991 (as 'GEF I') with an initial endowment of just over $1 billion for expenditures to secure global environmental benefits from global warming control, biodiversity conservation, and pollution control in international waters. In 1994 the GEF's resources were replenished ('GEF II') with an endowment of $2 billion. This chapter looks at the genesis of the GEF and some of the controversies surrounding its operation.

THE BEGINNINGS OF THE GEF

The GEF was created to deal with global environmental problems. Because of what in Chapter 1 we referred to as the public-good nature of the solutions to these problems, unilateral action by individual countries will not take place. The issue then becomes one of using existing institutions, or creating a new one. The resulting GEF was a compromise: a separate organization but built on the existing UN agencies – UNEP, the World Bank, and UNDP. Its funding had to be additional to existing sources of aid, otherwise developing countries would not have agreed to its existence – the GEF funds would have been at the expense of conventional development aid which has higher priority for developing countries. The issue of 'additionality' is dealt with in detail in Chapter 11.

The GEF could not be introduced as a ready-made institution. While the international agencies had vast experience of development aid, no one had previously addressed the issues of funding global projects, projects designed to secure a global benefit. Hence GEF was introduced as a pilot phase in 1990 (GEF I) to learn how to evaluate investments in four areas: global warming control, biodiversity conservation, conservation of stratospheric ozone (under the existing Montreal Protocol) and 'international waters' – seas and lakes shared by two or more nations. While the GEF was created as a new institution, the experience of the development agencies was clearly critical. Hence the tripartite management of the GEF.

In 1987 the Brundtland Report (*Our Common Future*) called for 'a significant increase in financial support' to deal with major environmental issues, and that the United Nations 'should clearly be the locus for new institutional initiatives of a global character'. The Commission actually suggested linking the new facility to the World Bank. The Bank, however, was not popular with many developing countries nor with international non-government organizations. It had been charged with causing, not reducing, environmental destruction through its involvement in development projects that gave scant attention or no attention at all to the environment, its advocacy of 'structural adjustment' – i.e. economic reform in borrowing countries – which was alleged to make environmental issues worse, not better, and its involvement in some major investments, especially hydropower dams, which had led to major social dislocation through population resettlement. This debate never subsided: the Bank's involvement in the GEF was and is controversial for many.

The World Resources Institute (WRI) – a think-tank and policy agency in Washington DC – had established an International Conservation Financing Programme (ICFP). The ICFP became the international forum at which these issues of 'new' financing were discussed. WRI was commissioned by the UNDP to undertake a study on new financing methods. Already some new approaches, notably debt-for-nature swaps, had emerged spontaneously. In 1989, WRI produced its final report calling for the establishment of an 'International Environmental Facility' with funding of $3 billion for five years. This was one of several funds the WRI recommended. While the final report did not mention the World Bank as a 'host' for the IEF, an earlier draft had. The IEF proposal was similar to the eventual pilot phase GEF but lacked the pilot phase concept and the global benefit orientation. There was a separate proposal for a 'Global Environmental Trust Fund' to deal with global warming control, but the GEF was to be financed through international taxes. The WRI report set much of the ground for the eventual GEF, but the report itself did not stimulate action.

In 1987 the World Bank introduced a central Environment Department to give guidance on integrating environmental concerns into Bank lending. An internal debate was going on as to the best way to achieve this and, to a lesser extent, the global issues were part of that debate. The Environment Department itself began releasing documents looking at new financing methods for dealing with global problems. As with the WRI document, reaction was muted, and there was some hostility to creating new funding sources and a separate agency even within the Bank, not least because of the fear that these new funds would not be new at all, but diverted from existing concessional funding for development. But by mobilizing support from outside the Bank, those arguing for the Bank's involvement in some sort of new environmental fund began to gather the upper hand. Knowledge of the WRI proposals, not then (1988) publicly published, also helped, and the UNDP was known to be agitating for a role in any new environmental fund. While technically funding different aspects of development, the Bank (which deals mainly with capital projects) and the UNDP (which deals mainly with capacity-building) have long been rivals. If the Bank did not take on board a new facility, UNDP might. Indeed, UNDP began to solicit support for an expanded environmental role for itself. At the same time, however, UNDP was strenuously distancing itself from the WRI report, despite having helped to commission it, perhaps because it limited UNDP's ability to pursue other proposals then circulating.

In 1989 various proposals were put forward for the creation of a new facility. The 'Hague declaration' of that year called for the creation of a fund for protecting the atmosphere. Prime Minister Rajiv Gandhi of India also called for a Planet Protection Fund funded by a levy of 0.1 per cent of the GDP of contributing countries. In September 1989 the French Minister of Finance presented a proposal to the World Bank Development Committee calling for a study of how to implement a new fund. More importantly, the French backed the proposal with an offer of funds, some 900 million francs over three years. By making the offer in the World Bank, the French proposal effectively ended UNDP's bid for leadership. Neither would UNEP succeed in any bid for leadership since its capacity to manage substantial new funds was in doubt. The French proposal was based on voluntary contributions. Other countries were pursuing the idea of obligatory burden-sharing arrangements. The World Bank was reportedly surprised at the French proposal (Sjoberg, 1993) and was not prepared for the resulting pressure to take action on establishing leadership for a new fund. Nor was there widespread agreement even among donors that the best place for such a fund was the World Bank. Nonetheless, by early 1990 the Bank had produced a discussion paper for a new fund focused exclusively on global environmental problems, rather than generally on environmental issues. The Bank had learned from discussions with donors that only the global focus would elicit additional financing, although concerns were expressed within the Bank that a global focus was not consistent with the Bank's charter which focused on development aid for local benefit. The Bank discussion paper also suggested the four areas of intervention: CFCs, global warming, biodiversity and international waters. The document proposed a tripartite management by UNDP, UNEP and the World Bank, to be known as the Implementing Agencies. The three agencies would meet as the Implementation Committee. Finally, it suggested a pilot phase rather than a permanent body. The building blocks for the GEF were in place.

The new proposals found favour among donors and, generally, among the developing countries. Funding was to be additional, but the US and Australia refused to contribute to a core fund. The US was opposed to funding new ventures based solely on global benefits, and particularly on climate change. UNDP was to deal with technical assistance and institution-building, its traditional concerns, UNEP would look after the links between the GEF, the Montreal Protocol, and the, by then, emerging conventions expected to come from Rio in 1992. The Bank would develop a work programme in association with UNDP and UNEP, and would manage the day-to-day running of the GEF.

In June 1990 the Interim Multilateral Fund of the Montreal Protocol was established with $160 million of funds to assist developing countries to substitute for CFCs. The fund was to increase to $240 million if China and India signed the Protocol. In September 1990 the Joint Declaration on the Global Environment was signed by the three agencies, and it was agreed that core funding for the new agency would be on a grant basis with some co-financing between the GEF and individual country finance being permitted on a concessional basis. In November 1990 the GEF was formally debated by national governments meeting in Paris. There it was suggested that the Interim Fund of the MP should be integrated with the GEF. The US continued its refusal to contribute directly to a core fund but declared its acceptance of the principle of a GEF. Its own contributions would run in parallel via US AID. A Scientific and Technical Advisory Panel (the STAP) was formed and the GEF began officially to function in June of 1991.

THE PILOT PHASE

The Pilot Phase of the GEF lasted from June 1991 to mid-1994. During this period the Rio Conventions were negotiated. It had already been agreed that financing under the Conventions would be linked in some way to the GEF. In May 1992, the GEF published *The Pilot Phase and Beyond* which had been commissioned by the participants to the GEF. It set out the Pilot Phase principles. These included:

- providing additional funding (on a grant and concessional basis) of the 'incremental cost' of interventions designed to secure global benefits. Incremental cost was defined as the extra costs of an activity, over and above the costs in some baseline plan, designed to secure global benefits;
- the GEF accepted that the local/global benefits distinction would be blurred in many cases;
- the GEF would be 'available' as the financial mechanism of the Rio Conventions should the Parties to such conventions so wish;
- the GEF aimed for cost-effectiveness;
- funding would be of 'country-driven' projects consistent with sustainable development; this raised the issue of how incremental costs might be affected by domestic policy distortions, i.e. the greater the distortion the greater the incremental cost; GEF financing would therefore be coordinated with 'appropriate national policies';
- the GEF would build on existing institutions, i.e. the World Bank, UNDP and UNEP;
- the GEF would be accountable and 'transparent'.

The document went on to discuss issues of governance and the future, suggesting a fund that would be replenished every three years. The Pilot Phase had a nominal $1.3 billion in the first three years. The 'Global Environmental Trust Fund' (GET) accounted for $860 million; co-financing funds for some $360 million, and the Montreal Protocol for $200 million. The USA and Australia did not contribute to the GET but set up separate arrangements. As a 'rule of thumb' the GEF was to allocate 40–50 per cent of its funds to global warming control; 30-40% to biodiversity, and 10–20 per cent to international waters. The Montreal Protocol Interim Multilateral Fund was separate. Box 10.1 shows how the funds were actually used during the Pilot Phase.

The fact that the Pilot Phase was designed as a learning process meant that the GEF did not have to have very detailed procedures for evaluating projects. There were many discussions of cost-efficiency,

Box 10.1
THE ALLOCATION OF FUNDS IN THE PILOT PHASE OF THE GEF, 1991–1994

Biodiversity	$333 million	(46%)
Global warming	$260 million	(35%)
International waters	$120 million	(16%)
Ozone	$ 4* million	(1%)
Multiple areas	$17 million	(2%)
Total	$733 million	

*funds not included in the Multilateral Fund which funds ozone projects

THE GEOGRAPHICAL ALLOCATION OF PILOT STAGE FUNDS

		Biodiversity ($m)	Global warming ($m)	Water ($m)
Africa	(16%)	76	25	16
Europe, Mid-East, North Africa	(21%)	62	49	43
Asia/Pacific, Latin America and Caribbean	(33%)	72	130	38
	(22%)	110	27	20
Global programme	(8%)	14	28	3
		334	259	120

The slight bias to Asia was the result of three major projects attracting significant funding.

Source: Global Environmental Facility, 1995, *Semi-Annual Report on the Pilot Phase to February 1995 Council Meeting*, Washington DC.

for example. In the climate context this was at least manageable since projects could be ranked on the basis of tonnes of carbon (equivalent) saved per dollar of expenditure. But what does cost-effectiveness mean in the context of biodiversity? What, for example, is the unit of biodiversity against which cost is compared? Much the same problem arose in the waters context. The GEF's Scientific and Technical Advisory Panel (STAP) addressed these issues, as did the GEF itself, but it seems fair to say that the Pilot Phase projects were not treated in any systematic way. This is reasonable given the 'learning curve' nature of the Pilot Phase, but more might have been done to develop clear criteria for project selection given the high chance that the GEF would be continued into an operational phase in 1994.

The kinds of projects supported by GEF during the Pilot Phase varied substantially. In biodiversity they ranged from management programmes for coastal wetlands, strengthening of protected areas, game ranching, forest restoration and programmes on genetic resources, through to marine pollution-reduction projects and aquatic weed control. In the global warming context, projects ranged from rehabilitating rangelands for carbon sequestration, reduction of coal-bed methane emissions, wind power, solar photovoltaics and energy conservation programmes, through to substitution of lighting by fluorescent lights and switching from coal-fired electricity to gas-fired electricity (the carbon content of gas being less than the content of coal). In international waters there were projects including reducing ship waste disposal in China and the Caribbean, pollution control in Lake Tanganyika, and 'engineered wetlands' for sewage treatment. Some projects sought to apply existing known technologies to problems, others sponsored new technologies to see how they might function in the developing country context. Some projects were controversial. 'Demand-side management' projects – i.e. energy conservation – were encouraged but it is arguable that these represent almost zero cost investments which the developing countries should carry out for themselves. How far the various projects succeeded remains to be seen: projects approved in the Pilot Phase have only just begun in many cases and it is too early to assess their rate of return in terms of global and local benefits.

THE INDEPENDENT EVALUATION

In December 1993 independent evaluators from UNEP, UNDP and the World Bank reported on the progress by GEF (UNEP *et al.*, 1993). Their report makes curious reading, not least because it appeared that limited consultation with the relevant agencies was carried out by the evaluators. Thus the report has a section on the Scientific and Technical Advisory Panel (the STAP) but no member of STAP appears to have been approached by the evaluators. Nonetheless, the evaluators touched on some issues of concern, despite revealing some lack of understanding of the basic concepts involved in GEF operations. Thus, the evaluators were concerned that:

● There was no clear rationale for the selection of the four focal areas for the GEF, although the public goods concept introduced in Chapter 1 would have explained the implicit rationale for them.
● There was no clear rationale for the suggested allocation of funds to the four focal areas. This is certainly correct.

- The Pilot Phase's concern to get roughly equal geographical balance in the distribution of funds was inconsistent with the goal of achieving the largest global benefits. This is again correct and had been pointed out by the STAP in its own discussions.

- The concept of 'incremental cost' had not been developed and was probably not very useful. Incremental cost is discussed in detail in Chapter 11, but the evaluators revealed lack of understanding on this issue since they appeared to think it had been used alone to determine funding. In fact a judgemental approach to global benefits had been used along with some very preliminary attempts to calculate incremental cost. Incremental cost cannot in fact be used on its own to determine project suitability.

- The distinction between local and global benefits is made too sharply by the GEF. There is substantial overlap. Again, it is not clear if this observation was carefully thought through, but it is certainly the case, as Chapter 1 observed, that biodiversity has mixed 'public and private good' characteristics that may make it appear difficult to define in terms of global benefits.

- STAP's own suggested guidelines for project acceptance were non-operational, i.e. not helpful in practice. There is some truth in this observation and it tended to reflect the fact that the STAP consisted of excellent scholars and internationally famous people who had, however, little experience of how project evaluation works in practice.

- There was no real way of knowing whether the GEF was truly operating with 'additional' funds. Again, this is true since it is not easy to say what donors would have given as aid had the GEF not existed.

- Project selection was 'haphazard' in the biodiversity area, and many of the projects would contribute 'only marginally' to global biodiversity conservation. Insufficient attention was given to institutional capacity to manage biodiversity. While a telling point in some ways, the GEF was effectively constrained to operate through individual nations advancing their own projects. The lack of familiarity with the concept of a global benefit certainly meant that many projects were 'old' projects, dusted off and thinly disguised as new ones.

- In the global warming context, the aim of achieving high cost-effectiveness ratios – i.e. high levels of reduction of greenhouse gases per dollar outlay – was 'only partially successful'. This appears to be due to the fact that many global warming projects were already in the pipeline and were not selected on explicit GEF criteria.

● On international waters, there was a concern that biological resource exploitation was neglected, that international waters were not defined, and that a system of priorities was not defined.

Overall, the evaluators felt that GEF's objectives needed a clear statement, that greater participation in the governance of the GEF was required and that the implementing agencies themselves needed to strengthen their management capability over the portfolio of projects. It also called for clearer criteria for the selection of projects.

GEF II

The Evaluators' report combined with continuing developing country and NGO pressure to make the GEF more accountable led to delays in getting the operational stage of GEF, GEF II, under way. New funding of $3 billion was agreed for the period 1994–1997. The additional problems were whether the new GEF would be confirmed as the financial mechanism for the two Conventions. A restructured GEF was developed, but even at the end of 1994 the first meeting of the Conference of Parties to the Biodiversity Convention was casting doubt on the GEF as the financial mechanism for biodiversity. Some countries continued to call for a separate agency and new funds, even though GEF's replenishment would not, apparently, have been available for a further new financial body (i.e. the GEF could have proceeded without being the mechanism for the Convention). The Conference of Parties finally did agree to the GEF as interim financial mechanism, retaining the threat that the GEF might not be 'permanent'.

THE CONVENTION ON BIOLOGICAL DIVERSITY

The Convention on Biological Diversity (CBD) was opened for signature in Rio in June 1992 and entered into force in December 1993. It had been the subject of negotiation since 1988. The Intergovernmental Committee on the Convention on Biological Diversity (ICCBD) was established in 1993 in order to prepare for the first Conference of Parties for the CBD in November 1994. Progress was slow and the Conference of Parties meeting lacked many of the worked-through documents the ICCBD was originally supposed to produce. At the time of writing, many of these issues remain unresolved.

The CBD itself can be summarized as follows. Its objective is the 'conservation of biological diversity (and) the sustainable use of its components' (Article 1) and the 'fair and equitable utilization of the benefits arising out of the utilization of genetic resources' (Article 1).

These objectives establish that conservation in its traditional sense is embraced and that this objective can also be achieved through sustainable use of biological resources. The 'fair and equitable' clause relates mainly to the exploitation of biological diversity as genetic information and for biotechnology, the argument being that the developing world does not 'capture the rents' from its biological resources when exploited by the rich world.

Each signatory country is to prepare a National Plan for biodiversity conservation and is to monitor biodiversity within its own borders (Article 6). The kinds of actions embraced include protected areas; sustainable development activity in areas adjacent to protected areas (to deter invasion of the protected area) and protection of threatened species. Article 11 makes an interesting reference to countries adopting 'as far as possible and appropriate' 'economically and socially sound measures that act as incentives for conservation and sustainable use of biodiversity'. This article is a rather watered-down acknowledgement of 'government failure' (see Chapter 5) as a factor in biodiversity loss, e.g. subsidies to deforestation. Article 7 also calls for the identification of policies which damage biodiversity, but it is clear that the idea of government failure was resisted since it would have placed responsibility for biodiversity loss on the national policies of the developing countries.

The CBD calls for resource owners to have access to technology based on the development of their biological resources. This is a clear indication that developing countries should be able to extract rents associated with their sovereign resources. This access to technology, including biotechnology, should be on 'fair and most favourable terms' consistent with the protection of intellectual property rights. This clause, Article 16, was the one that caused the USA the greatest worry and the Bush administration did not sign the CBD, despite the apparent caveat that intellectual property rights would be protected. The Clinton administration did sign the CBD.

The CBD calls for 'new and additional resources' to fund the developing country actions under the CBD. These resources would meet the 'full agreed incremental costs' of the actions. Incremental cost is discussed in detail in Chapter 11. As there are no targets at all in the CBD and no delineation of what biodiversity is important – simply the objective of conserving biodiversity – this clause could be interpreted as meaning that developed countries should fund whatever conservation measures developing countries choose to undertake. In reality, the financial mechanism is voted a fixed sum and must ultimately work down a priority list until those funds are exhausted.

Finally, the financial mechanism (as we have seen, the GEF) should be subject to the 'authority and guidance' of the Conference of Parties (COP). This contrasts with the Climate Convention's reference to 'guidance' only from the COP. Disputes continue as to the extent to which the COP will determine what gets transferred and to whom.

Overall, the CBD is remarkable for acknowledging the biodiversity problem and for putting it at the head of international environmental actions. It remains somewhat confusing in not making reference anywhere to the global benefits of biodiversity. The end result is that it gives no guidance on what biodiversity should be conserved in face of limited funds, i.e. it offers no guidance on priorities.

THE FRAMEWORK CONVENTION ON CLIMATE CHANGE (FCCC)

The FCCC seeks to achieve:

> the stabilisation of greenhouse gas concentrations in the atmosphere at a level that would prevent dangerous anthropogenic interference with the climate system (Article 2).

Little guidance is given on how to determine what this level is beyond saying that it needs to be achieved in a time-frame 'sufficient to allow ecosystems to adapt naturally to climate change, to ensure that food production is not threatened and to enable economic development to proceed in a sustainable manner'. Chapter 2 discussed alternative paradigms for climate change control. The precautionary principle is explicitly embraced in the FCCC to cover the fact that global warming is still not scientifically 'proven', i.e. action should be taken nonetheless.

Countries have 'common but differentiated responsibilities' for the protection of climate, meaning that climate control is a matter of common concern, but that the responsibility for action lies mainly with the developed economies. Action must be cost-effective, the mention of which is in contrast to the CBD where no reference is made to efficient conservation of biodiversity.

Countries must establish inventories of greenhouse gas emissions and must establish national plans for their control. Developed countries are to take the lead in securing emission reductions 'recognising that the return by the end of the present decade to earlier levels of anthropogenic emissions of carbon dioxide and other greenhouse gases ... would contribute to such modification' (Article 4). National plans should have the 'aim of returning individually or jointly to their

1990 levels these anthropogenic emissions'. This Article establishes the short-term targets for the developed economies, i.e. to get emissions back to 1990 levels by the year 2000, or better. There is even a let-out clause here since the same Article refers to the need for sustainable economic growth and implies that this should not be sacrificed in the effort to achieve the emission targets.

Parties to the FCCC may 'implement such policies and measures jointly with other Parties'. This clause allows for joint implementation, an issue dealt with in detail in Chapter 12.

The developed countries agree to meet the 'agreed full incremental costs' of implementing the FCCC in developing countries – the incremental cost clause.

Chapter 11

Incremental cost

INTRODUCTION

Under the 1992 Rio agreements on climate change control and the conservation of biological diversity, the developed world agrees to bear the 'incremental' costs that developing countries will face when implementing actions to secure global environmental benefits. The terminology of incremental cost followed on from its use in the earlier 1987 Montreal Protocol dealing with ozone layer depletion. The concept of incremental cost is clearly important since it appears to determine the flow of resources from North to South to secure global environmental benefits: the obligation of the developed world appears to be open-ended. Whatever the incremental cost is of achieving global benefits, the developed world appears to have agreed to pay it. On the other hand, Chapter 10 showed that the total of these resources has already been agreed for the first three years of the Global Environment Facility's operational phase. Incremental cost, whatever it means, appears unrelated to this grand total which was determined by political bargaining. In this 'fixed budget' context, incremental cost takes on a different purpose, that of helping to guide the allocation of the fixed budget among competing schemes. Partly because of these differences of interpretation, incremental cost has become a controversial concept. Yet, its economic interpretation is simple in concept. What, then, is incremental cost?

INCREMENTAL COST: THE INTERNATIONAL AGREEMENTS

The flow of funds that the developed world agrees to transfer to the developing world under the Montreal Protocol and the Rio Conventions is certainly related to the 'incremental cost'. Incremental cost is the additional cost arising from choosing an action that differs from the action that would otherwise have taken place. The situation that would have occurred is known as the *baseline*. The modified activity is then the *alternative* or *incremental activity* or *intervention*. The implication, then, is that the developing world will do something different (the alternative) to what they would have done (the baseline) because of the existence of an international agreement. The baseline activity could include 'doing nothing'. So, in concept, incremental cost is simple: it is simply the cost to developing countries of undertaking actions under the international agreements, i.e. actions they would not otherwise have undertaken. Developing countries would not otherwise undertake actions for the sake of the 'global good' for many reasons, not least the facts that they have severely constrained resources and different priorities for the use of those limited resources. If the issue is the choice between controlling greenhouse gas emissions and, say, sanitation, the developing country will choose the latter. As we saw in previous chapters, developing countries also tend to regard it as the responsibility of rich countries to pay for global benefits since, they argue, the rich countries are the main cause of their diminution.

None of the international agreements cited offers a definition of incremental cost. The Montreal Protocol (MP) as amended in 1990 (the 'London Revisions') states:

> The Parties shall establish a mechanism for the purposes of providing financial and technical cooperation, including the transfer of technologies, to Parties operating under paragraph 1 of Article 5 [developing countries whose annual consumption per capita of ozone depleting substances – ODSs – is less than 0.3kg] of this Protocol to enable their compliance with the control measures set out in Articles 2A to 2E of the Protocol [a list of control measures for individual ODSs]. The mechanism, *contributions to which shall be additional to other financial transfers* to Parties operating under that paragraph, shall meet *all agreed incremental costs* of such Parties in order to enable their compliance with the control measures of the Protocol. An indicative list of the categories of incremental costs shall be decided by the Meeting of the Parties.
> (Revised Article 10, emphasis and explanation [ ] added).

The Convention on Biological Diversity (CBD) states (Article 20):

> The developed country Parties shall provide *new and additional financial resources* to enable developing country Parties to meet the *agreed full incremental costs* to them of implementing measures which fulfil the obligations of this Convention (emphasis added).

The Framework Convention on Climate Change (FCCC) states:

> The developed country Parties and other developed Parties included in annex II shall provide *new and additional financial resources to meet the agreed full costs* incurred by developing country

Parties in complying with their obligations under Article 12, paragraph 1 [costs of inventories and information on greenhouse gas emissions]. They shall also provide such financial resources, including for the transfer of technology, needed by the developing country Parties to meet *the agreed full incremental costs* of implementing measures that are covered by paragraph 1 of this Article [sets of measures to control greenhouse gas emissions] and that are agreed between a developing country Party and the international entity or entities referred to in Article 11 [the financial mechanism], in accordance with that Article.

(Article 4.3. Emphasis and explanation [ ] added)

Both the Rio Conventions borrowed terminology directly from the amended Montreal Protocol. The term 'new and additional financial resources' refers to financial resources over and above existing or expected development aid, a clause also in the Montreal Protocol in slightly different language. The rationale for new resources was to ensure that existing development aid was not diverted to secure global environmental benefits which are not priorities for developing countries, an issue we return to later. On incremental costs, the phrase 'all agreed' incremental costs in the MP is replaced with 'agreed full' incremental costs in the FCCC and CBD. Both phrases reflect the tension between the developing countries' view that, whatever the cost of securing global environmental benefits, the entire cost should be met by the developed world; and the donor's view that financial transfers are not necessarily the same thing as incremental costs. We return to this distinction also.

NEW RESOURCES AND GLOBAL BENEFITS

The three agreements – MP, FCCC and CBD – have been discussed in terms of securing *global benefits*. These are benefits that accrue to the world generally, although the share of them that any one country secures can vary significantly. Thus some countries may be significant losers from global warming – small island states, for example – and others may actually be net gainers. Many countries will, on current evidence, not be at serious risk from the health risks of ozone layer depletion, but all will be at risk if enhanced UV radiation damages ocean productivity. Chapter 1 introduced the idea that the benefits of controlling greenhouse gas emissions and chlorofluorocarbon emissions, and the benefits of conserving biodiversity are *global public goods*. Recall that the essence of a public good is that its consumption by any one individual does not detract from the consumption of that good by another individual ('joint consumption' or 'non-rivalry'), and that if the good is provided to one individual it is generally difficult or impossible to prevent its provision to another individual ('non-exclusion'). The relevance of the global public goods concept is discussed shortly.

In all cases, the relevance of resource transfers from North to South is that those transfers act as incentives to cooperate. They are compensation for forgoing land uses and technologies that are inconsistent with environmental conservation of globally beneficial assets, but which land uses and technologies define the 'baseline' referred to previously. But the CBD and the MP do not in fact refer to global benefits at all. In contrast, it appears quite explicitly in the FCCC. Article 3.3 calls on Parties to take 'precautionary measures' to control greenhouse gas emissions:

> taking into account that policies and measures to deal with climate change should be *cost-effective so as to ensure global benefits at the lowest possible cost* (emphasis added).

Similarly, the April 30 1992 Participants' meeting approved a text on the future of the GEF (GEF, 1992). Principle IV states that 'The GEF would assure the cost effectiveness of its activities in addressing the targeted global environmental issues' – clearly indicating the global benefit focus and the principle of cost-effectiveness. Principle I states that 'The GEF would provide additional grant and concessional funding of the agreed incremental costs for achieving agreed global environmental benefits' – indicating the global focus.

Much of the dispute about incremental cost and the interpretation of the financial implications of the Rio Conventions rests on the fact that there are several explanations for the need for 'new and additional financial resources' for environmental conservation. Each explanation rests on assumptions about what motivations countries have to pursue environmental protection unilaterally and what motivations they have to pursue environmental protection collectively, i.e through international agreements. In turn, these motivations are determined by who gets the benefit from environmental conservation.

The global commons explanation

From the definition of public goods in Chapter 1 a vital implication follows: no one individual has an incentive to provide public goods since in so doing he or she provides it to others and he or she cannot charge others for the benefits generated. This is the fundamental rationale for a cooperative agreement. By cooperating and seeking 'mutual assurance' about the sharing of the costs of the agreement, global public goods will be provided. Otherwise, the risk will be that no one will provide them. What is true for individuals is also true for nations. The international agreement effectively establishes property rights in contexts where none previously existed, as with the stratosphere (ozone) and atmosphere (global warming). The case of biological diversity is less straightforward since the land and water on and in which it exists, are generally owned by sovereign nations. The issue here is how to attenuate those sovereign property rights in such a way that the benefits conferred by biodiversity on other nations can be realized.

The first explanation for the need for new and additional resources, then, is that no one country has an incentive to pursue environmental improvement that constitutes a shared benefit, and that, in order to induce cooperation to secure those benefits it is necessary to provide financial incentives to countries with limited resources. The global public good explanation is clearly appropriate for ozone layer protection: reduced depletion will benefit all because of the generally widespread nature of the health and ecosystem risks. Most people would argue that the benefits of reduced climatic change are also like this, although it is arguable that some countries may actually gain from climate change. The Convention on Climate Change itself refers to change in the Earth's climate and its adverse effects as 'a common concern of mankind' (FCCC, preamble). Biodiversity conservation is less obviously a clear example of 'global common property' because its conservation may provide significantly more benefits for some countries than others. On the other hand, if biodiversity is critical to life support systems generally, then 'everyone' will benefit from its conservation. The Convention on Biological Diversity chooses the same words as the Climate Change Convention in referring to conservation of biological diversity as 'a common concern of humankind' (CBD, preamble).

The global commons argument provides a rationale for an international agreement, but not for increased North–South transfers. After all, all countries could agree to contribute. But the South countries still have a low incentive to contribute if either of the following hold:

● they do not benefit much from global environmental resources, whereas the rest of the world does;
● they benefit from global environmental resources but those benefits have lower priority than the 'local' benefits of economic development. They can focus on only the high priority issues because they have limited capital resources;

Clearly, if the resources for solving these global commons problems come from existing North–South aid flows, South countries will lose development aid for the sake of the global benefit. On either of the arguments above, they will not cooperate in a global commons agreement.

On this analysis, new and additional financial resources are needed to secure the cooperation of the South countries in an agreement which is not high priority for them but which is a high priority for the North countries. (In the jargon, the finance is effectively a 'side payment'.)

Note that the global commons argument is consistent with South countries being not very concerned with global problems, or with them being very concerned but unable to contribute financially because of capital constraints. Put another way, it is consistent with South countries not wanting to take significant action, or with wanting to, but being unable to.

The validity of the argument for new resources therefore depends on:

1 the need for cooperative action;
2 the 'global commons' nature of the problem being addressed;
3 the relative priority of 'local' and global environmental problems for the poorer countries.

In the biodiversity context, 1 is correct, although the large potential for conservation being secured through the correction of domestic policies that harm biodiversity should not be overlooked (Brown *et al.*, 1993; see also CBD, Article 11).

Proposition 2 is open to question. Mittermeier and Bowles (1993) distinguish six categories of biodiversity conservation benefit: 'global intangibles' which include ecological values (biodiversity as a dynamic system) and geopolitical values (biodiversity as a means of preventing social, economic and political insecurity); major ecosystem functions such as watershed protection; regional market values; local market values; and household use values (non-marketed products). They then argue that:

> One can make the argument that global biodiversity ought to be conserved for its carbon sequestration function or its future biotechnological potential, but that misses most of the benefits that biodiversity provides. Of the six categories of biodiversity values ... only the first relates to a global benefit. Utilization of biodiversity principally provides national, regional and local benefits, not in the future, but right here and now.
>
> (Mittermeier and Bowles, 1993, p.15).

Other experts dispute this emphasis on national benefits. The Convention on Biological Diversity speaks of biodiversity conservation as 'a common concern of humankind' (Preamble). McNeely *et al.* (1990), for example, refer to biodiversity as both essential for economic development and as a global asset.

Proposition 3 above probably does state the view of many developing countries, i.e. that biodiversity conservation is *not* a local priority. This could be inconsistent with the Mittermeier and Bowles view, although it could be a matter of relative priorities.

The responsibility argument

As discussed in earlier chapters, the responsibility argument rests on the assumption that all countries are motivated to secure global environmental improvement for the benefit of all, but that the South countries *should not* contribute, even if they were able. This 'moral view' arises from ascription of responsibility for environmental problems to the North countries who are richer and who have higher environmental impacts per capita than poor countries. In other words, the problem has come about because of the behaviour of the rich countries. In so far as the cooperation of the poorer countries is needed to reverse, or slow down, the degradation, that cooperation requires financial inducement. New resources are required because South countries should not be expected to lose (from diverted aid expenditures) for something that is not their responsibility.

This argument has some appeal in the context of CFCs and global warming, although it is easy to dispute the extent to which *past* actions taken without apparent knowledge of the implications can be held to imply responsibility for current generations. It has less appeal in the biodiversity context since much of the world's biodiversity is, and always has been, concentrated in the tropical countries. Its rate of loss has also primarily been a function of land conversion to meet rising agricultural demands, although some losses are clearly due to urbanization, timber production, introduced species and trade in species (Brown and Pearce, 1994). This 'mix' of factors giving rise to biodiversity loss makes it less than obvious where 'responsibility' lies.

Obligation and local benefits

The third argument assumes that the main beneficiaries of conservation are the South countries, but that they either should not meet the cost, or cannot meet the cost. They should not meet the cost if responsibility for past and current problems rests primarily with the

North countries perhaps because of past policies of resource exploitation without adequate compensation for resources taken from developing countries. This view is reinforced by the presumption that biological resources have potentially very high development value if modern technologies for their exploitation – biotechnology – are applied. In effect, the purpose of an international agreement is to enable the sustainable exploitation of those resources for the economic benefit of the developing countries.

This view is consistent with the argument that South countries cannot meet the costs of biodiversity conservation and the North is 'obliged' to meet the cost in the same way as they are obliged to provide development aid. This obligation is recognized by North and South countries alike and explains the existence of development aid in the first place.

But why would new and additional sources of finance be required on this argument? The requirement for additional funds could be explained by the recent 'discovery' of the problems to which the funds are applied, i.e. new problems require additional finance, especially if the new problems have relatively low priority in South countries. Whether those funds should be 'new' in the sense of being *different* to development aid is, however, much more debatable. If, as many experts argue, biodiversity conservation is essential for *economic development*, then biodiversity conservation would appear to fit neatly into standard development aid. Development aid is aimed at improving national economic development and that can only take place if actions are taken that lead to national economic benefits greater than national economic costs. If this is true, additional funds may be justified because of the 'newness' of the problems, but the separation of those funds from conventional development aid is open to question.

Some explanation for separation of funds might be found in the 'non-market' nature of many of the benefits. Inspection of the Mittermeier–Bowles list of benefits shows that many of them are not expressed in the market-place, e.g. subsistence use of biodiversity and watershed protection. On this basis, separate funds are required because the relevant actions cannot be evaluated in quite the same way that conventional development aid projects are evaluated. This is not a particularly strong argument, however, given that major efforts are being made to incorporate non-market values into conventional development aid anyway.

The existence of a separate financial mechanism thus sits uneasily with new and additional funds if those funds are *solely* for development aid purposes. This suggests that the motivations for a separate fund arise from more than the concern with development benefits alone, wholly legitimate though that concern is.

Summary of arguments for new and additional funds

Two features of international agreements need to be distinguished.

The first is why an international agreement is needed at all. The most compelling answer to that question is that countries would not individually undertake actions to conserve biodiversity, reduce global warming and ozone layer depletion, whereas they would if there was a cooperative agreement. The 'failure' of individual action arises from the 'common property' nature of biodiversity conservation: i.e. its conservation is 'a common concern of humankind' in the language of the Conventions. This 'commonality' of concern is open to dispute, with some experts arguing that the benefits of biodiversity conservation arise mainly at the national level. The Convention on Biological Diversity does not develop the 'common concern' argument since it nowhere refers to the issue of *who* benefits from conservation. (It speaks of a broad range of environmental, economic and social benefits from investments to conserve biodiversity – CBD, Preamble). If benefits are mainly national, then an agreement is still required if developing countries cannot meet the cost of such conservation. Developed countries will need to meet at least part of the cost in order to assist developing countries to realize their own benefits. This is an extension of conventional development aid. If, on the other hand, benefits are common to all countries, then an agreement is necessary because even if developing countries had their own available finance, they would have no incentive to invest in biodiversity for the benefit of others.

The second feature of an agreement is how it is financed. Many international agreements do not involve resource transfers between countries, but the Rio Conventions do. This transfer is required either because the developing countries have no incentive to provide benefits for other countries, or because they are unable to finance conservation even though it is mainly for their own benefit. These arguments may be reinforced by views to the effect that the developed countries are more responsible for the existing state of damage than developing countries, or have responsibility for past uncompensated exploitation of resources, especially biological resources.

Which is the correct view? It is difficult to avoid the impression that, despite the absence of reference to shared benefits from biodiversity conservation in the Biodiversity Convention (beyond the 'common concern of humankind' statement), the existence of shared benefits is the major driving force of all the agreements.

GLOBAL AND NATIONAL PRIORITIES

The replenishment agreement for the GEF speaks of the GEF funding projects that are 'country driven and based on national priorities', although they must still represent 'the agreed incremental costs of measures to achieve global environmental benefits'. The terminology of global benefits thus secures open recognition as far as operational activities are concerned, but whether securing global benefits is consistent with national priorities remains an open question.

'Incremental cost', however interpreted, is only part of the overall equation determining what environmental priorities are addressed. It is part of the cost side of the equation, and it must, necessarily, be compared to a benefit part of the equation. Most environmentally beneficial activities tend to involve a cost of some sort. Those that do not – the so-called 'win-win' strategies – are clearly the first actions that should be taken. Indeed, 'win-win' strategies are likely to combine the features of securing global benefit and benefitting the host country as well in terms of developmental aims. If so, then the global/domestic benefit dichotomy referred to above need not be one of conflict.

But once win-win actions are used up, subsequent measures will involve a net cost. From the host country standpoint, then, no 'incremental' action under the agreements will be worthwhile unless it is better off with the action than without it. This is why incremental cost must include any foregone benefits from the baseline activity. In many cases the issue will not arise. The host country's benefit from, say, coal-fired electricity is the same as its benefits from gas-fired electricity. But the global environmental impacts are quite different due to the lower CO_2 content of gas. In this context, the host country will be no worse off with gas-fired electricity provided it is compensated for any incremental costs of adopting that technology. Indeed, it may be better off if gas-fired electricity produces fewer local pollutants (e.g. particulate matter) than coal.

In other contexts, the forgone benefits of the baseline activity will be relevant. This will be especially the case in biodiversity conservation. Since the objective of the CBD is biodiversity conservation, the global benefit of the actions can be measured by the degree of conservation secured. Various measures of the 'degree of conservation' are feasible, and it seems fair to say that there is still only limited agreement on how to set about determining biodiversity conservation priorities (e.g. see Myers, 1988, 1990; Dinerstein and Wikramanayake, 1993; Reid *et al.*, 1993a; Mittermeier, 1988; Mittermeier and Werner, 1990). Nonetheless, any rational strategy for biodiversity conservation has to make some comparison of costs and benefits. (Making that comparison implies nothing in particular about the units in which costs and benefits are expressed, but, clearly, costs will be in monetary terms). The local benefits of biodiversity conservation may be significant, but the local costs in terms of foregone baseline benefits could also be large. For example, conserving biodiversity through extension of protected area status for forests may deprive local people of previous open access to the forests, e.g. fuelwood, plants, wild meat, etc. In this case, incremental cost must include the value of these forgone benefits.

Since the CBD does not itself make any reference to global benefits, and since the GEF is charged with interventions that are consistent with national priorities, one literal interpretation of the CBD is that it is consistent with conserving *any* biodiversity, whether its importance is nationally defined in terms of benefits to the 'host' countries or globally defined. Pursued to its limit, then, this argument would require the developed countries to meet the incremental costs of conserving whatever biodiversity host countries choose to conserve. There are two elements here. The first is whether any conservation is warranted, or whether only some high priority biodiversity should be conserved. The second is whether the benefits should be measured in national or global terms.

While the CBD does not refer to priorities, the reality is that a finite sum of money has been allocated to the GEF, as financial mechanism, for conservation of biodiversity and global warming control. Unless all biodiversity has equal importance, it follows that more conservation will take place if cost-effectiveness criteria are employed, and less if they are not. The absence of cost-effectiveness criteria in the CBD should not therefore be allowed to dictate inefficient policies. Examples of inefficient criteria would include the idea that conservation funds should be distributed 'equally' across geographic regions. More importantly, it would be inefficient to focus on any biodiversity rather than on 'important' biodiversity. Cost-effectiveness must be implied by any rational strategy, regardless of whether it is openly embraced in the relevant international agreement or not. Cost-effectiveness only ceases to be relevant if funds are, in some sense, unlimited relative to the scale of the problem. But in the biodiversity context this is clearly not the case – the threats to the world's biodiversity are clearly growing, not diminishing.

If some form of prioritization is implied by the CBD, the second question is whose priorities? There are two views on the issue of global 'versus' host country (domestic) benefits.

The first view focuses on conservation as a development option. Biodiversity conservation takes place through conventional development aid. This is because it is argued that (a) biodiversity conservation will come about 'naturally' as developing countries develop and (b) conservation must be consistent with national priorities which in turn require that conservation be justified in terms of net national benefits to development. Resource transfers would then be related to the cost of achieving such nationally beneficial conservation measures. Cost is 'incremental' in the sense that it is over and above what countries would have spent on conservation measures, and these baseline expenditures are limited because of capital constraints. For costs to be incremental and for there to be net development gains to the country means that the country has not pursued a domestic policy of max-imizing the net benefits of conservation. If it had maximized net benefits it could not be facing the prospect of net development gains from further conservation. There is no reference in this view to global benefits.

The obvious problem with this view is – why set up GEF at all? Existing agencies deal with conservation measures justified in solely development terms. One response is that in choosing the GEF as the financial mechanism, participants were adopting an institution that had developed particular expertise in the relevant areas of intervention, and which did not have its origin in the Conventions. That is, while the Pilot Phase may have been 'globally oriented' there is no reason why the Operational Phase should be. But it is not clear what 'Pilot' and 'Operational' phases mean if the 'terms of reference' change from one period to the next. Moreover, GEF was set up in anticipation of the Rio Conventions. The same issue of cost-effectiveness also arises. If any conservation activity secures local, development-oriented benefits *and* global benefits, this must clearly be preferred to an activity securing local benefits only, or 'rest of the world' benefits only. In other words, it is important to ensure that 'global' means what it says – i.e. that it embraces host-country and rest-of-the-world benefits.

On the alternative view, then, the primary concern is to encourage the conservation of biological diversity of global significance, where 'global' means shared by developed and developing nations. National gains from conservation would therefore not be given pre-eminence. All countries would be expected generally to share in the global benefits and may be expected to gain purely domestic benefits as well. The rationale for this approach is that it gives justification for a separate financial mechanism, the GEF, which otherwise appears not to be present. It also embraces the fact that biodiversity conservation has global public good characteristics, whereas the 'domestic benefits only' approach plays down the significance of shared benefits.

A variant of the global benefits focus suggests that 'global' has a stricter meaning. It embraces shared developing and developed country benefits but only if they take on the characteristics of global public goods – goods that can benefit all nations without depleting the benefit by any one nation. Developing country benefits that are not shared would not then be relevant to priority assessment and, indeed, might be deducted from any measure of incremental cost calculated to achieve those global benefits. This issue is addressed below.

INCREMENTAL COST

Some basic concepts

Regardless of the interpretation of incremental cost (IC) in particular contexts, there are certain concepts that must be defined and understood at the outset:

- The notion of an *action*, which is taken here to mean any form of intervention designed to achieve a given environmental end. Thus an action might, for example, be an investment project, training, capacity-building, or a policy measure.
- The country undertaking the action is the *recipient* or *host* country and will typically be a developing country in the context of the Rio Conventions and the Montreal Protocol.
- Any country contributing to the central fund out of which resource transfers are made is a *donor* country.
- The *resource transfer* constitutes the actual payment out of the central fund to the recipient country.
- *The environmental benefit* may be measured in a number of different ways. Use of the term 'benefit' implies nothing about the units of measurement which might be ODP (ozone depleting potential) as with the Multilateral Fund of the Montreal Protocol; tonnes of carbon equivalent as under the Pilot Phase of the GEF for climate change protection investments; and so on.
- The environmental benefits may accrue solely to the host nation, in which case they can be termed *domestic benefits* or *national benefits*; or they might accrue to the rest of the world and not at all to the host country, in which case they might be termed *rest of the world benefits*; or they might accrue partly to the host country and partly to the rest of the world, in which case they might be termed *global benefits*. Global benefits are shared benefits, but some countries may benefit more from global benefits than other countries. In the climate context this is obvious: deltaic and island communities, for example, are likely to benefit more from global warming control. In the biodiversity context the same could apply: some countries may have a higher priority for conservation than other countries.

- Incremental costs are incremental to what otherwise would have been done. What would otherwise have been done is known as the *baseline* and the baseline that is relevant is the host country's baseline. Without the concept of a baseline, however hard it is to define and measure, and however it may change over time, the term 'incremental' in incremental cost has no meaning. Incremental always means incremental to the baseline.
- Incremental cost and the resource transfer are not necessarily the same thing, but they are related.

Certain very elementary rules can be derived provided a basic assumption is made, namely, that host countries will accept transfers if they are better off as a result (or at least no worse off), and donor countries will offer transfers if the benefits from the transfer exceed the cost of the transfer. For the moment, this second assumption is made quite independently of *who* receives the benefits from the action in question.

These rules can be looked at from two perspectives: that of the host country and that of the donor country:

The host country

Host countries are most likely to want all of the incremental cost paid as compensation if they expect to gain very little by way of domestic benefits or their share of global benefits from the action. In this case, the rest of the world is the dominant beneficiary, the host country gains little or nothing, and the host country will therefore either not agree to the action at all, or it may agree provided all its costs are offset by the transfer. Taking the extreme where the host country gains nothing from the action, and calling this the *zero domestic gain case*, we see immediately that, from the recipient's point of view, the resource transfer has to be at least as large as the size of the incremental cost. If the transfer just equals the incremental cost, then the host country should be indifferent between receiving a transfer and not receiving a transfer: it is neither better off nor worse off with the action;

Host countries will be most likely to accept less than the incremental cost of the action if the domestic benefits they secure from the action are large, or if their share of the global benefits is significant. Rationally, they will be prepared to bear some of the incremental cost if they think their domestic benefits, or their share of global benefits, 'exceeds' the cost they bear ('exceeds' means here that 'judged to be greater than', to avoid any implication that costs and benefits are in the same units). In this case the resource transfer is less than incremental cost. This might be called the *positive domestic gain case*.

Donor countries

Donor countries will not be willing to make transfers greater than the benefit obtained from the transfer. In the *zero domestic gain* case the transfer will therefore only be made if the rest of the world's benefits 'exceed' the transfer since, *ex hypothesi*, the host country gains nothing. In turn, we know that the transfer in this case must be at least equal to the incremental cost (see above). Hence the transfer only takes place if the rest of the world's benefits exceed the incremental cost. In these cases, transfers could be even greater than incremental cost, so long as they are below the benefits expected. In this way, host countries would gain, and so would the rest of the world. If the transfer just equals incremental cost, then the host country is no worse off, but the rest of the world is better off because of the transfer;

In the *positive domestic gain case*, donor countries will still only be willing to make transfers if benefits 'exceed' the size of the transfer. The benefits in question could be counted as domestic plus global benefits, or they could be rest of the world benefits only, or they could be global benefits only. There is nothing in the concept of incremental cost of itself to dictate who gains from the action. How the transfer relates to incremental cost, however, depends on two things: who gains, and how they gain. It is here that some of the controversy has arisen. This controversy is addressed shortly.

Incremental cost – a generic approach

On the basis of the concepts introduced above it is now possible to develop a generic approach to incremental cost. A more formal statement is set out later.

We begin with the assumption that both the donor community and the host community are concerned with the benefits of any agreement to them. Assume too that there are global benefits from the environmental action, say biodiversity conservation, where global benefit means common property benefits in the sense defined previously. Global also means that the benefit is shared between the host and donor community.

Then the donor's standpoint would be that any financial transfer is worthwhile if the rest of the world's share of global benefits exceeded the cost of the transfer. The host community's standpoint would be that they would accept the transfer if any national benefits they secure, plus their share of the global benefits, plus the financial transfer, exceed the cost to them of implementing the project (the incremental cost). Some simple rearrangement shows that this rule sets the minimum transfer at the incremental cost less any national benefits, and the maximum transfer at the level of the total global benefits obtained. Further reflection shows that the minimum transfer would leave host countries neither worse off nor better off under the agreement. The maximum transfer rule would leave them better off. Which rule is better is discussed in the next section.

Now suppose that there are no global benefits, or that they are sufficiently small to be ignored. Recall that the MP and CBD do not mention global benefits, although the MP has as its sole objective the securing of global benefits since ozone layer depletion is the opposite of a public good. Then the donors' standpoint would be the same as for any development loan or grant, namely that the benefits to the host nation should exceed the costs. And this will be the same requirement for the host nation. But the incremental costs in this case could still be shared, i.e. host countries could be expected to pay something, even though they cannot pay all the costs. Hence the minimum transfer will be some proportion of incremental cost, that proportion being determined by negotiation; and the maximum transfer would be incremental cost.

The generic rule for incremental cost that emerges is then:

● *When global and domestic benefits exist:* the financial transfer is at least equal to a proportion of incremental cost and is at most equal to incremental cost. In addition incremental cost must be less than the global benefits of the project. The absolute minimum is set by the size of incremental cost minus the domestic benefits.
● *When domestic benefits only exist:* the financial transfer is at least equal to some proportion of the incremental cost and is at most equal to incremental cost. In addition, incremental cost must be less than the domestic benefit of the project. The minimum size of the transfer is indeterminate, depending on negotiation.

The distinction between global benefits and domestic benefits was germane to the functioning of the GEF during its Pilot Phase (1991–1993). In its Pilot Phase the GEF certainly declared a principle of not funding activities where host country domestic benefits would exceed host country costs if the project was implemented. This is because such projects would normally qualify for conventional development aid – they contribute to national economic development. They were referred to as 'Type I' projects. Type II projects were ones where domestic benefits were less than domestic costs but global benefits exceeded the incremental costs. In practice, the Pilot Phase made it clear that the Type I/Type II distinction is not very helpful. One reason is that Type I projects could well have significant global benefits as well as domestic net benefits. If Type I is ignored, then potentially 'globally profitable' ventures might be rejected in favour of less cost-effective Type II projects (Wells, 1993). Clearly, this is directly similar to the debate over 'national' versus 'global' benefits.

Issues with incremental cost

A number of issues arise with this generic approach to incremental cost.

Can transfers be less than incremental cost?

Consider first whether the financial mechanism under the Conventions could in fact make transfers less than the incremental cost of the projects in question and still be consistent with the aims of the Conventions. We illustrate this issue with the CBD.

The institutional structure in Article 21 of the CBD is the financial mechanism, the GEF, which is in turn accountable to the Conference of Parties (CoP). Article 20.2 thus appears not to permit transfers less than full incremental cost unless agreed by the CoP, which is quite proper. Some interpretations of Article 20.2 suggest that in fact transfers must necessarily equal full incremental cost. They cannot be less. If so, a number of problematic issues disappear, but others arise. The issue that disappears is the role that domestic benefits play in determining transfers. They simply cease to be relevant, as the analytic rules for determining transfers show. All transfers are then equal to incremental cost.

Cost efficiency

The issue that arises, however, is how *cost-efficient* the transfers then become. For, if some proportion of domestic benefits is not deducted, transfers for each individual project will be larger than if they were deducted. Self-evidently, less biodiversity is then conserved for a given budget. The question is whether this outcome is consistent with the intentions of the Convention.

Those who favour the literal interpretation of the Convention would identify all transfers as being equal to incremental cost. They might accept that this is not cost-efficient, but would observe that there is no reference in the Convention to principles of cost-efficiency (in contrast to the FCCC, see above). A more middle-of-the-road approach would be that cost-efficiency is relevant, but has to be tempered by other considerations. This would hold also, for example, with respect to the geographical distribution of projects. Cost efficiency across the board might encourage a focus on just a few areas. This could also be held to be inconsistent with the focus of the GEF on country-driven activities.

Budget size

Another view is that emphasis on cost-efficiency diverts attention away from efforts to increase the overall size of the budget for biodiversity conservation. That is, incremental cost is whatever it costs to secure given commitments under the Convention, and the sum of all the incremental costs is then the budget required. There is, in a sense, then no need to consider priorities because the budget will always respond to whatever the priorities are in such a way that they can all be met. This is an unrealistic view, in part because endowments for the financial mechanism have already been made. They might indeed be revised upwards as the scale of the problem is recognized, but it seems unlikely that budgets will simply respond to whatever projects happen to be presented.

Net vs gross incremental cost

The analytical rules suggest a distinction between 'gross' and 'net' incremental cost. Gross incremental cost is the cost of meeting the global or domestic environmental objective relative to what the country would have done (the baseline). Net incremental cost is the gross cost minus some proportion of domestic benefit. This distinction can be found in several documents (Pearce and Barrett, 1995; King, 1993). But it has caused considerable adverse comment for being (a) at variance with the wording of the Convention (see above) and (b) for diverting the focus away from national priorities towards global priorities (Werksman, 1993).

Should domestic benefits be deducted? On the net cost interpretation, host countries are left as well off as they would have been had the Convention not existed, or slightly better off. On the gross cost interpretation host countries are over-compensated by the transfer, i.e. they are made better off than they would have been without the Convention.

There are arguments in support of both interpretations. If countries are no better off with the Convention than they are without it, why should they agree to host any project or policy change? To induce them to 'sign up' they will require an incentive and that incentive could be that they secure the national benefits from conservation. Moreover, the national benefits could be thought of as a kind of conventional aid flow. This might help overcome the objections that have been advanced against the net cost concept, as being indifferent to the primary concerns of the developing world. The national benefit 'bonus' is the price for accepting projects which meet the priority concerns of the North, not the South. Those priority concerns are in fact made very clear in the CBD itself. Article 20.4 states:

The extent to which developing country Parties will effectively implement their commitments under this Convention will depend on the effective implementation by developed country Parties of their commitments under this Convention related to financial resources and transfers of technology and will take fully into account the fact that economic and social development and eradication of poverty are the first and overriding priorities of the developing country Parties.

Moreover, the national benefits obtained will help to contribute to the sustainability of the project by providing an incentive to local people to comply with project objectives.

There appears to be no clear-cut case for either interpretation. Cost efficiency favours the net cost concept, but project sustainability and maximum cooperation favour the gross cost concept. The wording of the Convention points towards the gross concept. In practice, there are reasons for thinking that the two interpretations will not be very different.

It is necessary to ask what the national benefits are likely to be in the biodiversity context. They could be significant if, say, the creation of a national park encourages eco-tourism or enables local markets to be retained for medicinal plants, forest products and so on. Some recent case studies suggest that local conservation benefits may be important – for a survey see Pearce and Moran (1994) and Pearce *et al.* (1993). But, while the evidence is flimsy, it looks to be the case that the local benefits may be fairly small relative to the likely size of GEF interventions. This suggests that the netting out of local benefits may not alter the picture very much. If so, the net/gross cost distinction is more academic than real. But this conclusion is tentative and awaits far more effort on the economic valuation of national and global benefits.

Second, many domestic benefits that appear to be the outcome of the intervention may not be legitimately included in the calculation of the transfer. Suppose, for example, that the intervention results in less pollution. This benefits biodiversity, but it also benefits the host country's population at large. Now suppose that reducing pollution for the benefit of the population was not a national priority in the host country prior to the intervention. This amounts to saying it was not 'in' the baseline. If it was not in the baseline, then it should not be regarded as a benefit to the host nation in the context of the project. It is rather like a 'free good' that is not highly valued.

Alternatively, suppose pollution reduction was in the baseline, then its achievement in the project means that it is netted out – the alternative is always relative to the baseline. In other words, some of the *apparent* domestic benefits arising from GEF interventions are likely to make little or no difference to the calculation of incremental cost.

Probably the most useful point to make in these contexts is that, given the very rationale of the Convention, which is to conserve bio-diversity, ignoring the basic principles of cost-effectiveness will not be consistent with that rationale. This does not mean that cost-effectiveness is the only principle, but it is clearly a very important one. There is a real risk that focusing on very narrow legal interpretations will result in less conservation that could otherwise be achieved with the modest resources available.

AN ALGEBRAIC MODEL OF RESOURCE TRANSFERS AND INCREMENTAL COST

[This section may be omitted without loss of continuity].

The previous discussion gave an intuitive definition of incremental cost as the cost of securing (incremental) global benefits and which cost would not otherwise be incurred because of the absence of incentives to secure global benefits without an international agreement. We can now set out a more formal 'model' of incremental costs, linking the concept to resource transfers.

Assume to begin with that both the host and the donor community behave in their own best interests. Then the donor community will make financial transfers to the host community if:

$$[(1-\alpha)GB] \geqslant T$$

where GB is global benefit, $1-\alpha$ is the share of the 'rest of the world' (i.e. the world minus the developing country in question) in those benefits, and T is the financial transfer.

As argued previously, the host community will accept a project if and only if it is better off after the action than before, i.e. if:

$$[\alpha GB + DB + T] \geqslant IC$$

where DB is now the domestic or national benefit, IC is incremental cost, i.e. the cost of this particular action, and α is the share of the developing country in global benefits.

Hence the transfer must lie in the range:

$$(IC - DB) \leqslant T \leqslant IC \leqslant GB$$

Note the deduction of the item DB in terms of defining the minimum transfer.

Now suppose that it is not possible to demonstrate that there are any global benefits from biodiversity conservation. All conservation expenditures could then be treated like any other form of development aid. The rule would then be that donor countries would be willing to supply such aid if:

$$T \leqslant IC$$

and host countries would similarly be willing to accept aid on the basis that $IC \leqslant DB$. Host countries could be expected to pay some proportion of DB, say β, towards the cost even though they cannot meet all the incremental cost because they are capital-constrained. The general rule for the range of transfer cost would be:

$$(IC - \beta DB) \leqslant T \leqslant IC$$

The rule is similar to the global benefits rule, but the minimum transfer is now undefined.

A technical observation about this second rule is that it is redundant if host countries have already secured biodiversity conservation up to the point that they individually consider desirable. If this was true, then the extra benefits of more conservation must be less than the extra costs, i.e. $DB < IC$ for further conservation, thus breaking the basic requirement for a worthwhile investment. Hence this second rule applies *only if* host countries have insufficient finance from domestic sources to fund the amount of biodiversity conservation that they consider desirable.

The two rules may then be summarized as:

$$(IC - DB) \leqslant T \leqslant IC \leqslant GB$$

when global and domestic benefits exist, and:

$$(IC - \beta DB) \leqslant T \leqslant IC \leqslant DB$$

when domestic benefits only exist.

Note that if the Conventions are interpreted so that full incremental cost must always be paid, then the term DB in $(IC - \beta DB)$ and $(IC - \beta DB)$ in these equations disappears, and all transfers are necessarily equal to incremental cost.

THE MEANING OF COST

An important set of issues concerns the cost categories to be included in the calculation of incremental cost. The relevant costs are the sum of:

$$\text{Direct costs} + \text{Indirect costs} + \text{Opportunity costs}$$

Direct costs refer to the immediate capital costs and on-going operational costs of the measure taken to conserve biodiversity. Indirect costs are meant to refer to those costs that fall on other agencies because of the conservation project, e.g. the need to divert a road round a protected area. All outlays arising because of the conservation measure must be included as costs, regardless of who bears them.

The opportunity costs item is more difficult and more important in the biodiversity context. Since the compensation flows under the Convention on Biological Diversity are 'new and additional' there is no opportunity cost to those funds from the host country's standpoint. That is, the funds are dedicated to biodiversity conservation and would not be available but for the Convention. It cannot be argued then that the funds could have been used for some other developmental purpose. But there is an opportunity cost if the funds are used for measures which displace other economic activity. The most obvious example will be a national park or any measure which changes land use. At the other extreme, transfers of technology and capacity building are unlikely to have opportunity costs in this sense: they do not displace an activity in the host country, they simply add to existing opportunities.

The distinction between the zero opportunity cost of the incremental flow of funds and the potentially positive opportunity cost of the actual conservation measure needs to be borne in mind.

The next problem with the opportunity cost concept is how it should be calculated if an initial check determines that it is positive. Pursuing the national park example again, the park will involve changes in land use compared to what would have been the case without the CBD. Issues of determining the 'baseline' aside, the opportunity cost of conservation has two alternative measures:

a) what land users would have received by way of net gains to themselves;
b) what society would have gained by way of net gains.

The difference between the 'private' opportunity cost (item (a)) and 'social' opportunity costs (b) could be substantial because the rule, not the exception, in developing countries is that various land uses are subject to fiscal incentives such as taxes and subsidies.

Which is the correct opportunity cost? From the standpoint of economic efficiency, it is the social opportunity cost that has to be measured and, despite the presence of many sets of economic guidelines, this is not simple to estimate. But it could be argued that basing opportunity cost on social rates of return to, say, farming displaced by the national park, does not actually compensate the land users in question. The fact that certain farming practices may not be socially worthwhile on the land in question is small comfort for those who would have practised that land use. Equally, compensating land users for incomes lost, where those incomes included a subsidy element, is quite clearly inefficient and sends the 'wrong' signals to host countries. At one extreme, it would invite those countries to pay even larger subsidies in order that they be offset by even larger payments under the incremental cost concept.

Difficult though it may be to estimate in practice, it is the social opportunity cost concept that will be relevant.

THE BASELINE

To calculate incremental costs requires a baseline in order to answer the question: 'incremental to what?'. Establishing the baseline is difficult, partly because the baseline is never actually observed if the project is completed and partly because the baseline and the economics of the project itself will be affected by the policy background (see King, 1993).

To take an example, suppose we wish to calculate the incremental costs of establishing a nature reserve. Then we would need to consider how the land would have been used in the absence of the intervention. If the land would not have been used at all, then the only incremental costs that are relevant are the capital and operating costs of setting up the reserve. If the land would have been protected by the national government were the GEF not to intervene, then incremental costs would be zero – no compensation should be paid. Suppose, instead, that the land would have been developed, but only because of incentives created by the country's tax policy. Then a dilemma exists. If incremental costs are based on the country's 'optimal' development programme, then no compensation would be paid, and the land might be developed, even though it was both nationally and globally desirable that it not be. On the other hand, if incremental costs are calculated taking existing policies as given, then compensation would be paid and the biodiversity protected, but one might then worry that, had compensation not been paid, the country would eventually have abandoned the wasteful policy or, even worse, an incentive would be created for countries to threaten to distort their policies in order to gain even greater compensation.

This is not simply a matter of accounting. It is widely argued that national policy failures (policies which create distortions within a country or which fail to correct for market distortions within a country) are the main cause of biodiversity loss – more important than that associated with global market failures which the GEF and Biodiversity

Fund were set up to correct. If the Convention institutions effectively countenance national policy failures by basing incremental costs on actual or stated national policies, then it may be vulnerable to the criticism that it has exacerbated biodiversity loss. According to this view, the CoP should use leverage to provide incentives for countries to correct their national policy failures.

A middle ground would require that the CoP establish pre-conditions for compensation, and then calculate incremental costs based on the policy background which satisfies these pre-conditions. If the pre-conditions are that all national policy and market failures be corrected, then this approach is identical to basing incremental costs on the country's 'optimal' development programme. If the pre-conditions are so weak that no country could fail to satisfy them, then this approach is identical to basing incremental costs on current policy if that policy embraces distortions. An intermediate listing of pre-conditions would have the advantage of creating incentives for correcting domestic failures while at the same time ensuring that enough compensation is offered that countries actually want to parti-cipate in the scheme. Such a listing would also seem to be allowed by the Biodiversity Convention. Article 20 states that incremental costs must be in accordance with 'eligibility criteria' established by the Conference of the Parties. Clearly, then, the Conference of Parties will have to determine the ground rules for the baseline for incremental cost. This is likely to be some compromise between the 'optimal' and actual forecast land use programme for the host country. Useful reference points would be National Conservation Strategies where these already exist, and, of course, the conservation strategies proposed by the National Biodiversity Units under the Convention.

Even where clear biodiversity strategies exist, the baseline in the biodiversity context is likely to be far 'fuzzier' than in the climate change context. This is because most countries have forward looking electricity development plans because of the need to phase in invest-ments over long periods of time. In so far as greenhouse gas reduction policies impinge on the electricity sector, which most do, there is at least a reference point for some assessment of the baseline (although this should not be thought of as a simple matter – see King, 1993).

Biodiversity strategies, on the other hand, are often partly paper exercises only, not because of a lack of will on the part of host coun-tries, but because of lack of finance. Moreover, biodiversity con-servation is not an environmental priority in most developing countries – sanitation, water and energy are far further up the policy priority schedule. This raises another issue for the baseline concept. If the baseline is what countries *would have done*, is this what countries *would like to have done* (but cannot) or simply what they are *likely to do* (given limited resources)? National conservation strategies tend to be a mixture of both ideals and what is feasible.

There is no easy resolution of this issue in the biodiversity context and, once again, the idea of *negotiated incremental cost* is seen to be important.

CONCLUSIONS

The emergence of new environmental problems of global nature like climate change, loss of biodiversity, ozone layer depletion and pollution of international waters, has induced the international community to make available new and additional funds to address these problems. It has also required new international agreements (the Montreal Protocol, the Rio Conventions), the establishment of new institutions (the Global Environment Facility), and the formulation of a specific financing criterion, incremental cost.

Incremental cost is the cost to a developing country of achieving a given objective – global benefit – relative to a baseline situation in which that globally beneficial action would not be taken: either because of lack of funds, or because of its low relative priority, or for both reasons.

The determination of incremental cost is complicated by a number of factors. First, two different measures can be identified: gross incremental cost, which takes no account of domestic benefits a nation may derive from adopting a GEF project; and net incremental cost, which is the compensation flow, net of domestic benefits. Strictly speaking, incremental cost is always a gross measure, but the transfer may equal the net measure. The gross and net measures define the upper and lower limits within which the 'agreed' incremental cost stipulated by the Rio Conventions needs to be determined.

Second, consensus on baselines may be difficult to reach, both for lack of information and of clear country strategies, especially in the case of biodiversity; and for the risk of strategic behaviour of recipient countries. The extent to which policy distortions should be included in the baseline is also likely to be controversial.

Although gross incremental cost provides substantial incentives to recipient countries to comply with the conventions, it is in conflict with the objective of maximizing the cost-effectiveness of international transfers for the protection of the global environment. The latter is the stated purpose of a number of international protocols, including the Framework Convention on Climate Change and the instrument for the establishment of the Global Environment Facility (but, notably, not the Convention on Biological Diversity).

Regarding the determination of the baseline, the same type of contrast arises, between the need to induce recipient countries' compliance, and the purpose of meeting cost-efficiency targets. Respecting national priorities fosters international cooperation, and is explicitly requested by the Conventions. However, the baseline should not incorporate policy measures which are clearly detrimental to, say, biodiversity conservation or the reduction of greenhouses gases concentration, and which are therefore inconsistent with the fundamental purpose of the Conventions. Often some of those policies may be reformed at zero or minimal costs.

Chapter 12

Joint implementation

INTRODUCTION: THE MEANING OF JOINT IMPLEMENTATION

In the context of international environmental agreements, joint implementation (JI) involves a bilateral deal, or even a multilateral one, in which countries with high costs of pollution abatement or environmental conservation invest in abatement or conservation in a country with lower costs, and receive credit for the resulting reduction in emissions or increase in conservation. While JI is potentially applicable to any environmental objective, it is generally applied in contexts where one of the partners in the deal has a commitment – which could be legal or self-imposed – to reduce pollution emissions. A constraint on the trade is that emission reductions in the low-cost country, the 'host' country, must at least offset the avoided reductions in the 'donor' country. In the context of international agreements, the obvious potential attraction of joint implementation is that it reduces the global costs of meeting internationally agreed emission targets. It therefore contributes to cost-minimization. This is fairly self-evident: if the donor avoids cutting emissions of X tonnes at cost C, and invests in cutting emissions in the host nation by X tonnes at cost, say, 0.4C, then there are cost savings of $(1-0.4)C = 0.6C$ and no worsening of global environmental quality. However, the latter result, that global quality does not decline, can be guaranteed only if the obligation being traded is 'uniformly mixed', i.e. the damage being done does not vary with the location of the bargaining parties. Greenhouse gases are examples of such uniformly mixed pollutants: it does not matter *where* the reduction takes place since one tonne of a greenhouse gas does the same amount of global damage wherever the reduction takes place.

Once JI is extended to other pollutants and environmental damages, the guarantee of non-declining global quality cannot be provided without further restrictions on the trades. For example, acidifying pollutants, such as SO_x and NO_x, are not uniformly mixed pollutants. The amount of damage done varies according to the source of the pollution, the wind direction and the ecological and social character-istics of the destination of the pollutant. Thus a trade between one donor and one host could affect air quality and acidifying depositions in a third party country. Although it has not generally been entertained, trades could be undertaken between countries in conserving an environmental asset such as biological diversity. In practice, the 'value' of biological diversity is likely to be very site-specific and no satisfactory 'metric' exists yet for comparing reductions in different locations. Were such relative values, or 'exchange rates', to be developed and accepted, then JI could be applied in that context also.

Apart from cost savings, JI is widely held to be consistent with other objectives. First, JI could permit national emission targets to be more ambitious than the obligations under any agreement. This outcome is less predictable for sulphur: cost saving may well be at the expense of ecosystem protection because of the need to introduce constraints that give third parties some guarantee against being damaged by an agreement between two other parties.

JI can also permit a wider participation in any agreement. In the greenhouse gas context this may be very important since it can reduce the 'carbon leakage' problem whereby measures to reduce emissions among one set of countries result in increased greenhouse gas emissions in other countries which are not party to the agreement. This can come about because some measures, such as carbon taxes, raise the tax-inclusive price in the participating countries but depress the tax-exclusive price in other countries. Thus, other countries have an incentive to expand their use of fossil fuel energy, thus increasing greenhouse gas emissions.

In principle, then, JI can be applied to any international deal in which one or more of the Parties has emission targets, or, more generally still, to any international agreement in which the Parties have obligations to achieve some environmental goal. Nor is it necessary for there to be an international agreement: country A may trade with country B simply to achieve its own domestic environmental target. In general, however, discussion has focused on JI in the context of international agreements.

One way of thinking about JI is that it is the 'thin end of the wedge' towards a full international tradeable obligations scheme, or 'closed' joint implementation as it is sometimes called. Tradeability here means that anyone who does better than their target emission reduction receives a credit which can then be sold in the market place to others. In initial form, it is likely to involve trades in which just a few countries are involved, one donor and one or more hosts, but it is easy to see how it could be developed to embrace a wholesale trading system such as that being developed in the USA under the Clean Air Act Amendments of 1990. Most commentators appear to be agreed that the prospects for such a fully integrated global trading system are some way into the future. Others have questioned whether JI is a credible precursor to a full traded system.

Why does keeping down the cost of an international agreement matter? Some people argue that if there are obligations they should be met regardless of cost. Some would go further and argue that an expensive agreement in which the costs of compliance are high is just what polluters should suffer: cleaning up the environment should 'hurt' so that polluters are taught a lesson. Unfortunately, while such views may give comfort to those who expound them they tend to work directly against environmental improvement. The more expensive the agreement the less likely it is that the agreement will set strict objectives. And the less likely it is that those who bear the high costs will sign up to future agreements. Making international agreements expensive is therefore counterproductive from an environmental standpoint. There should be a strong interest in keeping compliance costs down.

THE ECONOMICS OF TRADING EMISSION REDUCTIONS

JI is, as noted, an instance of trading pollution reduction obligations. Tradeable, or 'marketable', permits are instances of market-based instruments for the control of environmental pollution and the conservation of natural resources. A market based instrument (MBI) approach to environmental policy makes use of the market-place, by modifying market signals in order to induce environmentally more friendly behaviour. The MBI approach regards traditional forms of regulation, based on 'command and control', as unnecessarily bureaucratic and inefficient. Two broad sources of inefficiency arise in the command and control (CAC) approach:

1 CAC requires the regulator to use up resources to acquire information that polluters already possess. For example, polluters know far better than government what it will cost to abate or clean-up waste emissions. Yet, under the CAC approach, governments must obtain this information.
2 Polluters vary in the ease with which they can abate pollution. Put another way, their costs of control differ. Under the CAC system each polluter has to achieve a given standard, subject usually to some consideration about 'excessive' cost. Control is not concentrated in the sources that find it cheapest to abate pollution. Yet, such a process of concentration would enable overall costs of compliance with the standard to be minimized.

The basic idea underlying tradeable permits is simple. First, an acceptable level of pollution is determined. This may be expressed as some allowable concentration of, say, lead in gasoline; a production or consumption target for chemicals, e.g. CFCs; or an allowable national emission level as is likely with carbon dioxide some time in the future. Permits are then issued for the level of emissions etc. up to the allowable level. If, say, 100 units of pollution is allowable, 100 permits each with a value of 1 unit of emission might be issued. There are various ways of determining the initial issue of the permits. Because of the disruption that might ensue by alternative allocations, a popular initial allocation is one based on historical emission levels. This is known as 'grandfathering': rights to pollute are based on past emission levels. While this is not the only way to determine the initial allocation, the experience so far with tradeable permits shows that it is important to find an acceptable formula for this initial allocation, and that grandfathering tends to be acceptable to all parties. Clearly, grandfathering does nothing to reduce pollution or excessive resource use unless either (a) the initial allocation is for less pollution than already takes place (i.e. quotas are allocated pro rata to existing emissions but the overall level is less than the current total), or (b) the initial allocation is reduced over time. Any polluter achieving lower pollution than the number of permits he possesses receives a credit. For example, polluter A has permits to emit 10 units of pollution but actually emits 8. The credit 2 is then tradeable. This works to the advantage of polluter A if reducing their pollution by 2 units is cheaper than the price they can get by selling permits equal to 2 units. In technical terms, there is an incentive to sell permits if the (marginal) abatement costs are below the ruling price for permits, and to buy if abatement costs are above the price of permits.

Once the initial allocation is made, polluters are then free to trade the pollution rights. It is this tradability that is the hallmark of the permit system since it is tradability that accounts for the main attraction of such a system – its role in keeping down the costs of complying with regulations. Basically, a firm that finds it comparatively easy to abate pollution will find it profitable to sell its permits to a polluter who finds it expensive to abate pollution. Essentially, it will sell the permit if it receives a price higher than the costs it will have to bear of abating pollution now that it has no permit. The high-cost polluter, on the other hand, will find it profitable to buy permits if the price is below what it will otherwise cost them to abate pollution. Both low- and high-cost polluters therefore stand to gain and this provides the incentive for them to trade. Moreover, by trading, the control of pollution will tend to be concentrated among those polluters who find it cheap to pollute. Permit-holding will tend to be concentrated among those who find it expensive to control pollution. Yet the overall environmental standard is safeguarded because nothing has happened to alter the overall number of permits and it is this that determines the level of pollution.

Clearly, such a description is simplistic, but it captures the essence of the tradeable permit system. Trade need not be between different polluters (external trading). It can be between different sources within a single firm (internal trading). The result is the same, however, because the firm will gain by concentrating abatement in its low-cost sources and concentrating permits in the high-cost sources.

Box 12.1 gives a numerical example of how tradeable permits might work.

Box 12.1
HOW TRADEABLE PERMITS WORK

Imagine two factories, A and B, which emit sulphur oxides into the atmosphere. Each has different costs of controlling emissions: the costs of controlling 1 tonne of sulphur oxides in factory A is $20 per tonne, and in factory B it is $30 per tonne. These marginal costs are shown by the height of the two blocks in the diagram. Assume that overall emissions are 5 tonnes from each of A and B. Now suppose the regulator uses a command-and-control solution and requires that A and B each reduce emissions by 1 tonne, a total reduction of 2 tonnes. The cost to A is $20 and the cost to B is $30, so that overall compliance costs are $50. Emissions are now 10 tonnes minus the reduction, i.e. 8 tonnes.

Instead of using the CAC approach, the regulator could issue permits for 8 tonnes of sulphur oxides emissions. A and B are both 'equal' polluters because each emits 5 tonnes of pollution. The regulator therefore decides to allocate the 8 tonnes allowance equally between A and B: each gets permits for 4 tonnes of sulphur oxides (the 'grandfathering' solution – see text). But the regulator allows trading to take place. This means that the permits will acquire a market value because they can be bought and sold. Let the resulting market price be $24 per tonne sulphur, as shown in the diagram. A can reduce a tonne of sulphur at a cost of only $20. It will therefore pay factory A to reduce emissions below the number of permits it has. That is, although A need only reduce by 1 tonne (from 5 to 4) it gains by reducing more than this, say to 3 tonnes. This gives him a credit of 1 tonne which he can trade with B. B will happily buy the permit because it will allow him to avoid cutting emissions at all. The end result is that A cuts by 2 tonnes and B does not cut at all. But this is what the regulator wants – an overall cut of 2 tonnes. So, the level of environmental quality is as good as it would be under the CAC approach.

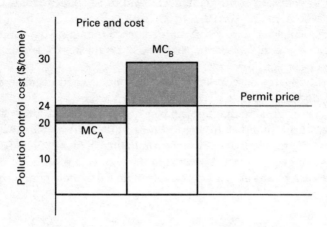

But, interestingly, both A and B have gained through the permit trade. The relevant sums are (− shows a cost, and + shows a benefit):

	Factory A	Factory B
Total cost of reducing emissions by 1 tonne: no trade	20	30
Actual control costs with trade	40	0
less sale of permits	24	0
plus purchase of permits	0	24
Net costs with trade	16	24
Gain from trade	20–16 = 4	30–24 = 6

Notice that the gain from trade, 4 + 6 = 10, is the difference between the marginal costs.

INTERNATIONAL AGREEMENTS AND JOINT IMPLEMENTATION

JI has found a firm place in a number of recent international agreements.

The Montreal Protocol

JI is enabled under the Montreal Protocol on the control of chlorofluorocarbons (CFCs). Article 2 (5) of the 1990 Revisions to the Protocol states:

> Any Party may, for any one or more control periods, transfer to another Party any portion of its calculated level of production [of CFCs], provided that the total combined calculated levels of production of the Parties concerned for any group of controlled substances does not exceed the production limits set out in those articles for that group

thus permitting trade in production quotas.

Article 2(8a), which deals with the European Community, states that:

> Any Parties which are Member States of a regional economic integration organisation ... may agree that they shall jointly fulfil their obligations respecting consumption under this article provided that their total combined level of consumption does not exceed the levels required by this Article

effectively placing a 'bubble' over the EC, i.e. a ceiling on EC CFC emissions but within which individual countries can vary their emissions by trading with each other.

The Framework Convention on Climate Change

Article 4 (2a) of the Framework Convention on Climate Change (FCCC) states that:

> developed country Parties and other Parties included in Annex 1 may implement ... policies and measures jointly with other Parties and may assist other Parties in contributing to the objective of the Convention

Annex 1 countries are the developed economies and the economies in transition, and these countries have generally recognized, if vaguely worded, obligations to cut emissions of greenhouse gases to their 1990 levels by the year 2000. Non-annex 1 countries – the developing countries – have more general obligations.

JI is not defined in the Convention, (along with another and related critical economic concept – incremental cost – see Chapter 11), and the criteria for determining JI are to be established by the Conference of Parties at their first meeting in 1995. Until then the Intergovernmental Negotiating Committee (INC) is the forum for discussions about the meaning of JI in the context of the FCCC.

JI takes on a wider meaning in the FCCC since it may also be the foundation for more general global partnerships in achieving sustainable development.

The Second Sulphur Protocol

JI is also permitted under the Second Sulphur Protocol of the 1979 Convention on Long Range Transboundary Air Pollution, signed by the main European countries in June 1994. The Protocol covers the UN Economic Commission for Europe region, i.e. Europe and the economies in transition. Article 2(7) states:

> The Parties to this Protocol may, . . . in accordance with rules and conditions which the Executive Body shall elaborate and adopt, decide whether two or more Parties may jointly implement the obligations set out in Annex II. These rules and conditions shall ensure the fulfilment of the obligations set out in paragraph 2 . . . and also promote the achievement of the environmental objectives set out in paragraph 1

Annex II of the Protocol sets out the targets for SO_x emission reductions in each country that is party to the Protocol, and which targets are derived from computerized models of emissions, transportation and deposition in the UN Economic Commission for Europe area. The inclusion of JI is interesting. The Second Sulphur Protocol is based on mathematical models of the transfer of acid rain pollution within Europe and the 'critical loads' for sulphur. A critical load is like a threshold: below it no damage is done. Above it damage is done, although the concept says nothing about the way in which damage then varies with the 'excess' deposition of the pollutant. The models on which the Protocol is based are cost-minimizing models, i.e. they secure a given target of reducing the excess depositions of sulphur at the lowest cost for the UN ECE region as whole. Given 'optimal' achievement of the resulting emission targets, which vary by emitting source, JI would have no role to play. This is because JI works when costs differ between emitting sources. If JI was to be carried out repeatedly, then these cost differences would be 'traded away' until the point came when no further trades are possible. This will be the minimum cost point. But if the Protocol already achieves minimum cost then trades will not be possible. It follows that JI is redundant if the Protocol works perfectly.

The inclusion of JI in the Protocol is a recognition of the need to ensure cost-efficiency in a context where (a) actual targets will diverge from the optimized ones, and (b) emissions, depositions and costs are the subject of remaining uncertainties. This underlines one of the virtues of international bargains: once the institutions are established, inclusion of clauses that enable bargains to take place will 'iron out' the inefficiencies that are always present in negotiated legal solutions.

The Rhine 'Salts' Treaty

A 1993 Protocol to the 1976 Convention on the Protection of the Rhine Against Pollution by Chlorides enables the Rhine riparian states to engage in joint funding of downstream measures in The Netherlands to divert chlorides to the North Sea rather than requiring upstream polluters to remove them at source.

COST EFFICIENCY

[This section may be omitted without loss of continuity].

Just how far JI will result in significant cost savings is difficult to say. Self-evidently, cost savings arise because the marginal costs of abatement are assumed to vary between host and donor nations. But it is not clear how safe this assumption is.

Cost savings in the sulphur context: Europe

One of the ways of estimating the cost savings associated with JI is through computer simulation models. In the context of the Second Sulphur Protocol in Europe such models exist and some of them have been utilized to estimate cost savings associated with JI. In the sulphur context, unlike the carbon dioxide context, the effects on 'third parties' are important. Suppose two countries agree a JI bargain. Because the bargain will enable one country to maintain higher emissions than would otherwise be the case, and the other country to lower its emissions, damage to countries who are not party to the agreement may occur. This is because damage from sulphur emissions is dependent on the location of the sources of emission. We noted this did not apply in the carbon dioxide case. Related to this third party problem is the issue of 'emission exchange rates'. If country A was obliged to cut emissions by X tonnes, but does a JI deal with country B so that it no longer cuts by X, what reduction should there be in country B's emissions ? It could be X tonnes, in which case the 'increase' in A is exactly offset by the decrease in B. We can say that the 'exchange rate' is 1 since X/X = 1. This is indeed how trades are carried out under the United States sulphur trading scheme (see below). But the exchange rate need not equal 1. Indeed it should be equal to the reduction in emissions in country B needed to offset the emissions increase in country A, *allowing for the damage done by each of the emissions changes.* These are 'damage-related exchange rates'.

Another approach is possible. For cost minimization to occur the marginal costs of control should be equal in the two bargaining nations. (This is because if they are not, we can save more cost by reducing emissions in the country with lower marginal costs). So, one way of defining exchange rates is to set them equal to the ratio of the two marginal costs before trade takes place. So, we have two approaches to determining exchange rates: one based on damages and one based on costs of control. (If the system is 'optimized' in the benefit-cost sense, then they are the same since marginal damages would equal marginal costs of control). There are various intermediary results, depending on what constraints are imposed on the JI deals. For example, one constraint arising from concerns over third party effects would be to ensure that sulphur depositions in third party countries do not increase at all.

With trading schemes employing such exchange rates, how much would cost savings be? After all, if the savings – which are the dominant motive for JI – are small in practice, it may be not worthwhile to establish complex JI schemes. Computer simulations for Europe suggest that schemes that do not have the constraint on third party effects, and where the exchange rates are based on marginal costs of control, could save 18–19 per cent of the costs of the Second Sulphur Protocol. This is significant. When constraints on third party effects are introduced, the cost savings are reduced dramatically to perhaps a little under 1 per cent of the Protocol costs. Given the uncertainty in the figures, such results need to be treated with caution. But they do suggest one underlying factor: the more restrictions there are on trade between countries,the lower the cost savings. This is as we would expect.

Cost savings in the sulphur context: USA

In the USA the 1990 Clean Air Act Amendments established a national programme for sulphur trading. But there was a limited experiment with trading emission permits prior to this. The US Environmental Protection Agency had in fact begun experimenting with pollution permit trading in 1974. We would expect the actual experience of permit trading to result in no decline in environmental standards and a reduction in the costs of compliance compared to what would have been incurred in a CAC system. By and large, this is the experience of the early trading experience in the USA.

Some terminology is needed to understand the US system. *Netting,* introduced in 1974, is a procedure whereby a firm can create a new emissions source provided it offsets the resulting emissions by reductions elsewhere in the same plant. Netting always involves *internal trading,* i.e. the firm is not allowed to acquire permits from outside. *Offsets* were introduced in 1976 in areas where the Clean Air Act standards had not been met ('non-attainment areas'). Stringent rules applied to new sources would have meant that such areas could attract little or no new industry. However, by offsetting the new source by even greater reductions in existing sources, these areas are allowed to acquire new industry. Such offsets can be obtained by internal and external trading, i.e. from buying up permits from within the same source or from other firms. *Bubbles* are perhaps the most famous part of the US tradeable permits system. They were introduced in 1979. A 'bubble' is a hypothetical aggregate limit for existing sources of pollution (whereas netting and offsets relate to new sources). Within the overall bubble limit firms are free to vary sources of pollution so long as the overall limit is not breached. Bubbles are allowed to extend beyond a single firm, but in practice bubbles have tended to be placed round single firms. *Banking* was introduced in 1979 and operates just like a bubble but through time, i.e. the firm is allowed to bank credits and use them at some stage in the future.

Box 12.2 summarizes the US experience and shows the effects on cost savings and on environmental quality. Box 12.2 reveals the following:

- Nearly all trading was internal. Only the offset system resulted in moderate external trading. While the bubble system does permit external trading, hardly any occurred. This appears to be due to the high costs of acquiring information about other firms' willingness to trade, and the costs of obtaining the regulator's permission to trade.
- The cost savings were probably considerable, with a minimum of $1 billion and perhaps as much as $13 billion having been saved.
- Banking was hardly used at all.
- The extensive use of netting compared to bubbles, even allowing

---

Box 12.2
EARLY USA EXPERIENCE WITH TRADEABLE PERMITS

	Bubbles Federal	State	Offsets	Netting	Banking
Number of trades	42	89	2000	5000–12000	< 120
Cost savings ($US million)	300	135	large	525–12300	small
Air quality impact	zero	zero	zero	probably insignificant	probably insignificant
Nature of trade: internal	40	89	1800	5000–12000	< 100
external	2	0	200	0	< 20

Source: R. Hahn and G. Hester, 1989, 'Where Did All the Markets Go? An Analysis of EPA's Emissions Trading Program', *Yale Journal of Regulation* 6 (1), Winter 1989, 109–153. See also Hahn, 1987.

---

for the predominance of internal trades, is surprising since bubbles apply to existing sources whereas netting applies only to new or modified sources.

Explaining the less than hoped-for level of trading activity in the early US permits system so far is not easy. Companies such as Armco, Du Pont, USX and 3M have traded permit credits, but the take-up was otherwise quite low. Commentators have suggested five main reasons:

1   New sources were subject to far stricter regulations about emissions quality. This means that firms are keen to adopt any offsetting procedure when a new source starts up. Netting is the appropriate procedure in these cases and this does much to explain the dominance of netting in the US system. Moreover, existing sources inherited abatement equipment, bought before the bubble policy was introduced in 1979, so that the costs of adjustment under a bubble policy were high.

2   Uncertainty about pollution credits. There was considerable uncertainty about just what emission credits ensue under the banking legislation. Firms were not always sure how the regulator

will determine baseline emissions and hence how emission credits will be determined. This uncertainty is heightened when other firms' credits are the subject of the trade (i.e. when external trading is involved). Firm A has to be sure that firm B really will reduce emissions to create credits that can be traded. In contrast, internal trading involves far greater certainty because the firm is dealing only with itself.

3 It is more expensive to acquire information about external trading since firm A needs to find out what other firms have banked credits, and the price at which trade is likely to take place. Similar problems have arisen in other countries where attempts have been made to establish waste exchange information services.

4 Firms will not trade with other firms because of the prospect of permit prices rising. Permits will be hoarded as long as the expected price rise is greater than the cost of hoarding, i.e. greater than interest rate.

5 Hoarded permits can be used as a deterrent to new entrants.

Permit trading is the central feature of a more recent US Clean Air Act in the context of acid rain control. Regulators claim they have learned from the experience of the previous tradeable permit systems and that most of the problems should be avoidable in the new system. It is known that abatement costs per tonne of SO_2 vary substantially across states. Rico (1994) suggests that in the year 2000 a traditional command-and-control programme applied to the US target of 10 million tonnes p.a. SO_2 reduction would cost some \$3.2–4.9 billion p.a. compared to costs with allowance trading of \$1.1–2.1 billion, a saving of perhaps 60 per cent.

Cost savings in the climate context

In the climate change context, RISO (1992) suggest marked variations in CO_2 control costs between European countries. However, the variation is not in the direction that might be thought, namely lower costs in generally poorer countries. Abatement costs turn out to be lower, for example, in Germany, UK and Denmark than in Greece, Portugal and Spain. Barbier *et al.* (1991) found substantial variations in costs of CO_2 control between countries. Jackson (1994) argues that the assumption of significant cost differentials between countries is unfounded. First, there is more scope for 'negative cost' reductions in the developed economies – so called 'win-win' reductions from e.g. energy conservation. Moreover, the scope for JI gains is, he argues, limited once one looks at actual abatement cost curves.

Whether the evidence supports the assumption of marked cost

differentials between countries or not is not a serious blow to JI as an 'enabling' concept under the FCCC. Essentially, all the agreements cited permit JI if participants find it profitable to engage in it. It is not mandated in any sense. Hence if profitable opportunities exist they are likely to be exploited provided countries are aware of actual cost differentials. On the other hand, if cost differentials are small, or are 'perverse' in the sense that less developed countries have higher costs than developed countries, then JI does not hold out the prospect for major cost savings.

Even if cost differentials are significant, the potential for profitable trade is limited by transaction costs. Information on transactions costs is also difficult to evaluate. As noted above, the 'thinner' the market, the higher are transaction costs likely to be. This suggests that there is a 'chicken and egg' problem in that the true cost-saving benefits of JI will not be realized until large-scale trading occurs, while large scale-trading cannot occur until it has been demonstrated that JI results in significant cost savings.

OBJECTIONS TO TRADING POLLUTION REDUCTIONS

Objections to the idea of trading pollution rights have been raised by various 'interest groups': environmentalists, industry, and government.

Environmentalists' objections tend to focus on two main issues: whether environmental quality is sacrificed under a tradeable permits system, and whether it is morally right to 'permit' pollution even for a price. Box 12.2 shows that the environmental quality argument has little or no foundation. The second objection has to be countered by an educative process. All regulatory systems 'permit' pollution if by pollution is meant waste. No economic process is waste-free. The issue has therefore to be one of whether a tradeable permits system somehow permits more waste than a CAC system. As we have seen, there is no reason at all for this to be the case. It is significant that many environmental organizations now welcome tradeable permits. In the climate change-context, however, a number of critics have argued that JI could threaten the commitment of the rich countries to their own targets, i.e. they fear that JI is seen not as an *additional* opportunity for pollution reduction but as a means of escaping making the reductions in their own countries. An extension of this argument is that countries paying for emission reductions will be transferring their technology to the developing countries, expanding their sphere of technological influence (Climate Network Europe, 1994).

The US experience suggests that certainty about the regulatory system is highly valued. With CAC systems the firm is, by and large, clear about the nature of the regulation and what is and what is not permitted. This is also true for CAC systems that are less rigid, such as the UK system in which there is considerable scope for flexible adjustments in light of dialogue with the Inspectorate of Pollution. As European Community Directives play an increasingly important role, however, we might expect more and more 'standard setting' to replace the system of negotiation over achieving standards.

Regulators will naturally be sensitive to the concerns of both environmentalists and industry. Nonetheless they will also have their own concerns, primarily arising from the costs of considering, formulating and implementing any departure from the established CAC approach. It is worth remembering that the CAC mode of thinking is ingrained in environmental regulation in most countries, reflecting as it does the experience of over 100 years of public health, workplace and environmental legislation. Anxiety also tends to increase the less is known about the new system.

Regulators and industry are also likely to be concerned about the administrative costs of any regulatory system. Under a tradeable permits system, the administrative costs could be very high if there are a great many polluters. Where there are comparatively few the costs of administration are low, but a new problem arises in that one or two polluters may corner the market in permits and refuse to trade them. This would act like a barrier to entry for new firms and the permits could therefore contribute to non-competitive behaviour.

A potentially forceful objection to JI is that it will reduce pollution-reducing technological innovation in the developed economies, i.e. the developed economies will seek first to exhaust conventional technology in the developing world before turning to the need to develop new technologies in the rich world. In the climate context this could be important since the technologies in question are the renewable technologies, the transition to which has a wider justification.

According to some commentators, a problem in the climate context is that the FCCC does not permit, at the moment, any 'currency' in which full traded JI deals can take place. This is because the developed economies have targets while the developing countries do not. In a full trading scheme recall that the country selling permits has to honour the regulations on pollution emissions, but under the FCCC, developing countries have no targets and hence have nothing to honour. This is why the discussion on JI has typically been focused on 'open' JI deals, those where A pays B to reduce emissions in order to get a credit against A's own targets.

PROBLEMS WITH JOINT IMPLEMENTATION

If the cost conditions are right, JI promises significant cost savings in the context of climate change control and perhaps in contexts such as sulphur control as well. Why then does it cause controversy?

The problems appear to fall into several categories. The following list is far from comprehensive (for other questions see Jones, 1993):

1   whether there is in fact much scope for trade: this is the issue of (i) whether costs of control vary significantly between trading countries and (ii) transactions costs (this issue is addressed above);
2   in the climate context, the relationship between JI and developed country obligations under the FCCC;
3   who should trade;
4   the determination of cost; and
5   sinks vs emission reductions.

We address issues 2–5 briefly.

JI AND NATIONAL OBLIGATIONS

It is easy to see that, from some standpoints, JI looks like an attempt by the developed countries to 'offload' their problem on to developing countries. This is the issue of whether or not JI should result in 'credits' for the donor country which are then set against its national target under the FCCC. If the credits are allowed, then the developed countries save costs by not reducing their own emissions as much as they otherwise would have done. Low cost abatement options are then taken up in the developing countries. Objections to such credits being counted appear to range from the purely practical to the moral. At the practical end of the spectrum is the concern that developing country low-cost options would be used up so that developing countries would face only high-cost options in the event that they signed up to their own emission targets at a future date. At the moral end of the spectrum is the view that global warming is the result of developed country profligacy, and that JI would postpone the radical changes in 'consumption' needed in the developed world. A purely legalistic view correctly interprets the Convention as allowing JI against current emission reduction commitments. Equally, if JI is not to count against existing commitments, its likely scope will be fairly restricted since few countries have an incentive to go beyond their commitments. It is easy to overlook the fact that even with JI it is the donor country that is paying for the emissions reduction. Similarly, if JI brings benefits to the host country, those benefits will be forgone if JI is interpreted as being additional to national commitments. For these reasons, arguments that JI can be introduced on a voluntary basis without credits being counted against current commitments would seem injurious to the prospects for JI.

Who trades?

The common perception is that JI under the FCCC is about trade between developed countries and developing countries, and trade between developed countries and the economies in transition (Annex 1 countries in the FCCC). The obvious problem with this view, which would exclude inter-developed country trade, is that the developing countries do not have targets under the Convention. As such, it is not possible to say what they would have done if the JI deal did not take place. But determining what they would have done, the so-called 'baseline', is important since a credit for emissions reduction has no meaning unless it can be demonstrated that a genuine reduction has taken place. It is necessary to know that the emissions reduction under the JI deal is 'genuine', i.e. does not involve emissions reductions that would have taken place anyway. This argument has been used by Klaassen (1994) to declare that non-signatories to the Second Sulphur Protocol should not be permitted to engage in JI deals. Including non-signatories results in delays and high transaction costs. This appears also to be the experience with the Montreal Protocol (Klaassen, 1994) and is underlined by the fact that only one in ten proposed trades under the past US sulphur trading system was accepted in the form originally proposed. In other words, anything that opens the way for difficulties with authorization should be avoided or minimized. Determining baselines will be a critical problem. Because of the problems of defining the counterfactual baseline, Bohm (1994a) argues that JI has the potential for being genuinely cost-reducing if the deals are between FCCC Annex 1 countries (developed plus transitional economies) but not if the deals are between developed and developing countries. This is because Annex 1 countries have (fairly) well-defined emissions, base years and emissions targets, whereas this is not true for developing countries. All Parties to the Framework Convention are obliged to publish national programmes showing climate change mitigation measures and these could, in principle, be the means for determining the baseline in developing countries. There remains the problem of knowing if national programme statements themselves contain a degree of manipulation of true baselines.

Notice that the 'moral' objection to JI noted above largely disappears if trades are between Annex 1 countries only.

Offsetting this view is the fact that including non-signatories will enhance the comprehensiveness of any agreement and thereby maximize cost-savings. How far this is a serious concern in the FCCC context, however, is open to question since the vast majority of greenhouse gas emissions emanate from signatory countries (Jones, 1993).

The other issue with who trades is whether trades occur between nations or companies, or both. The answer seems fairly clear that companies should be involved, and Box 12.2 above has shown that this is already the case outside the terms of the FCCC.

The determination of cost

What cost do donors pay? The theoretical answer is that they pay the *incremental cost* (see Chapter 11) incurred by the host country in implementing the JI deal. Incremental cost is always the cost of doing something that the host country would not otherwise have done. What it otherwise would have done produces the *baseline cost*. Unfortunately, whilst conceptually simple, incremental cost (IC) is difficult to evaluate in practice. Both the Rio Conventions and the Montreal Protocol speak of 'agreed full incremental cost', but none of them defines the concept. It may be, however, that such definitions, while needed for the Convention generally, are not needed for JI.

The problem of the baseline has already been alluded to. It is only readily determined if countries have pre-established national plans. Jones (1993) suggests that no attempt should be made to determine the baseline or even a common methodology on costs. But if so, it is difficult to see how it can be determined whether or not the JI deal has actually honoured the overall environmental objective, namely that greenhouse gas emissions should not increase. A JI deal might otherwise simply sanction a reduction that would have taken place anyway. This is particularly relevant for deals between Annex 1 countries involving economies in transition where structural change is likely to reduce greenhouse gas emissions in the baseline anyway. Some idea of the baseline therefore seems essential.

Incremental cost may also not define the actual transfer between donor and host, despite the implication of the FCCC that what is transferred, as funds or technology, is the 'full' incremental cost. This is because JI may involve the host country in securing some incremental domestic benefits that would not be present in its baseline. There are three options. First, any incremental domestic benefits (IDB) could be deducted from incremental cost so that the transfer (T) is given by $T = IC - IDB$. Second, IDB could be ignored, in which case the host country secures a net benefit at least equal to IDB (at least, because the host country also gains its share of benefits from the reduction in global warming), and T = IC. Third, some fraction of IDB could be deducted, as is perhaps implied by the term 'agreed' full incremental costs, so that T = IC − αIDB. As Chapter 11 noted, the FCCC provides no guidance on this issue of benefit deductibility. Clearly, if IDB is deducted fully, then the host country has no real incentive to adopt a JI deal: it is neither better off nor worse off with the deal. On the other hand, most deals involving technology switching will bring updated capital equipment into being and the benefits of such investments are unlikely to qualify as IDBs.

However, whereas incremental cost needs to be addressed in the context of the FCCC as a whole, it is far from clear that operational guidelines are needed on it for JI deals. This is because JI is a fairly explicit bargain between host and donor. They will therefore 'agree a price' at which the deal will take place. Issues such as incremental domestic benefits may well enter into those bargains, but there is no real need for an explicit set of guidelines on how to estimate incremental cost in this context. The transfer, T, will simply be agreed between parties, each of whom knows whether or not it is to their advantage.

Sinks vs emissions reductions

In principle, a JI deal could involve augmenting a sink or securing an emissions reduction. Chapter 9 listed a number of deals which are, in effect, joint implementation deals. They are generally of the kind where emissions are traded for afforestation, reforestation or efficient forest use. It is sometimes argued that the uncertainty surrounding the true measure of carbon fixed will simply add to the monitoring costs of JI and hence make JI less attractive. As such, it has been suggested that they be omitted omitting them from JI deals under the FCCC at least for now. Against this, one has to ask why it is that the private deals have opted for this option. A cynical view might be that such deals are capable of manipulation by all parties in their own interests. Certainly, JI carries with it the risk of threat situations when the baseline is not readily identifiable. Thus a host country might refuse to afforest and thus claim that 'no afforestation' defines its baseline. It can then attract an afforestation JI project and claim that newly planted trees are a genuine contribution to carbon fixation. The situation might be worse still if JI is extended to 'avoided deforestation', with threats to deforest being rewarded by JI deals. The donor agent also has an incentive to exaggerate the extent of host country emissions reduction or fixation since it gains more by way of its own emissions increases that will be allowed. But actual deals to date seem to have been motivated more by a concern to operate at a manageable level, to demonstrate JI in a context where the donor does something different to its normal operations (effectively making the baseline more credible), and to generate ancillary development benefits. Forestry projects appear to meet these conditions more readily than, say, fuel-switching investments.

CONCLUSIONS

Clearly, joint implementation is far from being straightforward in its application. The particular problems that arise may be summarized as those of: designing compatible incentives for the revelation of 'genuine' trades; monitoring; determining who trades and what the gains from trade are; and providing assurances to the developing world that JI is not a mechanism whereby the rich world can escape its own obligations. The issue is whether these problems are worth solving and that can only be resolved by securing a clearer idea of what the gains are to each party: the cost savings to the donor and the world at large, and the developmental gains to the host countries. We might end on the general reflection that if we ignore the cost savings argument, or if we allow too many restrictions to be placed on JI deals, we may risk reducing the incentives of the developed country parties to commit themselves seriously to strengthening the existing Conventions, and to any new ones that may have larger benefits to developing countries. As with all things, compromise has to be the outcome.

References

Alfsen, K., H. Birkelund and M. Aaserud, 1993, *Secondary Benefits of the EC Carbon/Energy Tax*, Research Department Discussion Paper, No 104, Statistics, Norway, Oslo.

Allen, J. and D. Barnes, 1985, The Causes of Deforestation in Developing Countries, *Annals of the Association of American Geographers*, 75(2).

Ayres and Walter, 1991, Global Warming: Abatement Policies and Costs, *Environment and Resource Economics*, 1(3): 237–270.

Barbier E., J. Burgess, D. W. Pearce, 1991, Technological Substitution Options for Controlling Greenhouse Gas Emissions, in R. Dornbusch and J. Poterba, *Global Warming: Economic Policy Responses*, MIT Press, London and Cambridge, 109–160.

Barker, T., 1993, *Secondary Benefits of Greenhouse Gas Abatement: The Effects of a UK Carbon/Energy Tax on Air Pollution*, Energy Environment Economy Modelling Discussion Paper No.4, Department of Applied Economics, University of Cambridge.

Binswanger, H., 1989, *Brazilian Policies that Encourage Deforestation in the Amazon*, World Bank, Environment Department, Working Paper no. 16, Washington DC.

Birdsall, N. and D. Wheeler, 1991, 'Openness Reduces Industrial Pollution in Latin America: the Missing Pollution Haven Effect', Paper Presented to World Bank Symposium on International Trade and the Environment, Washington DC, November.

Blum, E., 1993, Making Biodiversity Conservation Profitable: a Case Study of the Merck INBio Agreement, *Environment*, 35(4), May.

Bohm, P., 1994a, On the Feasibility of Joint Implementation of Carbon Emissions Reductions, Department of Economics, University of Stockholm, *mimeo*.

Bohm, P., 1994b, Making Carbon Emissions Quota Agreements More Efficient: Joint Implementation vs Quota Tradeability, Department of Economics, Stockholm University, *mimeo*.

Brown, K. and D. W. Pearce (eds), 1994, *The Causes of Deforestation: The Economic and Statistical Analysis of the Factors Giving Rise to the Loss of the*

Tropical Forests, University College Press, London, and the University of British Columbia Press, Vancouver.

Brown, K., D. W. Pearce, T. Swanson and C. Perrings, 1993, *Economics and the Conservation of Biological Diversity*, Global Environment Facility, Working Paper No.2, Washington DC.

Burgess, J., 1991, *Economic Analyses of Frontier Agricultural Expansion and Tropical Deforestation*, MSc dissertation presented to the University College, London.

Burgess, J., 1992, *Economic Analysis of the Causes of Tropical Deforestation*, London Environmental Economics Centre, Discussion Paper, 92–03, November 1992.

Capistrano, A. and C. Kiker, 1990, *Global Economic Influences on Tropical Broadleaved Forest Depletion*, The World Bank, Washington DC.

Cervigni, R., and D. W. Pearce, 1994, *North–South Resource Transfers, Incremental Cost and the Rio Environment Conventions*, Centre for Social and Economic Research on the Global Environment, University College London and University of East Anglia, Working Paper 95.

Climate Network Europe, 1994, *Joint Implementation from a European NGO Perspective*, Climate Network Europe, Brussels.

Cline, W., 1992, *The Economics of Global Warming*, Cambridge University Press, Cambridge.

Constantino, L. and D. Ingram, 1990, *Supply–Demand Projections for the Indonesian Forestry Sector*, FAO, Jakarta.

Cropper, M. and C. Griffiths, 1994, The Interaction of Population Growth and Environmental Quality, *American Economic Review: Papers and Proceedings*, May, 84(2): 250–254.

Cuesta, M., G. Carlson, and E. Lutz, 1994, *An Empirical Assessment of Farmers Discount Rates in Costa Rica and Its Implications for Soil Conservation*, Environment Department, World Bank, Washington DC.

Dean, J., 1991, *Trade and the Environment: a Survey of the Literature*, Background Paper prepared for the 1992 World Development Report, World Bank, Washington DC, *mimeo*.

Deacon, R. and P. Murphy, 1994, *The Structure of an Environmental Transaction: the Debt-for-Nature Swap*, Resources for the Future, Washington DC.

Dinerstein, E. and D. E. Wikramanayake, 1993, Beyond Hotspots: How to Prioritize Investment to Conserve Biodiversity in the Indo-Pacific Region, in: *Conservation Biology* 7(1): 53–65.

Dixon, R., K. Andrasko, F. Sussman, M. Trexler and T. Vinson, 1993, Forest Sector Carbon Offset Projects: Near-Term Opportunities to Mitigate Greenhouse Gas Emissions, *Water, Air and Soil Pollution*.

Fankhauser, S., 1995, *Valuing Climate Change*, Earthscan, London.

Fankhauser, S. and D. W. Pearce, 1994, The Social Costs of Greenhouse Gas Emissions in OECD, *The Economics of Climate Change*, Paris, 71–86.

Freeman III, A.M., 1986, On Assessing the State of the Art of the Contingent Valuation Method of Valuing Environmental Changes, in R.G. Cummings, D. Brookshire and W. Schulze (eds), *Valuing Environmental Goods: an Assessment of the Contingent Valuation Method*, Rowman and Allenheld, Totowa, 148–161.

Gamez, R. *et al.*, 1993, Costa Rica's Conservation Program and National Biodiversity Institute (INBio) in Reid, *et al.*, 1993b.

GATT, 1989, *United States – Section 337 of the Tariff Act of 1930, Report of the Panel*, L/6439, November 7.

GATT, 1990, *Thailand – Restrictions on Importation of and Internal Taxes On Cigarettes*, Report of the Panel, DS10/R, October 5.

GATT, 1991a, *United States – Restrictions on Imports of Tuna, Report of the Panel*, DS21/R, September 3.

GATT, 1991b, *On Environment, Economy and GATT*, GATT Briefing, No. 5–6, March.

Global Environment Facility, 1992, *The Pilot Phase and Beyond*, GEF Working Paper Series No 1, GEF, Washington DC.

Global Environment Facility, 1992, *Memorandum of Understanding on Norwegian Funding of Pilot Demonstration Projects for Joint Implementation Arrangements Under the Climate Convention*, GEF, World Bank, Washington DC, *mimeo*.

Godoy, R. and R. Lubowski, 1992, Guidelines for the Economic Valuation of Non-Timber Products, *Current Anthropology*, 33(4): 423–433.

Grais, W., J. de Melo and S. Urata, 1986, A General Equilibrium Estimation of the Effects of Reduction in Tariffs and Quantitative Restrictions in Turkey in 1978, in T. Srinivasan and J. Whalley (eds), *General Equilibrium Trade Policy Modelling*, MIT Press, Cambridge, Mass.

Grossman, G. and A. Krueger, 1991, *Environmental Impacts of a North American Free Trade Agreement*, Working Paper No. 3914, National Bureau of Economic Research, Cambridge, MA.

Grut, M., J. Gray, and N. Egli, 1991, *Forest Pricing and Concession Policies: Managing the High Forests of West and Central Africa*, Technical Paper No.143, World Bank, Washington DC.

Hahn, R. and G. Hester, 1989, Marketable Permits: Lessons for Theory and Practice, *Ecology Law Quarterly*, 16(2): 361–406.

Hahn, R., 1987, The Market for Bads: EPA's experience with Emissions Trading Programme, *Regulation*, Nos 3/4.

Hardin, G., 1968, The Tragedy of the Commons, *Science*, 162: 1243–48.

Hines, C., 1990, *Green Protectionism: Halting the Four Horsemen of the Apocalypse*, Earth Resources Research, London.

Hodgson, G. and J. Dixon, 1988, *Logging Versus Fisheries and Tourism in Palawan*, East West Centre, Occasional Paper No.7, Honolulu, Hawaii.

Hyde, W. and R. Sedjo, 1992, Managing Tropical Forests: Reflections on the Rent Distribution Discussion, *Land Economics* 68(3): 343–350.

Hyde, W. and R. Sedjo, 1993, Managing Tropical Forests: Reply, *Land Economics* 69(3) 319–321.

Jackson, T., 1994, Asessing the Cost Effectiveness of Joint Implementation under the Climate Convention, in Climate Network Europe, 1994, *Joint Implementation from a European NGO Perspective*, Climate Network Europe, Brussels.

Jones, T., 1993, *Operational Criteria for Joint Implementation*, OECD, Paris, June.

Kahn, J. and J. McDonald, 1994, Third World Debt and Tropical Deforestation, in Brown and Pearce, *The Causes of Tropical Deforestation*, 1994.

Katila, M., 1992, *Modelling Deforestation in Thailand: the Causes of Deforestation and Deforestation Projections for 1990–2010*, Finnish Forestry Institute, Helsinki, *mimeo* (first draft).

Katzman, M. and W. Cale, 1990, Tropical Forest Preservation Using Economic Incentives: A Proposal of Conservation Easements, *BioScience* 40(11): 827–832.

King, K., 1993, *The Incremental Costs of Global Environmental Benefits*, Global Environment Facility, Working Paper No. 5.

Klaassen, G., 1994, *Joint Implementation in the Second Sulfur Protocol: a Tempest in a Teapot?*, International Institute for Applied Systems Analysis (IIASA), Laxenburg, Austria.

Kramer, R., E. Mercer and N. Sharma, 1994, *Valuing Tropical Rain Forest Protection using the Contingent Valuation Method*, School of the Environment, Duke University, Durham, NC, *mimeo*.

Krause, F., W. Bach and J. Kooney, 1989, *Energy Policy in the Greenhouse*, Earthscan, London.

Kumari, K., 1994, An Environmental and Economic Assessment of Forestry Management Options: A Case Study in Peninsular Malaysia, Chapter 6 of K. Kumari, *Sustainable Forestry Management in Malaysia*, PhD Thesis, University of East Anglia, UK.

Kummer, D. and C.H. Sham, 1994, The Causes of Tropical Deforestation: a Quantative Analysis and Case Study from the Phillippines, in Brown and Pearce, 1994, 146–158.

Leonard, H.J., 1984, *Are Environmental Regulations Driving US Industry Overseas?*, The Conservation Foundation, Washington DC.

Leonard, H.J., 1988, *Pollution and the Struggle for the World Product*, Cambridge University Press, Cambridge.

Leonard, H.J., 1991, *Economic Instruments and the International Location of Industry: Evidence Regarding Whether Industry Will Move to Low Cost Pollution Havens*, Business Council for Sustainable Development, Workshop on Economic Instruments, London.

Low, P., 1991, *Trade Measures and Environmental Quality: Implications for Mexico's Exports*, Paper Presented to World Bank Symposium on International Trade and the Environment, Washington DC, November.

Low, P. and A. Yeats, 1991, *Do Dirty Industries Migrate?*, Paper Presented to World Bank Symposium on International Trade and the Environment, Washington DC, November.

Lovejoy, T., 1980, A Projection of Species Extinctions, in G. Barney, (ed), *The Global 2000 Report to the President*, Council on Environmental Quality: Washington.

Lucas, R., D. Wheeler, H. Hettige, 1991, *Economic Development, Environmental Regulation and the International Migration of Toxic Industrial Pollution: 1960–1988*, Paper Presented to World Bank Symposium on International Trade and the Environment, Washington DC, November.

Lugo, A., R. Schmidt and S. Brown, 1981, Tropical Forest in the Caribbean, *Ambio* 10(6).

MacArthur, R.H. and E.O. Wilson, 1967, *The Theory of Island Biogeography*, Princeton: Princeton University Press.

McNeely, J., K. Miller, W. Reid, R. Mittermeier, T. Werner, 1990, *Conserving the World's Biodiversity*, IUCN and World Bank, Gland and Washington DC.

Maddison, D.J., 1994, *The Shadow Price of Greenhouse Gases and Aerosols*, Centre for Social and Economic Research in the Global Environment (CSERGE), University College London and University of East Anglia, Norwich, *mimeo*.

Mahar, D. and R. Schneider, 1994, Incentives for Tropical Deforestation: Some Examples from Latin America, in Brown and Pearce (1994), 159–171.

Mittermeier, R. A., 1988, Primate Diversity and the Tropical Forest: Case Studies from Brazil and Madagascar and the Importance of the Megadiversity Countries, in: E.O. Wilson (ed.), *Biodiversity*, Washington D.C., National Academy Press.

Mittermeier, R.A., and I. Bowles, 1993, *The GEF and Biodiversity Conservation: Lessons to Date and Recommendations for Future Action*, Conservation International, Washington DC.

Mittermeier, R.A., T.B. Werner, 1990, Wealth of Plants and Animals in 'Megadiversity' Countries, *Tropicus* 4(1): 4–5.

Morredu, C., K. Parris, B. Huff, 1990, Agricultural Policies in Developing Countries and Agricultural Trade, in I. Goldin and O. Knudsen (eds), *Agricultural Trade Liberalization: Implicatuons for Developing Countries*, OECD, Paris, 115–157.

Mutti, J.D., and J. Richardson, 1976, Industrial Displacement Through Environmental Controls: the International Competitive aspects, in J. Water (ed), 1976, *Studies in International Environmental Economics*, Wiley, New York.

Myers, N., 1979, *The Sinking Ark. A Look at the Problem of Disappearing Species*. Pergamon: New York.

Myers, N., 1988, Threatened Biotas: 'Hot Spots' in Tropical Forests, *The Environmentalist* 8(3): 187–208.

Myers, N., 1989, *Deforestation Rates in Tropical Forests and Their Climatic Implications*, Friends of the Earth, London.

Myers, N., 1990, The Biodiversity Challenge: Expanded Hot Spots Analysis, *The Environmentalist* 10(4): 243–256.

Newcombe, K. and R. de Lucia, 1993, *Mobilising Private Capital Against Global Warming: a Business Concept and Policy Issues*, Global Environment Facility, Washington DC, *mimeo*.

Nordhaus, W., 1991a, To Slow or Not to Slow: the Economics of the Greenhouse Effect, *Economic Journal* 101(407): 938–948.

Nordhaus, W., 1991b, A Sketch of the Economics of the Greenhouse Effect, *American Economic Review, Papers and Proceedings*, 81(2): 146–150.

Nordhaus, W., 1994, Expert Opinion on Climate Change, in *American Scientist*, January–February.

OECD, 1994, *Integrating Environment and Economics: The Role of Economic Instruments*, OECD, Paris.

OECD, 1993, *Agricultural Policies, Markets and Trade: Monitoring and Outlook 1993*, OECD, Paris.

Panayotou, T., 1993, *Green Markets: The Economics of Sustainable Development*, Institute of Contemporary Studies Press, San Fransisco.

Panayotou, T., 1994, Conservation of Biodiversity and Economic Development: The Concept of Transferable Development Rights, in C Perrings *et al.*, *Biodiversity Conservation: Policy Issues and Options*, Amsterdam, Kluwer Academic Press (forthcoming).

Panayotou, T. and S. Sungsuwan, 1994, *An Econometric Study of the Causes of Tropical Deforestation: The Case of Northeast Thailand*, in Brown and Pearce, 1994, 192–210.

Palo, M., G. Mery and J. Salmi, 1987, *Deforestation in the Tropics: Pilot Scenarios Based on Quantitative Analyses*, Metsatutkimuslaitoksen Tiedonantaja nro. 272, Helsinki.

Pearce, D.W., 1991, *Blueprint 2: Sustaining the World Economy*, Earthscan, London.

Pearce, D.W., 1993, *Blueprint 3: Measuring Sustainable Development*, Earthscan, London.

Pearce, D.W., 1995, Joint Implementation: a General Overview, in C.P. Jepma (ed), *The Feasibility of Joint Implementation*, Kluwer, Dordrecht, forthcoming.

Pearce, D.W., N. Adger, D. Moran, R. Cervigni and K. Brown, 1993, *Mexico Forestry and Conservation Sector Review: substudy of economic valuation of forests*, Report to Latin American Technical Department, World Bank, Washington DC.

Pearce, D.W., G. Atkinson and R. Dubourg, 1994, The Economics of Sustainable Development, *Annual Review of Energy*, 19: 457–474.

Pearce, D.W. and S. Barrett, 1995, *Incremental Cost for Biodiversity Conservation*, Global Environment Facility Working Papers, forthcoming.

Pearce, D.W. and I. Brisson, 1994, BATNEEC: the Economics of Technology-Based Standards, with a UK Illustration, *Oxford Review of Economic Policy* 9(4).

Pearce, D.W. and D. Moran, 1994, *The Economic Value of Biological Diversity*, Earthscan, London.

Pearce D.W., A. Markandya and E. Barbier, 1989, *Blueprint for a Green Economy*, Earthscan, London.

Pearce, D.W and Ulph, D. 1995, *A Social Discount Rate for the United Kingdom*, Centre for the Social and Economic Research for the Global Environment, University College London and University of East Anglia, Working Paper 95–01.

Pearce, D.W. and J. Warford, 1993, *World Without End: Environment, Economics and Sustainable Development*, Oxford: Oxford University Press.

Peck, S.C. and T.J. Teisberg, 1993, Global Warming Uncertainties and the Value of Information: An Analysis using CETA, *Resource and Energy Economics*, 15(1): 71–97.

Perrings, C., 1992, An Economic Analysis of Tropical Deforestation, Environment and Economic Management Department, University of York, UK, *mimeo*.

Peters, C.M., A.H. Gentry and R. Mendelsohn, 1989, Valuation of an Amazonian Rainforest, *Nature* 339: 655–656.

Phillips, D., 1994, The Potential for Harvesting Fruits in Tropical Rainforests: New Data from Amazonian Peru, *Biodiversity and Conservation* 2: 18–38.

Raven, P., 1988, Our Diminishing Tropical Forests, in E.O. Wilson (ed), *Biodiversity*, National Academy Press, Washington DC, 119–122.

Reid, W.V., 1992, How many species will there be? In Whitmore, T.C. and J.A. Sayer, *Tropical Deforestation and Species Extinction*, London: Chapman and Hall, 55–74.

Reid, W.V. and K.R. Miller, 1989, *Keeping Options Alive: The Scientific Basis for Conserving Biodiversity*, Washington DC, World Resources Institute.

Reid, W., J. McNeely, D. Tunstall, D. Bryant and M. Winograd, 1993a, *Biodiversity Indicators for Policy Makers*, World Resources Institute, Washington D.C., October.

Reid, W.V., S. Laird, C. Meyer, R. Gamez, A. Sittenfeld, D. Janzen, M. Gollin, C. Juma, 1993b, *Biodiversity Prospecting: using Genetic Resources for Sustainable Development*, World Resources Institute, Washington DC.

Reinstein, R., 1991, *Trade and Environment*, US State Department, Washington DC, *mimeo*.

Reis, J. and R. Guzman, 1994, *An Econometric Model of Amazon Deforestation*, in Brown and Pearce, 1994, 172–191.

Repetto, R. and M. Gillis, 1988, *Public Policies and the Misuse of Forest Resources*, Cambridge University Press, Cambridge.

Rico, R., 1994, The US Allowance Trading System for Sulfur Dioxide: an Update on Market Experience, *Environmental and Resource Economics*, Special Issue on Acid Rain (edited by G. Klaassen and D.W. Pearce), forthcoming.

Rijsberman, F. and R.J. Swart (eds), 1990, *Targets and Indicators of Climate Change*, Stockholm Environment Institute, Stockholm.

RISO, 1992, *UNEP Greenhouse Gas Abatement Costing Studies*, RISO National Laboratory, Denmark, August.

Robinson, H., 1988, Industrial Pollution Abatement: the Impact on the Balance of Trade, *Canadian Journal of Economics* 21(1).

Rowbotham, E., 1994, *The Tuna Case and Extrajurisdictional Protection Under the GATT/WTO*, Centre for Social and Economic Research on the Global Environment, University of East Anglia and University College London, *mimeo*.

Rudel, T. 1994, *Population, Development, and Tropical Deforestation: A Cross-National Study*, in Brown and Pearce, 1994.

Ruitenbeek, H.J., 1992, The Rainforest Supply Price: A Tool for Evaluating Rainforest Conservation Expenditures, *Ecological Economics* 6(1): 57–78.

Sagoff, M., 1993, Environmental Economics: an Epitaph, *Resources*, 111: 2–7.

Schneider, R., 1992, *Brazil: an Analysis of Environmental Problems in the Amazon*, Report No. 9104–BR, World Bank, Latin American and Caribbean Region, Washington DC.

Sedjo, R., 1988, Property Rights and the Protection of Plant Genetic Resources, in J.R. Kloppenburg (ed), *The Use and Control of Plant Genetic Resources*, Duke University Press, Durham.

Sedjo, R., 1991, *Towards a Worldwide System of Tradeable Forest Protection and Management Obligations*, Resources for the Future, Washington DC, *mimeo*.

Shafik, N., 1994, *Macroeconomic Causes of Deforestation: Barking up the Wrong Tree*, World Bank, Washington DC.

Shoven, J., and J. Whalley, 1984, Applied General Equilibrium Models of Taxation and International Trade: an Introduction and Survey, *Journal of Economic Literature* XXII, September: 1007–1051.

Simpson, D., R. Sedjo and J. Reid, 1994, Valuing Biodiversity: an Application of Genetic Prospecting, Resources for the Future, Washington DC, *mimeo*.

Sittenfield, A. and R. Gamez, 1993, Biodiversity Prospecting in INBio, in Reid et al, 1993b.

Slade, M., 1991, *Environmental Costs of Natural Resource Commodities: Magnitude and Incidence*, Department of Economics, University of British Columbia, Vancouver, July, *mimeo*.

Sjoberg, H., 1993, *First Time Round: Creating the Global Environment Facility*, Global Environment Facility, Washington DC.

Southgate, D., R. Sierra and L. Brown, 1989, *The Causes of Tropical Deforestation in Ecuador: A Statistical Analysis*, LEEC Paper 89-09, London Environmental Economics Centre, London.

Southgate, D., 1994, *Tropical Deforestation and Agricultural Development in Latin America*, in Brown and Pearce, 1994, 134–145.

Southgate, D. and M. Whitaker, 1994, *Economic Progress and the Environment: One Developing Country's Policy Crisis*, Oxford University Press, Oxford.

Stevenson, G., 1991, *Common Property Economics*, Cambridge University Press.

Tietenberg, T., 1991, Economic Instruments for Environmental Regulation, in D. Helm (ed), *Economic Policy Towards the Environment*, Blackwell, Oxford. 86–110.

Titus, J.G., 1992, The Cost of Climate Change to the United States, in E.W. Miller and L.M. Rosenfeld (eds), *Global Climate Change: Implications, Challenges and Mitigation Measures*, Pennsylvania: Pennsylvania Academy of Science.

Tobey, J., 1990, The Effects of Domestic Environmental Policies on Patterns of World Trade: an Empirical Test, *Kyklos* 43(2) 191–209.

Tol, R.S.J., 1994, *The Damage Costs of Climate Change: Towards More Comprehensive Calculations* (revised version), Working Document W94, Free University Amsterdam, forthcoming.

Turner, R.K., 1992, Sustainability: Principles and Practice, in R.K. Turner (ed), *Sustainable Environmental Economics and Management*, Belhaven Press, London, 3–34.

UNCTAD, 1991, *Environment and International Trade*, Report by the Secretary General of UNCTAD, Geneva.

UNEP (United Nations Environment Programme), 1991, *Montreal Protocol, 1991 Assessment: Report of the Technology and Economic Assessment Panel.*

UNEP (United Nations Environment Programme), UNDP (United Nations Development Programme), and the World Bank, 1993, *Report of the Independent Evaluation of the Global Environment Facilty Pilot Phase*, December.

Vatn A. and D. Bromley, 1994. Choices Without Prices Without Apologies. *Journal of Environmental Economics and Management* 26: 129–148.

Vincent, J., 1993, Managing Tropical Forests: Comment, *Land Economics* 69(3) 313–318.

Vincent, J., 1994, The Tropical Timber Trade and Sustainable Development, in Brown and Pearce, 1994, 298–308.

Walter, I., 1973, The Pollution Content of American Trade, *Western Economic Journal* 11: 61–70.

Walter, I., 1982, *International Economic Repercussions of Environmental Policy: an Economist's Perspective*, in S. Rubin and T. Graham, 1982, *Environment and Trade: the Relation of International Trade and Environmental Policy*, Allanheld, Osman, Totowa NJ, 22–45.

Wells, M., 1993, The Global Environment Facility and Prospects for Biodiversity Conservation, paper submitted to *International Environmental Affairs.*

Werksman, J., 1993, *Incremental Costs Under the Climate Change Convention: the International Legal Context*, Foundation for International Environmental Law and Development, London.

Wilson, E.O., 1988, The Current State of Biological Diversity, in E.O. Wilson (ed), *Biodiversity*, Washington: National Academy Press, 3–20.

World Bank, 1987, *World Development Report 1987*, Oxford University Press, Oxford.

World Bank, 1992, *World Development Report 1992*, World Bank: Washington DC.

Yezer, A., and A. Philipson, 1974, *Influence of Environmental Considerations on Agriculture and Industrial Decisions to Locate Outside of the Continental US*, Public Interest Economics Center for the US Council on Environmental Quality, Washington DC.

Index